LEAVING THE CASINO

Jessica Lackey

SPARK Publications
Charlotte, North Carolina

Leaving the Casino
Stop betting on tactics and start building a business that works
Jessica Lackey

Designed, produced, and published by
SPARK Publications
SPARKpublications.com
Charlotte, North Carolina

Interior illustrations by Hollie Arnett
Author photo by Danielle Cohen LLC
Rocket p. 7 M_Videous

Printed in the United States of America

Hardback, August 2025, ISBN: 978-1-953555-88-5
Paperback, August 2025, ISBN: 978-1-953555-89-2
E-book, August 2025, ISBN: 978-1-953555-92-2
Library of Congress Control Number: 2025913764

*For the business owners building root by root,
season by season.*

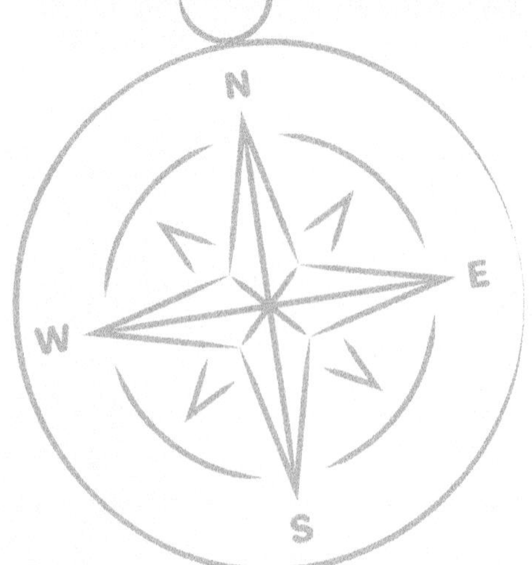

Table of Contents

Part II: The Big Decisions—
Your Strategic Business Foundations

Drawing you in with the sounds of Stripe notifications buzzing and highlight reels ringing, the Entrepreneurial Casino pulls you deeper into the maze of exciting games and promised payouts.

Introduction: Breaking the Spell

IT'S JUST ANOTHER MORNING, a year into trying to build my full-time consulting practice.

I open my eyes, grab my phone, and do what every entrepreneur swears they'll stop doing: I check social media before I've even left my bed. The first thing I see is a parade of promises screaming for my attention, as if each one holds the golden ticket to my entrepreneurial dreams:

"The secret strategy the top 1% of entrepreneurs don't want you to know!"

"Want a 6-figure business while working 10 hours a week? Here's how!"

"You don't need more clients, you need THIS system."

"This one mindset shift doubled my income overnight."

I scroll faster, hoping to escape the barrage, but it's like a slot machine I can't stop pulling. Each post promises more than the last, and I feel a familiar mix of skepticism and hope. What could they possibly teach me in a photo carousel that will help me break the laws of physics and double my business revenue overnight? But also … *is* there a secret they have that I need to know?

Still in bed, I open my email. My inbox? Even worse.

"Your path to 6 figures starts here 🚀"

"Make more, work less: the proven formula."

"My foolproof 3-step plan to scale your business."

It's not just emails—it's an endless carnival of urgency and scarcity. Countdown timers tick away on webinar registration pages.

Video testimonials loop with wide-eyed entrepreneurs gushing about how *this* course finally changed their life.

And the courses themselves? They're everywhere, with titles so shiny they practically sparkle:

"Course Creator Pro: Launch Your First 5-Figure Program in 30 Days"

"Millionaire Mindset: Reprogram Your Brain for Wealth and Success"

"Zone of Genius Mastery: Focus On What You Love and Make Bank"

It's not even 8 a.m., and I already feel dazzled and disoriented—surrounded by flashing lights, bold promises, and a constant hum of opportunity. Everywhere I turn, someone is shouting, "This is your big win! Don't miss it!" It's intoxicating and overwhelming all at once.

But then I check my bank account transactions—and the glossy promises start to blur.

A $300 course on how to sell a digital course *(to the email list that I don't even have, for which there's a different product to solve that problem also listed on my credit card bill).*

A $2,000 mastermind with a mentor who promised personal attention *(but that feels like a glorified group chat).*

A $30 subscription to a community and course hosting platform *(because I needed a place to host the course and community that's crickets, see above).*

An $800 Zelle payment to my assistant who helps organize community events and upload said courses *(of course, I haven't really utilized her in a few months now).*

For all the energy and money I'm pouring into my business, I'm starting to wonder if the only thing I'm building is someone else's empire.

I feel a weight settle on my chest. *How did I get here? I have an MBA from Harvard, was trained at one of the top consulting firms in the country, worked for name-brand companies … What the hell am I doing?*

That's when it hits me: I've stepped into the Entrepreneurial Casino. And, like so many others, I've been playing a game I didn't even realize was rigged.

Drawing you in with the sounds of Stripe notifications buzzing and highlight reels ringing, the Entrepreneurial Casino pulls you deeper into the maze of exciting games and promised payouts.

All of this marketing is designed to capture your attention and convince you that you're only one investment away from your dreams. There are no windows, no clocks, no cues to remind you of the world outside—except for the countdown timer on the checkout screen reminding you to finalize your purchase. Everywhere you go, you're met with smiling dealers and the encouraging roll call of strangers in Facebook groups cheering their wins.

For a moment, you feel the thrill—the promise of something more, something better, just one spin, one hand, one roll away. But beneath the glamour and adrenaline, there's a subtle undertow. The game is tilted in the house's favor and is never as simple as it seems. Yet still, you stay and play … because what if your dreams really *are* just one viral post away?

But there is a way out. *We can leave the Casino.* And I'm going to show you how—after I tell you how I ended up trapped there myself.

Let's go back a few years to understand how even a business-savvy (yet newbie) entrepreneur fell for the empty promise of the Casino.

THE CORPORATE MIRAGE

I started my career with the odds in my favor. Trained as an industrial engineer in undergrad and grad school, I became skilled at embedding operational efficiency and optimization into businesses and systems. My early professional life was built on problem-solving at its highest level, first at McKinsey & Company and later at Harvard Business School, where I learned to diagnose issues, craft strategies, and implement solutions across a variety of industries. By my early thirties, I had landed at Nike, climbing the corporate ladder and being labeled "high-potential talent." On paper, I was thriving.

The corporate world can be dazzling. It promises status, security, and prestige. It seduces you with its mirage of success: private offices, impressive titles, and the sense that you've "made it." I believed in that promise, and I chased it hard. I played the game, dressed the part, and followed the rules. I told myself the paycheck and upward mobility were worth it—even as the long hours piled up and the relentless demands took their toll on my personal life and relationships.

But as I climbed higher, the cracks in the illusion began to show. Behind the glossy veneer of corporate success was a relentless machine fueled by profit over people. The focus wasn't on meaningful impact or authentic leadership: it was on quarterly earnings, office politics, and surface-level performance metrics. The expectation to sacrifice my soul for the bottom line felt unavoidable, like an unspoken contract I'd signed without reading the fine print.

The more I gave, the more the corporate world took. My health began to falter, subtle at first, then impossible to ignore: the stress, the constant striving, the sacrificing of friendships and hobbies for weekend work and late nights. It all began to wear me down. I was doing everything I thought I was supposed to do, yet I felt hollow.

The corporate mirage I had been chasing wasn't the oasis it had promised to be.

After over a decade of the "perfect-on-paper" professional life, I had a breakdown. A literal week where I bawled in my boss's office and on colleagues' shoulders, crumbling under the stress. It was exquisitely clear that I no longer wanted to reach the next rung on the ladder, or even the rung I was on. I didn't want to waste my energy on the endless status games: pushing PowerPoints around, preparing for never-ending meetings, protecting my team during hiring freezes and layoffs, or struggling to speak my truth without being labeled "bossy" or "cold." I saw clearly how much time and energy I'd spent on portraying an image of success rather than cultivating something rooted and real.

I had to walk away. I needed to leave the corporate world, not because I couldn't handle it—though that was becoming increasingly precarious—but because I didn't *want* it anymore. The mirage had faded, and I realized I had to find something more aligned, work that didn't ask me to sacrifice myself for accomplishments within an organization that never really cared about me.

So, I turned my eyes to entrepreneurship. I originally set out to side hustle as a life coach as a first step in creating my pathway out of corporate.

And what I experienced was eye-opening.

WALKING INTO THE ENTREPRENEURIAL CASINO

When I started building my own business, I thought I'd see entrepreneurs taking a different approach—something more intentional, more authentic, and more human than the corporate world I'd left behind. I believed I was stepping into a space where creativity and individuality thrived.

Instead, I walked straight into the *Entrepreneurial Casino*. Of course, I didn't know it at the time.

At first glance, it felt exciting. Everywhere I looked, I saw promises of freedom, independence, and limitless income potential. The Casino was buzzing with opportunities—playbooks, proven formulas, and foolproof roadmaps. Every guru had the "secret" to six-figure launches, seven-figure businesses, or passive income streams that would let you work four hours a week while sipping margaritas on a beach.

The Entrepreneurial Casino is a multibillion-dollar industry built around the dream of entrepreneurship, focused on selling quick and easy solutions to grow your fame and fortune. The influencers selling you these solutions are experts at using every marketing tactic in the book to ensnare you—scarcity, urgency, social proof, even sex appeal. It's the course-based version of diet pills: fast promises of big results with little effort. This makes the tech platforms the *ultimate* winners of this game—you pay big bucks to advertise while your attention and data are commoditized and sold to the highest bidder.

The deeper I wandered into the Casino, the more it felt like I'd traded one mirage for another. The formulas promised to be foolproof, but they often relied on advantages I didn't have, like early-adopter momentum, large teams, or preexisting fame. The guarantees weren't built on solid ground but on half-truths and flashy facades.

And when their strategies didn't work? I was told to try again. Just invest a little more. Take the next course, upgrade to the premium mastermind, "fix my mindset," and the oasis of success would finally be within reach.

The same mechanisms that had kept me hustling in my corporate career—dangling the next promotion, the next bonus, the next growth opportunity—were alive and well in the world of online entrepreneurship. Only now, they were dressed up in "founder" jargon and repackaged as freedom. I'd left one game of relentless striving only to find myself in another. I was in a constant loop of comparison, buying into some shiny new growth hack and becoming frustrated that "the dream" always seemed out of reach. And as I started to see the pattern, I realized I hadn't broken free at all.

The Casino doesn't teach you how to build a business—it teaches you how to *play business*. Complex funnels, big teams, and expensive marketing campaigns are framed as essentials, even when they have nothing to do with the stage or structure of your actual business.

The house rules are clear: The only way to win is to keep investing.

When that doesn't work, the fallback plan is to become an influencer—teaching others how to build the same broken model. Entrepreneurship started to look like a multilevel marketing (MLM) scheme, where the real money comes not from selling products but from recruiting others or selling sales coaching on the side. Ever seen a health influencer who couldn't make their business profitable suddenly pivot to teaching other health influencers how to grow their businesses?

I quickly realized that every gamble I made in the Casino—the courses, the masterminds, the shiny tools—was padding someone else's pockets. This wasn't what I had envisioned. I hadn't left corporate to play a new version of the same game.

The more I built up my own business, the more I dug into the Casino and its games. But I noticed time and again that what I was being sold didn't align with what I knew about how businesses *actually work*. The Casino was soulless, filled with stale air and stuck in a constant loop of artificial entertainment.

Just like the free drinks in a casino aren't really free, a "free" summit ticket is often just bait for a high-ticket upsell. Success stories feel more like outdated decor—shiny testimonials from years ago, from a different program that worked in a completely different market. Influencers sell you social media success instead of the more relational business development that worked for me in my corporate and consulting life. Meanwhile, these same entrepreneurs are burning out, and the stories they post in Reddit threads or discuss in private conversations tell a very different story from their polished Instagram feeds.

It became clear to me: The only way to win wasn't to play by the house rules but to step away from the table altogether. Sure, with enough time and upfront capital, you can beat the house, just like the sophisticated card counting teams (*aka the big content creators*).

But the real win doesn't lie in playing the casino's game.

The real win is learning how the system works and choosing to build something different—something real—and walking out the door with your integrity, vision, and business intact.

LEAVING THE CASINO

Because I've had such a variety of experiences—engineering, consulting, big corporate businesses, the startup world, and building my own business (first as a life coach and then as a fractional COO)—I can see across all of the different floors of the Casino.

The boss babes and manifestation girlies on Instagram showing off their luxury lifestyles.

The Twitter/X and YouTube bros promising that you can have six-figure revenue months just by writing content for one hour a day.

The B2B marketers turning LinkedIn into a sea of homogenized and flattened expertise that always leads with a "hook." *(Feels like a hook, line, and sinker to me.)*

But I can use my experience to curate what ***does work*** in business and turn a torrential sea of information and shoddy promises into frameworks and tools specifically designed for small, knowledge-based businesses (like the ones I've built myself). The skills I honed in corporate strategy—diagnosing systems, analyzing trade-offs, and building sustainable solutions—are the same tools that can be applied to help entrepreneurs create profitable and sustainable businesses without sacrificing their values or well-being.

I've worked one-on-one with over 60 entrepreneurs, from consultants and healers to coaches and service providers, both in the online business ecosystem and in person, serving larger businesses. Moreover, I've helped hundreds of business owners through my programs and membership.

B2B, B2C, B2B2B, B2SMB, B2GOV—I've worked with about every *B* of business in my career.

My knowledge is hard-won from personal experience. I've tried most of the business models on the **delivery side:** serving as an independent consultant, a subcontract consultant, part of a boutique consulting firm, a success/support coach for larger businesses, and a fractional COO for multiple seven-figure organizations. Now, I'm building a business with more of a **creator style** as a course creator and community leader who markets via a weekly newsletter, a podcast, a YouTube channel, and this book. From my years of launching to my time spent running a consultative sales process with organizations, I've done and seen so much as an expertise-based business owner in the arena with you.

This book is for those of you whose business is based on deep knowledge and experience in a specific topic, subject, or process. I call us **expertise-based business owners** or **experts-turned-entrepreneurs:** the coaches, consultants, creatives, community leaders, educators, and anyone else selling knowledge, a skill, or a community based around a niche. You're here because you have a gift you want to share with the world or a craft you want to grow a business around. You haven't set out to build the next billion-dollar empire, but you do want a business that works—one that becomes more powerful and easier to run over time and is predictably profitable, purposeful, and designed specifically for you.

While this book is focused on service providers, its principles can also benefit product-based businesses, retail shops, or even SaaS founders who want to grow sustainably without scaling endlessly. You want to stay grounded, maintain control, and build something that feels real and fulfilling. And you might have been burned by the Casino's promises too.

If you're here, you probably believe that building a sustainable business is not about tactics or quick fixes; it's about diving deep into the business you actually want to build. It's about understanding how business works—from the foundations up—and creating systems that work together, compound over time, and deliver results aligned with the life you want to live and the business you want to run.

In growing my own business, I realized that I had to allow it to work like nature: laying deep roots, allowing for seasons of growth and rest, and focusing on sustainability, not competition.

I wrote this book because the advice most business owners encounter either assumes you want to scale to infinity or leaves you floundering with surface-level tactics that don't address the unique challenges of running a small, expertise-based business. Books and trainings are often designed for product founders, SaaS companies, or e-commerce entrepreneurs with larger teams—not those of us selling our own time, knowledge, and skills. So many high-level motivational courses could have been a short blog post, leaving you with lots of "inspo" and not much else.

Books like *Company of One* by Paul Jarvis have started the conversation by giving us the "why" behind deliberate business design. I walk in the footsteps of other business thinkers, such as Tara McMullin (*What Works*), Blair Enns (*Win Without Pitching*) and David C. Baker (*The Business of Expertise*), and internet colleagues, like Paul Millerd (*The Pathless Path*) and Khe Hy (*Khe Hy*), who have informed my approach, offering insights into sustainable growth, reframing success, and prioritizing what matters. I've also learned from a variety of others who will be cited in the book as well.

This book holds the answers, frameworks, and perspectives I wish I had when I started, and which I paid a price to learn. I hope this book is the permission slip you need to do things differently—your own way.

WHAT THIS BOOK AIMS TO DO

This book isn't designed to push you toward hustle or despair. It's here to help you build a real business—one that reflects your values, works for you, and operates within the size and style parameters you've deliberately chosen. It's not about quick wins or five-step blueprints; it's about addressing the foundational questions that every expertise-based business owner faces. It's a guide to navigating the trade-offs, understanding the frameworks, and making intentional decisions about growth that fit your business and lifestyle.

You'll walk away from this book with not only a deeper understanding of *what* to do but also the *why* and *how* behind those decisions. This guide will equip you to step away from the shiny distractions of the entrepreneurial space through agency, authority, and acumen as you navigate building your business.

With a business designed for you, you'll be able to breathe the fresh outside air, enjoy sunrises and sunsets, and connect with nature.

WHAT TO EXPECT

The book is divided into two parts.

Part I: The Big Questions—Your Business Values and Vision

Before you can make decisions about your business, you need clarity on what you're ultimately building. Part I addresses the fundamental questions every expertise-based business owner needs to answer:

- What kind of business do you want to run?
- What does success look like for you?
- How do you align your business with your personal values, strengths, and boundaries?
- What is "enough" for you in your business?

We'll interrogate the default societal scripts about impact, influence, and income to help you create a vision for your business that's rooted in what you actually want—not what someone else told you to want.

Part II: The Big Decisions—Your Strategic Business Foundations

Once you've answered the Big Questions, it's time to get practical. Part II dives into the core decisions every business owner must make:

- How to price your services for profit and sustainability
- How to design offers that work for both you and your clients
- How to approach marketing and sales in a way that feels in alignment
- When and how to hire—or decide not to

Instead of falling back on the Casino's tropes, this section gives you actionable frameworks, strategies, and tools to navigate these Big Decisions with confidence and clarity, based on the Big Questions you've already answered.

WHY THIS BOOK MATTERS

This book is a resource for those of you who don't want to chase infinite growth but do want to build something meaningful, sustainable, and deeply aligned with who you are. It's for the small business owner who is tired of being sold cookie-cutter solutions and is ready to build their business on their own terms.

This work matters because when our businesses are rooted in values and sustainability, they create ripples that extend far beyond the bottom line. They build communities, strengthen individuals, and set an example of what's possible when we step away from extractive systems. This book isn't just about building a business for you; it's about contributing to a healthier entrepreneurial ecosystem that connects us with each other, even at the "cost" of scale or profit beyond what we need.

My goal is to give you the tools, insights, and confidence you need to leave the Entrepreneurial Casino and build a business that's rooted in the solid foundation of your expertise, driven by your values, and designed for the life you want to lead.

THE BIG QUESTIONS

Your Business Values and Vision

What kind of business are you actually running? What stage are you in? What role does this business play in your life? Part I introduces the Big Questions to help you filter out the noise from online entrepreneurial influencers, determine what you want from your business, and articulate the values underpinning it to ensure all of your decisions align with *your* vision.

EVERYWHERE ONLINE, THE BUSINESS "SECRETS" and strategies you're sold are based on a specific image of success, a vision for *your* future where you make money while you sleep or sip mai tais on the beach.

While this advice is positioned as generally applicable to your business, it's not—it's people who built a business one way telling you how they did it and how you can do it exactly like them. Instead of giving you navigational tools, the advice and strategies they promote assume that you're walking the same path to the same destination. If you don't have your own vision in mind, you can get trapped in the mirage of fulfillment they create for you and ultimately end up with a business that you don't want or one that doesn't actually work (and doesn't work *for you*).

Plans come after purpose, so lay strong foundations by figuring out why you're building this business and what you want from it.

ANSWERING THE BIG QUESTIONS

The Big Questions serve as a way to set your internal compass and navigation beacons by framing the purpose of your business in your life. They will help you align all business decisions with the present and future you actually want, not with the image of success that's been sold to you.

What business do you really want to run, and what is your desired impact style? What are your desires, capabilities, interests, and values, and how do those inform the design of the business you want to build? Finally, what responsibility do you want to carry?

The answers comprise the filter through which you evaluate any and all business advice: "Does this strategy or secret even apply to the type of business I want to run?"

When it comes to the Big Questions, only *your* answers matter. Everyone comes to business with different circumstances, family situations, health conditions, internal and external motivations, strengths, skill sets, and values. A one-size-fits-all playbook doesn't allow you to decide what role you need your business to play in your life. Without centering on where you're coming from and where you're going, you could end up building a business you don't even want.

But when your path forward is clear, every step gets you closer to your goal—instead of lost and trapped in someone else's mirage.

CHAPTER BREAKDOWN

What Business Are You Really Running?

In a world filled with online course creators and YouTube sensations, not all businesses and business models are created equal—and not all advice is appropriate for every type of business. Answering this question will help you solidify your business model so that you can stop taking advice that doesn't apply to you.

What Stage of Business Growth Are You In?

Even good advice is bad if it's not a fit for your stage of business. Answering this question will help you determine what your focus and priorities should be based on where you are now.

What Impact Do You Want Your Business to Have?

We're told that we need to serve lots of people, accumulate lots of followers, and have a lot of customers and quantifiable influence to be successful—but this route is not the only way for your business to have impact. Answering this question will help you decide whether your goal is to have intimate or broad impact.

What Responsibility Do You Want to Hold in Your Business?

A business with a large team, a community, and long-term client commitments has greater responsibility burdens than a single-person operation selling short-term products. Answering this question will help you make decisions about your business based on the responsibility you want to carry.

What Is Enough?

We're sold the idea that we can and should have it all—all the freedom, all the time, and all the money we can get. But each of these comes with trade-offs, and the cultural value of "more is always better" may not align with how you really feel. Answering this question will help you get in touch with what is really enough for you—and what the trade-offs may be—so that you can optimize your business for the life you want.

HOW TO READ PART I

I suggest reading through and seeing what questions surprise or trigger you, answering what you can at the first read. Some questions will require homework and even struggle. Unwinding societal stories about impact, "enoughness," and responsibility takes time—and spreadsheets!

As you encounter these questions, notice where your stories and desires deviate from the script. Then come back and sit with those questions once it's time to face important business decisions.

Because your responses will be based on your values, life circumstances, and goals, they may change over time. Revisit these questions every year or at important junctures in your business journey, like when you're considering hiring or changing your pricing, as we'll discuss in Part II.

Remember, the only way to answer these questions is to undergo internal reflection, which you can't do when you're constantly distracted by the noise and temptation of the deluge of advice found on social media and YouTube and in email marketing. Set aside some time to spend with these questions, and you'll realize that this introspection takes less time than you think.

You already know what you want—you just have to bring it to the surface and articulate it.

It is worth it.

Without doing so, you'll spend inordinately *more* time taking advice that doesn't move the needle and costs you time, money, and sanity.

*You already know what
you want—you just have to
bring it to the surface and
articulate it.*

Knowing your business model can allow you to filter for the strategies, methods, and plans that are designed for your style of business. It helps you understand how your business actually works.

CHAPTER 1

What Business Are You Really Running?

I'M A CREATOR. *A freelancer. A solopreneur. An entrepreneur. A consultant. An agency owner. I run a small business.*

I hate to break it to you, but these are not business models, and they don't help you make any important decisions for your business beyond how to introduce yourself.

One freelancer might work with one or two companies on retainer for years, yet another might work on a different project every month. One consultant might lead a small firm of experts, generating millions of dollars through projects, while another might make all of their money through books, courses, and high-profile speaking engagements. One creator might sell thousands of low-priced courses, while another sells a few units of a high-priced membership. While the titles these entrepreneurs use might be the same, the underlying businesses they are running are very different.

Knowing your business *model* can allow you to filter for the strategies, methods, and plans that are designed for your style of business. It helps you understand how your business actually works—how many customers you need, what prices you should charge, what your marketing and sales strategies should look like, how your team size and structure should be formulated, and what profit structure and revenue levels you require.

Adopting secrets for someone else's model is not just a waste of time—it could set you back and even cost you. But do you ever hear business influencers talking about this issue? Of course not. That would be too nuanced!

There are generally two different categories of business models, under which fall several archetypes. The first category is **delivery-based business models,** where you are delivering a service to clients, either through hands-on work or as an advisor. Your revenue is largely tied to the number of clients you have the capacity to serve and your pricing structure.

The second category is **creator-based business models,** where you're monetizing attention and audience size through courses, programs, communities, sponsorships, or speaking engagements. Your revenue is largely tied to how large your audience is and the format you choose to charge in.

Delivery models often require fewer clients at a higher price per customer, leading to more relational marketing strategies—but also more time spent on client work! And while creator models might give you more freedom and flexibility on your calendar thanks to the lack of client delivery and meetings, you're frequently beholden to a more intense publishing cadence and higher marketing expenses to reach a larger audience.

The specific models that fall under these two categories are ordered on my **Business Model Spectrum** based on the number of people you'll impact or serve. The size of the audience you need to reach to make your business successful differs even among models in the same category.

The revenue and profit potential isn't limited on either part of the spectrum. While there's lots of lore about million-dollar, one-person creators who sell courses, there's an equal (or maybe even greater)

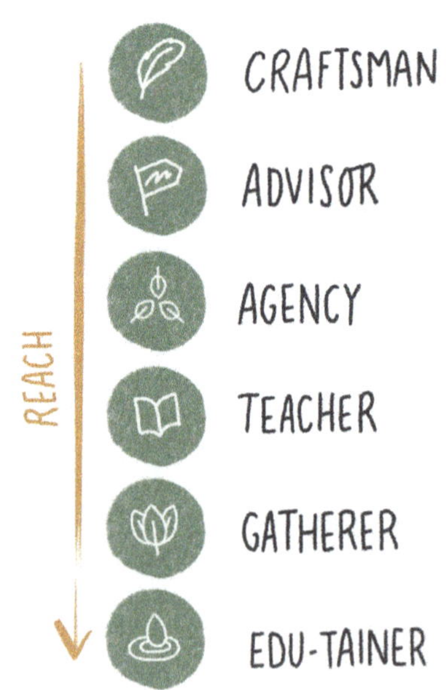

number of seven-figure individuals and small firms who deliver work to their clients quietly, without a huge social media following. Because they don't need a huge audience—just the right client base—you won't hear about them on social platforms, but you will hear about them in entrepreneurial development groups catering to more local or established businesses.

The boutique consulting firm specializing in the apparel and footwear supply chain, with high-six-figure advisory contracts. The executive coaching firm billing over a million annually with Fortune 500 firms, with a five-figure average engagement cost. The high-end accounting firm reaching that million-dollar annual revenue milestone with a team of less than ten people.

How do I know these firms make money? They've been past clients.

And you don't have to choose between either a delivery- or creator-style model: A consultant who does primarily project work might also sell books or do speaking as a marketing tool. Or an "Edu-Tainer" who largely monetizes through a paid newsletter might also host events or do one-off consulting engagements.

You're likely going to lean toward one model over another. However, knowing your primary business model and where you generally fall in along the spectrum will help you choose the appropriate strategies for your business and decide where your time and energy should be spent.

Your position on the spectrum can change over time as you realign with new values or responsibilities, gain influence and expertise, and face life changes. There's no right or wrong model. This isn't just about revenue and the way you spend your time—it's about how you want to relate to your work and the world and what you spend your time and money on in your business.

The following section outlines the delivery- and creator-based categories and the specific business models that fall within them. The overviews cover how each model can make money and include real-life examples of businesses making over $100,000 a year to demonstrate that it can be done. In addition, each outline includes *what you get—* the perceived benefits of each model—and *what you give,* or the requirements to run this business model. These aren't styled as pros and cons because you may look at some of the requirements, such as leading a team or running a certain style of marketing, and decide that this is exactly the type of business you want to run. Alternatively, you might consider those requirements and decide that the model is not an investment you're interested in making.

Your choice of business model will guide the trajectory of your company. If you don't know what model you want to run now, the rest of the Big Questions you answer later on in this book will help you establish where you want to be on the Business Model Spectrum. I suggest reading through each chapter in Part I before making any plans—as we grow your sustainable business from the roots up, we'll consider all the things that matter most.

THE DELIVERY MODEL BUSINESSES

In delivery-based business models, the focus is on providing a service, either through yourself or through a team. These models are characterized by comparatively fewer customers, with deeper and potentially longer-term relationships. They can be dismissed as "trading time for dollars" business models but can be wildly profitable even if they are not as scalable. Yes, you might be creating for clients or creating content to market your business online, but the focus is on client engagements, not content.

Delivery-Based Models:
- **The Craftsman:** Performing a service directly with or for a client
- **The Advisor:** Providing a service that helps a client solve a problem or achieve their goals
- **The Agency:** Delivering either Craftsman or Advisor services through others

The Craftsman

Short Description: Performing a service directly with or for a client

Inspiration: Bookkeeping/tax prep, ghostwriting, copywriting, graphic design, video editing, virtual assistant/online business manager services, web design, handcrafted artifact creation, fractional C-Suite services (e.g., chief operating officer, chief of staff, or chief marketing officer)

The Craftsman prides herself on delivering a craft. She enjoys doing the work and doesn't want to delegate it to someone else. A lot of advice disparages the Craftsman model, asserting that Craftsman work is just recreating a job—but instead of working "9–5" you're working "24/7."

However, done thoughtfully, working directly with clients on your own terms is many people's dream. Compared to other models, you'll spend a higher percentage of your work time delivering your Craftsman services, meaning you'll have less time for marketing. You'll want to construct your business to cultivate longer-term relationships with clients and referral partners. Exceptional client delivery and a strong relationship network that leads to recurring client work and referrals is your calling card.

What You Get:

- You get to do the work you got into business to do!
- You aren't managing anyone else—it's just you.
- You can construct a business with a high level of flexibility in how you deliver your services, as much of your work is done on your own time instead of delivered "live" with clients in meetings.
- Being a Craftsman allows for more flexibility in your schedule and finances. Want to take a month off? You can do so without worrying about keeping a team utilized as in an Agency model (assuming you've got a cash buffer or can schedule projects for later in the year).

- You probably work with people you know, like, and trust without having to do much true cold selling.

What You Give:
- You still have to market and sell! This can be tricky if you're spending almost all of your work time delivering services for clients.
- Based on your pricing and the number of projects or clients you can take on at once, there's a limit on your revenue. This revenue ceiling might be high, but it's still a ceiling.
- There is a limit to how many clients you can serve from both a time and energy perspective because the work is so hands-on.
- Since this model relies on delivering services, if you're not working, you're not making money. However, this constraint can be navigated with different offer structures, particularly with longer-term clients.
- Craftsman work, especially long-term work, is often priced at an effective price per hour lower than that of strategic advisory work. But because the deliverable is tangible, the sales process is often easier.
- Craftsman work can be lonely when you work on your own.

Examples:

Rachel is a book editor and book coach. She works with expert entrepreneurs on their writing craft, process, and practice. Rachel primarily sells book editing and writing coaching / developmental editing services for expertise-based entrepreneurs. She's often editing one major manuscript at a time and working with 5–10 clients at various stages of their projects. Between her editing projects at $30,000 and a monthly retainer for seven clients at $1,500 per month, Rachel can make over $150,000 per year. And because her clients are with her for the long term, she spends almost no time (or money) on marketing. She gets to fully profit and flexibly spend her days with her dogs and her editing.

Courtney is a copywriter. She works on project-based website and brand copy with one client a month, charging $6,000 per project. She also works with two retainer clients, doing ongoing sales copywriting for marketing campaigns, at $1,500 per month per client. Courtney can

make more than $108,000 per year, especially once her referral pipeline
starts bringing in clients and she sees repeat business from her previous
project-based copywriting customers.

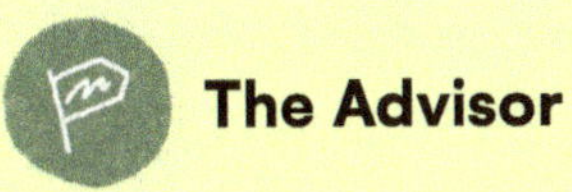

The Advisor

Short Description: Providing a service that helps a client solve a
problem or achieve their goals

Inspiration: Financial advising, 1:1 coaching, consulting, strategy
sessions, marketing strategy development

The Advisor finds joy in guiding clients through a transformation. She
loves consulting and advising on their work, adding value in short bursts.
Much of the client transformation happens between sessions.

As an Advisor, you'll often attract these clients and build your
reputation through branded models or frameworks, demonstrating
your intellectual property and expertise. You're most likely not doing
ongoing "in-the-business" or production-style work for your clients (e.g.,
copywriting, graphic design, or editing), though you're probably creating
strategic deliverables like coaching notes, financial or marketing plans, or
project roadmaps.

What You Get:
- You're positioning yourself in the "strategy" category, meaning you
  can often charge a higher effective rate.
- You have fewer delivery hours, so you can take on multiple clients at
  a time at reasonably premium price points.
- You're spending less time on delivery for each client, so your
  calendar is less committed to "in-the-business" work.
- You get to be hands-on with your clients and be more flexible or
  nimble in your delivery style or approach. While more scalable
  Creator models might let you serve more people, you can dial

in the "how you work" and your processes by delivering the transformation live with clients. (Personally, I can't imagine ever fully delivering my work through asynchronous courses or highly scaled offers.)

What You Give:
- Advisor work—especially project-based Advisor work—often has an end point, so there can be high income variability, with high-highs and low-lows. You must always be marketing and selling to maintain your client roster.
- As an Advisor, you will also hit a capacity limit here until you determine if and how you want to add leverage through a team or second business model.
- Similarly to Craftsman models, if you aren't working, you're not getting paid. Advisor models can be more forgiving than Craftsman work, though, especially depending on how you structure engagements.
- Running an Advisor business can be lonely. Without external motivation, it can be difficult to prioritize your efforts to work *on* your business when you're busy working *in* the business with clients.

Example:
For the first four years of entrepreneurship, my primary business model was the Advisor model. I worked with expertise-based business owners to help them build or refine their business foundations. My primary offer was biweekly consulting calls plus asynchronous document review, voice memo access, and light systems implementation (e.g., adding things to their task manager for their team). At $1,000 per month per client, I could make $180,000 with a roster of 15 clients at a time. Some were with me for three months and others for three years. That meant I was directly delivering with clients in meetings for 7–12 hours a week and answering voice memos and doing light implementation work for another 5–10 hours a week.

Some Craftsmen and Advisors choose to morph their business into the Agency model. In this model, someone else is delivering the service, while you—as the Agency owner—run the firm, including the marketing, sales, team management, and high-level client strategy.

You've moved from delivering a service or advising to bringing on a team to do all or some of the client delivery work. You may or may not still be involved with day-to-day client delivery, but your role shifts to company and client strategy creation, intellectual property development for your firm, and business development to keep the client roster full and your team sufficiently utilized.

The first move is to shift to the Advisor role for your clients, with more junior team members taking on Craftsman work like managing projects and producing deliverables. As your firm grows, you can move further out of ongoing delivery, bringing on seasoned team members who handle end-to-end project management while you manage business development and partnerships. (Think a consulting or law firm's rainmaking partners.)

The dream is to have a business that works without your being involved in the everyday execution. However, once you bring on people—either in client-facing roles or behind-the-scenes support—the responsibility and the role radically shift. You are paying people, which means that your role changes to business development: bringing in the projects and work to fully utilize your team.

What You Get:
- You have more flexibility with your time because you are no longer taking on the routine client work.

- You can step away from the business, freeing up time to think big thoughts and focus on strategy.
- Your business can become more profitable because you have more capacity to deliver higher revenue levels and return a profit on the work that your team delivers.
- You can work on larger-scale projects or more projects than you could by yourself.
- You have more time to invest in developing your firm's signature methods, approaches, processes, and tools to ensure you can scale your results through others.

What You Give:

- Agency owners have to love *(or learn to embrace)* running and managing a team. While the appeal of agency life is building a team that can run without you, you actually can't delegate team management!
- Marketing and sales are nonnegotiable, particularly if you have full-time staff. When your team is underutilized, without projects or ongoing billable commitments, their salary comes from your business profit or your owner's pay. And until the business really is large enough to run or drive sales and marketing without you, business development is your primary job.
- Quality control for your deliverables is a huge focus. You'll need rock-solid systems, processes, and training in place so that your clients are getting the same level of service and outcomes from your team that they would get if they worked directly with you—otherwise, churn will quickly become a problem.
- You'll have to figure out the backstop for employee management issues, like covering parental leave or a team member out sick. Often, the backstop is you as the business owner.

Example:

Jamie runs a virtual CFO, accounting, and tax planning firm. She has a team comprising two bookkeepers, a tax analyst, a tax strategist, one other CPA, and herself as the CFO. Her firm brings in about $700,000 a year in revenue through a combination of those services, but the payroll is ~$350,000 a year, not including her own salary. Jamie pays herself $100,000 a year in salary and $50,000 a year in owner distributions, and the rest is spent on marketing, software, the firm's office, tax payments, and building a cash reserve. Her firm's client roster of around 50 clients across all services is with them for the long term, so now that the business has been built, marketing is designed to keep their roster full and replace departing clients.

THE CREATOR MODEL BUSINESSES

In creator-based models, the focus is on creation—creating and distributing content around your point of view. What distinguishes the models from each other is the way in which you intend to make a business (aka monetize) from that content or that viewpoint.

Compared to delivery-based models, creator-based models require larger audiences with potentially fewer to no "clients," as you may not work with people directly. Also, these models are seemingly more scalable because you are not trading your time for dollars, for you or your team.

However, your primary work is marketing. Until you have an audience large enough to support the business you want to run—views, sponsorships, community members—the vast majority of your work is unpaid marketing. It takes time to build your audience and assets up to a level (a size of channel or audience) where you're paid to create or paid for your creations.

Once you've achieved this kind of scale, you can build more leveraged offers, like selling a course that requires less delivery time—but the path to get there can be brutal, and you may not like what having to create for hundreds of thousands of people you don't know requires from you!

Creator-Based Models:
- **The Teacher:** Directly selling courses, trainings, or tools and templates, delivered through recorded content or live interaction
- **The Gatherer:** Selling a member-to-member community or live events
- **The Edu-Tainer:** Monetizing your audience directly (user subscriptions) or indirectly (sponsorships, ads, keynote speaking)

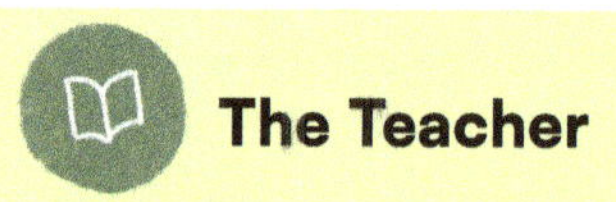

The Teacher

Short Description: Directly selling courses, trainings, or tools and templates, delivered through recorded content or live interaction

Inspiration:

Content Only: Tools, templates, digital or physical books, self-guided or evergreen courses, content-only memberships, curated resources

Content + Interaction: Cohort-based programs, course-based platforms with a lightly moderated online group, group programs with hot seat coaching, teacher-led masterminds, content-based courses with office hours

The teacher guides clients to either an outcome or deeper learning through skills, content, or a framework. You'll make your money by growing your audience via content and selling related products (e.g., templates, tools, courses, books, or self-guided or cohort-based programs).

I consider group coaching, teacher-based masterminds, and cohort-based courses to fall under this model. In group coaching/mastermind models, the live calls are most often a live discussion of course/program concepts instead of 1:1 client-led transformational coaching (which would be Advisor work). You may even have a community as part of an online program, but the primary draw is the course or content, with the community being a wonderful way to embed the learning.

You have to balance three priority areas: content development, student experience, and audience growth. In content development, you'll devote time to distilling and curating your insights into salable content, as well as designing the learning experience so that your customers get results. While you aren't "delivering" for clients in a 1:1 setting, you trade off that time in delivering the student experience: setting up onboarding, progress check-ins, and offboarding processes; creating accessible delivery for different learning styles; and hosting live sessions. You'll need to train anyone delivering your material. Particularly if there's a specific outcome that can be "achieved" (and therefore enrollment ends), you'll need a continued inflow of students so that the third pillar of your time is spent building your audience.

What You Get:

- Your revenue is no longer capped by the number of hours you have and the price you can charge (the implied price per hour). You're selling your knowledge in a one-to-many model.
- With less time spent on delivering, you have more free time to create content and teachings. *Free* white space on your calendar!
- People who thrive as teachers truly love to educate others. They are interested in putting their point of view out there—willing to be visible. Some people love that, and some people hate it.

What You Give:

- To serve more people, you have to have more people to serve! This means you have to have a larger network or audience to make the math "math."

- In addition to marketing to get this audience and learning how to grow your audience, you're also spending additional unpaid time up front developing assets and content that are not immediately salable.
- Process gaps that are forgivable in a one-on-one model aren't an option with groups or in asynchronous settings. The materials have to be codified, onboarding must be lower touch, and your methods have to work when you're not communicating with clients individually or personally delivering work with a high-touch service. The results and the transformation must be delivered in a less customized fashion.
- You have to spend a lot of time and energy making and upkeeping systems and tech, depending on the size of your program.
- You have to be skilled at holding space for groups, deciding how you'll facilitate a small group vs. a larger group (especially if you're transitioning from 1:1 services).

Example:

Jane helps creators monetize through content, courses, and creative digital products. She has low-priced courses (under $100), medium-priced courses (~$500), and a high-priced signature program ($3,000), all delivered as self-guided courses. On a given day, Jane might sell three to four $100 courses and one medium-priced course, and every few days, she sells a signature program (for an average of $1,000 per customer, assuming some are repeats). Jane can make over a million per year in revenue but spends a large portion of her money on advertising, with as much as 50% of her revenue going to ad costs.

Jane has also been in business for a decade, amassing an email list of 20,000 subscribers. With those purchase rates, assuming a total of 800 customers in a year, that's about 5% of her list buying in a given year. *(If your list was at 1,000, you might sell to 50 customers—a revenue of about $50,000 in total, a very different number!)*

While her calendar is free of calls, Jane spends time every day with her daily revenue generation routine: emailing her email list, setting up and managing ad campaigns, posting on social media, creating podcasts and other long-form content, updating email automations and campaigns, and creating new course content.

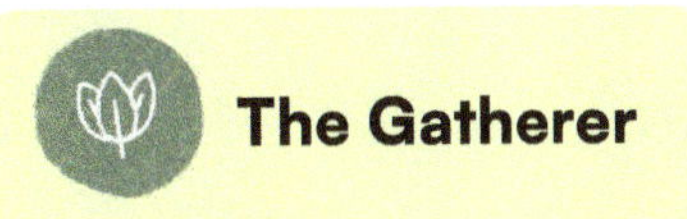

Short Description: Selling a member-to-member community or live events

Inspiration: Interest-based communities (e.g., around mindful productivity or shipping your creative projects), communities of practice (e.g., a community for independent consultants), retreats, events/conferences, community-organized masterminds

The Teacher is a hub-and-spoke model, where people are learning from you. In contrast, in the Gatherer model, people have a relationship with each other facilitated by you, brought together by your premise and your promise.

Gatherer models can involve online or in-person communities, retreats, or events. Often, there is no prescribed outcome, simply a premise around which to gather people who want to learn, share, or connect more about the subject. There are rhythms and rituals to a community and places where they connect. While the selling point of a community might be to provide content or promise a transformation, the reason participants continue to come back is the relationships—specifically, the relationships are with each other as much or more than with the host/facilitator.

Often, the Gatherer is looking for a place to belong, where their interests can be shared without the pressure of needing to have all the answers or be the "guru." They get to participate as much as lead.

In this model, your primary focus is on how to structure the community, build rituals and rhythms, and ensure engagement while maintaining a strong culture and norms—and, at the same time, attracting new members. In the Gatherer model, three forces are at play: designing engagement for the individual, designing engagement for the existing community, and designing methods to attract and onboard new members without substantial churn or community degradation. All three have to work in concert for a community experience to be beneficial to all.

People stay for a long period of time, so as the leader, you have to consider how to avoid getting bored of the same content year in and year out—and how to make sure you keep engagement high for that length of time. Moreover, since members are often coming and going, you are always managing churn. Seeing people leave can take its toll on your nervous system, especially if they are long-time members or have become friends.

What You Get:
- Because there is no natural end point, people may stay in communities like this for a really long time or return month after month for events. These types of communities can compound and build membership value and numbers over time.
- As the long-term value lies in members' relationships with each other, and not with the leader, there's less pressure to create new content to keep the value of the community high (as in a teacher-based model like a content subscription).
- Over time, there's less focus on you having to show up and add value—the value is in the other members showing up and participating.

What You Give:
- This model requires intentional, well-executed community cultivation. You can't just promise one person something; you have to think about design that adds value at varying levels of community engagement.
- The leader must set the tone and work to facilitate connection. So while you're not delivering, you're behind the scenes designing the experience to make this model sustainable.
- The value—both for members as well as revenue—often increases with more people.
- In-person experiences do come with hard costs of event space and/or food.
- Designing experiences that bring people together requires awareness of adult learning, community design, and content and community moderation. How are you brokering mutual value and stewarding a code of conduct? How are you keeping legacy members engaged while welcoming new members and maintaining culture?

- Particularly in a society where community is not always valued, it can be hard to get people to justify spending money on relationship building.

Examples:

Jay leads a community for established creators looking to become stronger creators and business owners. His primary offer is a $2,000/year membership, with a community forum, live events, and access to all of his courses. With 200 members, that membership model brings in $350,000/year, as some members joined with legacy pricing. In addition, Jay supplements his income through a lower-priced membership (the Gatherer), digital products (the Teacher), and sponsorship revenue (the Edu-Tainer model, discussed next).

Meghan leads trainings, events, and a community to help women embrace rituals and a connection to nature. While she runs a hybrid model, her primary model is the Gatherer. Fifty humans gather in the community for new and full moon gatherings and regular rituals ($44/month, $26,000/year), and the community meets each summer for a retreat (seventy-five participants at $595 for $45,000 gross revenue). The model is supplemented by single-ticket purchases to new moon meditations and a cohort-based Circle Leader Training ($750 per person, thirty people per year) for a total estimated gross revenue of slightly over $100,000—before paying expenses for the retreat camping site and the community moderators and guest teachers.

The Edu-Tainer

Short Description: Monetizing your audience directly (user subscriptions) or indirectly (sponsorships, ads, keynote speaking)

Inspiration: Speaking, monetized video/audio/written content through ads, affiliates, sponsorships, brand partnerships, or user subscriptions (paid newsletters, Patreon model)

As an Edu-Tainer, you make your money by truly monetizing your audience, either indirectly (through sponsorships, ads, affiliate revenue, or keynote speaking opportunities) or directly (through user donations, subscriptions, or royalties). In the purist model, your audience does not get contact with you directly, either through courses or live events. You're making money based on the size of your audience. While it takes a long time to build a platform—or luck, if you go viral—you're afforded a lot of creative freedom once that platform is built.

People who thrive as Edu-Tainers have the stomach to play the audience-building, speaking-circuit, or book-building game. They are relentless in their development and creating to truly build a following. They're willing to invest in storytelling and presentation skills and become very skilled at marketing. They have to be good at wielding influence and building relationships, which will lead to jumps in their revenue and influence.

But the Edu-Tainer model can be a grind. If you're not constantly writing, publishing, or making content, at some point, the audience will get bored, and what you've built will fade away without other business models supplementing the work. You have a lot of autonomy with Edu-Tainer work, but there's always something to do—it's just not on your calendar.

What You Get:
- You get paid *(directly or indirectly)* for your creativity: creating videos, writing, or speaking. You can make a living as a YouTuber!
- The Edu-Tainer is a high-intensity model. Outside of your sponsored content or keynote speeches, there are technically no other deliverables you owe to a client.
- This model requires but also brings a high level of perceived impact. If you're a speaker or you monetize your audience, thousands (or hundreds of thousands) of people will know about you!
- If you love to perform, this is the model for you. You'll be getting likes, applause, and cheers.

What You Give:

- Unless you're famous or very good at speaking, the Edu-Tainer model can be hard to sustain—you're monetizing attention without a back-end business engine that can continue to make money from the attention you've captured over a longer-term period.
- The production value required for high-end content is expensive, and there are many moving pieces in the business. Most Edu-Tainers hire at least some content creation and business operational support—editors, producers, managers, PR, and marketing leaders—which means the money needs to keep coming in to cover payroll.
- Your money is often dependent on others who are indirectly paying: conference organizers, sponsors, and ad networks. What happens when the algorithm changes? You lose revenue and might be unable to get it back. What happens when a pandemic decimates public speaking? Be prepared to pivot.
- The more you publish, the more you get paid (usually). The schedule for speaking or publishing can be intense.
- It can be hard to sustain this level of attention, for yourself and for your audience: Your next book or talk might not sell as well, you might get bored of your content and burned out from making videos, or you may want to take a break from writing your paid newsletter but feel guilty because of your subscribers.

Example:

Emily is an author, public speaker, and podcaster. She has a lot of ways to bring in money: three paid Substacks ($20/month for 300 paying subscribers, for $72,000), book royalties ($5 per copy sold, 1,000 copies per year, for $5,000), and two podcasts with sponsors ($125 per sponsor/ placement, for $10,000). The more asynchronous side of her business brings in about $90,000. However, Emily's main revenue driver is keynote speaking ($10,000 for each engagement), which is only now starting to rebound from the COVID-19 pandemic. Emily has felt pressure to grow the podcast (which is hard!) and has a strict publishing schedule—but on the flip side, she gets to spend a large chunk of her days taking care of her health.

THINK YOU NEED TO BE A SCALED BUSINESS TO MAKE MONEY?

Just because an agency or creator-model business is more "scalable" doesn't mean it's necessarily more profitable. In this section, we'll discuss how the profit and revenue profiles of each model type break down by the core variables that impact your profit.

You're probably in business to pay yourself with owner's pay, which should fluctuate between 40% and 60% of your total revenue based on your business model.

You'll have taxes, mostly paid through either payroll or estimated taxes on your profit.

You'll have profit, which you'll choose to hold in the business for buffer, reinvest in the business, or apportion as your owner distribution.

But all of that is impacted by operating costs, which can eat away at your profit and owner's pay if not managed well.

The three core variables that tend to impact your proportion of profit and owner's pay include the costs to deliver your service, run your business, and market your business. The cost of your personal development, especially early-stage coaching and consulting, is a bonus variable that requires a longer conversation.

Costs of Service Delivery

The costs of service delivery include the cost of the team delivering the work. If you're using a solo delivery-based model, that is your time as part of your owner's pay. But if you're an agency, you'll have to add the cost of the team members involved in delivering client work. Even creator-based models may have a cost of service delivery if your team leads live calls or manages a community.

For businesses with teams, this category is often the highest expense, at potentially 30% or more of your revenue.

Costs of Operating Your Business

These costs include technology, software, accounting, legal, customer service, and administrative support expenditures. If you have a low number of clients or recurring revenue and expenses, you don't need heavy-duty systems or a large team to help you.

But if you're running a creator-based business that sells courses or products, you'll need software to host your products and sale pages, run your community, and email your audience. And as you grow, you'll want a team that handles back office tasks like product/course setup and customer service.

Depending on the complexity of your business, these costs often start at 5%–10% of your total revenue.

Costs of Marketing Your Business

Marketing is the sneakiest cost because it's so variable.

If you're running a delivery-based business? Your marketing expenses can be lean, especially if you work with a limited number of recurring clients. As you shift to a larger delivery-based model, you might invest in a marketing strategy like podcast pitching, speaking, or content creation support.

Where this gets interesting is in the creator-based models, where you need to continually reach new audiences. Social media, search engine optimization (SEO), and business collaborations are nominally free ways to get organic reach but often require a team to help create content or manage collaborations as you grow.

But if you need to drive thousands of people to your work, you may require a paid customer acquisition strategy, including ads, sponsorships, ad or sponsor management, and referral/affiliate fees. Those costs can run in the thousands per month in management fees alone.

Costs of Personal Development

If you're in the Entrepreneurial Casino, you're consistently sold the idea that investing in yourself is the only way to grow your mindset and your business. While it might seem that the fast path to cash is buying course after course or investing in a four- or five-figure mastermind (at least, that's what their marketing says!), none of that is necessary to build a sustainable business.

Am I always learning from someone? Yes, I am, as I find mentorship, community, and education incredibly transformative to my business. However, I am looking at what I can realistically plan to return from that investment and whether it is appropriate given my business revenue and costs. I encourage you to do the same.

Costs of Taxes

Finally, taxes. If your business makes money (including enough to pay yourself), you must pay taxes. And if you're not paying taxes, you aren't making money, and the tax authorities and banks don't like that so much if you ever need to show proof of profit. Work with your financial professionals to set aside the appropriate amount for taxes, using tax-advantaged strategies.

How These Business Elements Come Together

Inspired by Mike Michalowicz's Profit First model,[1] we have general expense ranges for the revenue in your business.

For businesses making $0–$250,000 per year (which likely don't have full-time employees), the ratios suggested for distributing the revenue in your business are as follows:

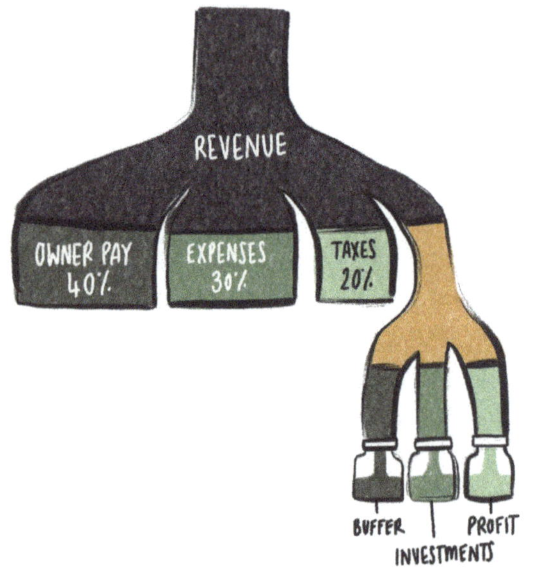

- 5%–10% profit/ investments/buffer
- 15%–20% taxes
- 20%–30% expenses (the four costs of delivery, operating your business, marketing, and development)
- 40%–50% owner's pay

1 Mike Michalowicz, *Profit First: Transform Your Business from a Cash-Eating Monster to a Money-Making Machine*, revised and expanded edition (Portfolio, 2017), 62.

This gives you a solid framework for how to stay profitable, pay yourself, and generate long-term wealth, which is the goal of running a small business.

While not as scalable, the Craftsman model (for a solo service provider) is very profitable. You can take home 60%–65% of your revenue—but you'll want to keep your expenses leaner than the Profit First guidelines suggest because your revenue likely can't increase quite as much.

We start to see the owner's pay for other models hover between 30% and 50% of your revenue.

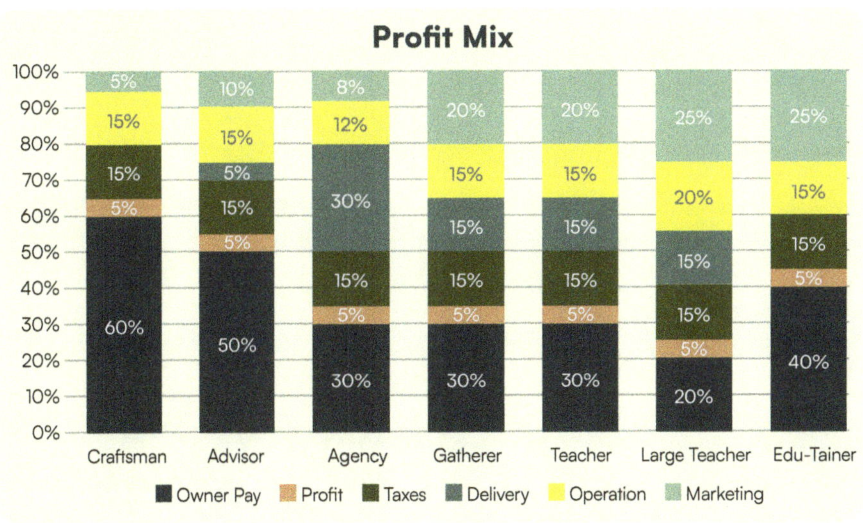

Teacher models can be modest (running small high-priced groups or cohorts) or very large in scale, serving thousands of students with courses and programs. If you're not careful, those models can hemorrhage cash. You've likely heard the stories about the "million-dollar launch," which drains cash (sometimes *a lot* of cash) because of payouts to the copywriter, launch team, affiliates, and ads.

The following chart shows what your target revenue needs to be in order to make ~$50,000 in post-tax owner's pay, based on these percentages.

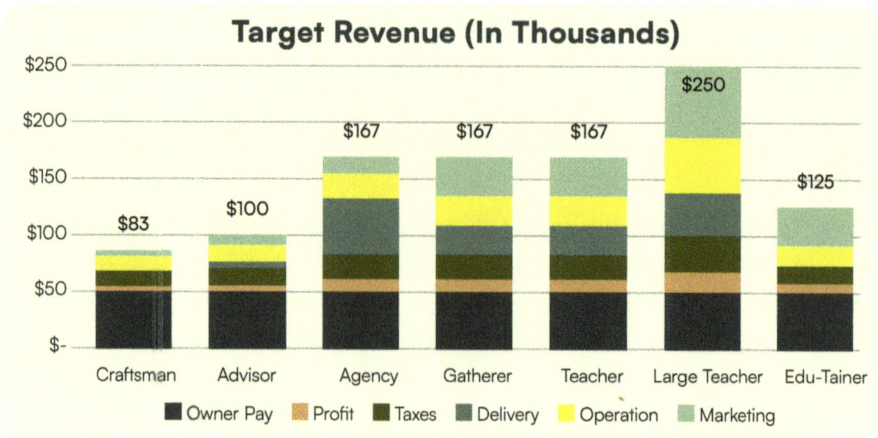

While you can generate $50,000 in owner's pay with around $80,000 in revenue as a Craftsman, I've seen Agency models struggle to have sustainable owner's pay under about $170,000 in revenue.

And Teacher businesses that rely on paid marketing need to generate $250,000+ in revenue to make the same amount of take-home pay once you account for the costs of marketing and operations (unless you're willing to do it all yourself).

HYBRID MODELS AND CHANGING OVER TIME
Benefits and Costs of Hybrid or "Multiple" Business Models

You may choose to run multiple models. A Gatherer can have a community but also work as an Advisor and sell courses as a Teacher. Consultants who primarily make their revenue through delivery can also earn money through books, courses, and speaking.

Of the examples I've included in this chapter, a few are running multiple models:

- Emily (the Edu-Tainer) makes additional money by offering an asynchronous coaching service (the Advisor) and runs a community (the Gatherer).
- Meghan (the Gatherer) has a cohort training program (the Teacher).
- Rachel (the Craftsman) arguably does a lot of Advisor work as part of her book coaching / developmental editing service.

- In my own business (primarily the Advisor), I have a group training program for emerging entrepreneurs and a content membership (the Teacher)—plus, long term, revenue from this book (the Edu-Tainer)!

However, running multiple business models, particularly if they are on different parts of the spectrum, can diffuse your efforts and increase the overall business costs. It's important to remember that there's a cost–benefit trade-off when you add or shift models. Each distinct model increases the overall cost and complexity of your business.

Going after audience growth and content creation to fuel a creator-model business is a whole different focus than the deep relationships, hands-on client work, and delivery process and system building that comprise the hallmark of a delivery-model business.

And if you're not sure of your "primary" business, it's easier to buy into the hype from the influencers in the house.

Do you *need* that academy on how to build a digital course and that expensive course platform software? Do you *need* that training on creating Instagram Reels and repurposing content all over social media? Not if you're in the smaller-volume delivery-model business, with a smaller number of clients and required audience size.

If you're going after a creator-model business, then you cannot ignore the requirement to get a lot of exposure to a lot of new audience members, often through a lot of front-end effort and publishing. (Delivery-model businesses can get by with an intimate network of referrals and may never publish content!)

In my own business, I am *stretched* across time, complexity, and team costs.

I'm fully running a **creator-model business**: finding time to create content for my own marketing platforms (a YouTube channel, weekly newsletter, and podcast), guest teaching on others' platforms to grow my audience and influence, creating curriculum and course material, and managing the membership, from tech to calendaring events. And, of course, the expenses that go along with this model, because I don't have the time or expertise to do these well: a podcast pitching agency, book coach, YouTube editor, and tech team that sets up the waitlist, checkouts, and onboarding sequences. (None of which I would need if I was just doing 1:1 coaching with clients!)

And I'm also fully running a **delivery-model business:** actively delivering with clients 15–20 hours a week in between live calls, follow-ups, and asynchronous support. While this model is typically high profit, the clients on the delivery side help offset the costs of running the creator-style business.

The marketing work I'm doing for my creator-model business fuels my delivery-model business, so it's not totally separate, and the work compounds.

It feels like I'm building two businesses because I actually am! Every week, I'm managing the deliverables and cadence of two different businesses, putting a nontrivial effort into allocating my own time and directing my team. I constantly feel the pressure to take on more clients on the delivery side than I might otherwise prefer to fund investments on the creator side.

Changing Models Over Time

The models you choose may evolve over time. Edu-Tainers may wait until their platform is large enough to add on a community, teaching program, or individual sessions. Craftsmen and Advisors might shift toward Agencies or scale their knowledge and intellectual property to the Teacher and Edu-Tainer models through courses, books, and speaking (like me).

Once you've built authority and a community that rallies around your message, the options open up.

But at each stage, it's critical to always know your primary spot on the spectrum and the purpose of each business model.

Are the course, cohort, and community the "offshoots" of my client work? Or is client work (one-off coaching calls, etc.) the "offshoot" of my creator work? For example, trying to make money with this book to cover my mortgage is different from using this book as a marketing asset for high-priced consulting.

These answers guide how you market and price different offerings and assess revenue and profitability.

THE SECRET THIRD MODEL: THE BRAND MODEL

Once your delivery process and/or intellectual property is sufficiently defined and your authority and audience are established enough, you may pivot to the third model: the brand model. This continues to help you build resilience as you sell to other organizations, which then sell to their customers.

In this model, you or your firm no longer deliver services, teach to groups, or lead a community. Instead, you rely on others to do this for you.

- **Licensing:** You license your frameworks and toolkit to licensees who use the materials in their organization or business and pay you a fee. Your job is to continue to build brand awareness and deepen intellectual property. This can be used to sell frameworks that others monetize, tools or assessments that others use and pay you for, or materials and programs that other organizations use internally. For example, Mike Michalowicz, mentioned above, has one licensee service provider firm attached to each one of his books.[2] He writes the book and creates the method, and a partner organization works directly with clients.
- **Franchising:** You might also choose to franchise, selling your proprietary frameworks and helping others start up their own businesses within a defined geographic location.
- **Certification Programs:** Instead of you delivering the work or teaching the curriculum, you certify others to deliver or perform the topic, and get paid for both the education to get certified and usually some kind of ongoing usage rights. StoryBrand, founded by Donald Miller, offers the StoryBrand Guide program, which includes a two-day certification framework, tools, and an exclusive license to use StoryBrand materials.

SUMMARY

Even if it's not completely defined, identify your primary business model at this present moment. Catalog how many different models you're currently trying to run and where they fall on the Business Model

---

2 Jay Clouse, host, Creator Science, episode 236, "Mike Michalowicz Wants You to Pay Yourself First," January 8, 2024, 50 min., 30 sec., https://podcast.creatorscience.com/mike-michalowicz/.

Spectrum. Recognize what you give and get from each one as you establish your future business model(s) and determine which ones you can drop from your portfolio.

Use the questions and examples presented in this chapter to determine both your near-term and your long-term desired model, and remember that this decision may shift once you've gained more experience, authority, and influence. These insights will help you filter the strategies presented in future chapters.

Reflection Questions 

1. What is your primary business model now, and is it a delivery or creator model?
2. How many business models are you currently running, and where do they fall on the Business Model Spectrum?
3. What activities are you doing today that might not line up with your business model?
4. What factors are most important to you in determining your long-term business model (including team size, schedule flexibility, impact profile, and marketing strategy)?
5. What is your desired future business model or set of models?
6. What is your ideal mix of business models, and how much variety feels sustainable for you?
7. What is one small adjustment you could make now to bring your current model closer to the one you want?

It's important to remember that there's a cost–benefit trade-off when you add or shift models. Each distinct model increases the overall cost and complexity of your business.

Building a sustainable business with real roots takes longer than the overnight success the entrepreneurial influencers are touting.

CHAPTER 2

What Stage of Business Growth Are You In?

ONCE YOU'VE DECIDED WHAT KIND of business you want to run, the second filter is understanding the stage you're at—some advice is good for bigger businesses, but that same advice will be ineffectual at best for a smaller business. At worst, it'll cost you time, energy, and money. Even if a strategy is solid for your *style* of business, as discussed in Chapter 1, it may not apply to your *stage*.

The actions you take to build your business at the starting point differ from the decisions you'll make to scale or strengthen it later on. It's important to know not only where you want to go but where you are now—without judgment.

This chapter will cover the five stages of business, how to know which you're in (based on your revenue, the number of clients served, and the growing pains you're facing), and how to think about decision-making at each stage.

Verne Harnish, author of *Scaling Up*, says $1 million is the first "valley of death" for small business owners. But for expertise-based businesses, thresholds significantly earlier than that require your navigation.

I delineated the five stages discussed in this chapter based on my background knowledge of delivery- and creator-based businesses. They are not based on the time you've been in business. On the surface, it may seem disheartening that you've been in it a long time and are not past the early stages. The Casino sells us this dream that building a business is fast and easy and should happen effortlessly.

But these stages are inspired more by nature. Building a sustainable business with real roots takes longer than the overnight success the entrepreneurial influencers are touting. It can feel shameful that we're not there yet. But only by acknowledging where you are can we do what needs to be done to grow those strong roots—instead of going viral and flaming out.

This framework for growing a business is inspired by the life cycle of a tree. It starts with the seed of an idea—a spark. As we move from seed to sprout to sapling to tree, we're both rooting down and rising up. We're putting in place the foundations that feed back into the process. We're growing as we see real fruits of our labor—some still small and green, some ready to eat. At each stage, you can't grow the topline (more results) without investing in strong foundations and systems and more personal and business capacity to support those results.

This process is not linear—it is cyclical. You might go through these stages multiple times and seasons. You might get to a certain stage of business and then decide to strip it down and reset in a different direction, with a different client or business structure.

Many other business growth frameworks are visualized by a linear process or ladder, assuming that the only direction is up and that the goal is to keep growing. However, with this framework, there is an option to scale but also an option to sustain—to stay at a place that works for you.

And, at some point, you may choose to wind down a product, market, or arm of your business. Just as nature has a period of closure, so do businesses. Constant growth forever and ever is a trick played on us to keep us paying—it's not how nature, or business, works. The seeds you plant for your past business will serve the growth of your next one, if that's the path for you.

SEED

At the Seed stage, you have the beginnings of an idea, the spark of a business. You think you know what's going to work, but no one knows what a seed will become! The goal in this stage is to test, explore, and get as much practice delivering your craft, articulating your message, and doing your work as possible.

You might be working another job or sunsetting your current business; this may be your first business or your tenth. Your idea will likely be general: "I wish I could make a business that did this" or "I want to be a copywriter, work with finances, work with people." At this point, you have a belief about what you'd like to do or who you'd like to work with but haven't fully formed or tested that idea yet.

The tendency at this stage is to rush to figure it all out—to know exactly what you're going to do and immediately become "polished and professional."

But what we're not taught or modeled is that this is a stage of exploration and experimentation. At this stage, you really don't know what works yet! You want to plant your idea in many forms, formats, and audience types and uncover the most fruitful ground for the seed to sprout in.

The goal of the Seed stage is to work with as many people as you can—even in a way that's not scalable for the long term—to get a sense for what type of work you want to do, with whom, and how. The goal is not revenue. Trying to optimize for pricing, packaging, positioning, or revenue at this stage is counterintuitive unless you're sure this is the only option. Your idea is a hypothesis that you're testing out with real humans.

What's hardest at this stage is that growth almost always comes from connecting with people, having real conversations, and doing things across marketing and delivery that don't scale while being bombarded with advice that puts barriers *between* you and doing work with people.

"Define your million-dollar offer!"
"Build that list!"
"Grow your biz by being consistent on social media!"
"Don't do work for free!"*

As you get more established, I agree with this advice. However, building your portfolio with a mix of free or lower-priced projects will accelerate your business-building efforts by demonstrating results and increasing your own skill and confidence.

At some point, developing a consistent offer suite will help you standardize your business, and scalable messaging and leveraged distribution will help you reach more people. But at the Seed stage, your business isn't there yet!

At this stage, people also tell you to "go all in" on your business: "Build your side hustle in 90 days!" But this stage often lasts much longer than people expect, and the financial pressure to optimize for revenue and sales can put too much strain on you. I encourage a bridge job or part-time work for most people at this stage. You don't need to make art full time to be an artist!

It can be really hard to fight this simple advice—but keep reading and we'll cover it all in Part II.

At the Seed stage, anything that keeps you from talking to humans and solving problems with your service or content is a problem. You don't need to invest tens of thousands into certifications or mastermind programs. You don't need to spend your time behind a computer screen or on social media or other digital marketing.

What you really need is to talk to humans. Solve their problems. Refine your thinking about the problems, your solutions, and your point of view. Start getting paid for that service or through that content. There are entire bodies of work, including my own programs, on how to navigate this stage through thoughtful experimentation and find ways to reflect and capture your insights (which is out of scope of this book). But rest assured, this is the stage where consistently planting seeds—practicing your craft as often as possible—will yield much more fruitful results than trying to architect anything perfect.

Perils at This Stage

Resist the urge to feel disappointed when something doesn't work in your business. In my own business, my first few proposals for fractional COO work didn't go anywhere—I hadn't learned who my best-fit client was yet! I felt like everything was hard because I was doing everything for the first time and I had to do it all by myself: It was my first time setting up my newsletter (and then re-setting it up), my first time leading sales calls that went sideways.

I look back on my early writing and cringe a bit—I didn't know my perspective and my voice yet. I was parroting my teachers instead of expressing my own point of view. I even hid my authority, feeling ashamed of my corporate and engineering background thanks to some of the more spiritual, nontraditional spaces I was in. I felt like having been trained in business by capitalist paragons was actually a liability and something to minimize.

And I fell prey to the many courses and programs promising that I could easily build my list, sell courses, and grow through social media. Yes—I, too, fell into the online influencer matrix.

You're Ready for What's Next

You'll be ready to move into the **Sprout stage** once you've worked with ten or so clients, with at least a handful having paid you. Celebrate the fact that you've overcome the first hurdle, which is finding that first paying client!

At this point, you're starting to notice some initial patterns and trends as to who you like to work with, how you like to work, and the topics you tend to reference most regularly. Your voice and point of view are starting to emerge. Not all clients you've worked with have been a fit, but you're still learning the rhythms of running your business.

To move to the Sprout stage, you're treating your business like a business, consistently dedicating time to building it every week.

You're still encountering some business obstacles for the first time and continuously creating new business systems, so you might wonder, "When will I stop feeling like a newbie?" But take heart in the fact that you've gone from a dream to something that has generated revenue.

SPROUT

You've been consistently planting seeds, and those seeds are sprouting into more and more clients. You have a business with growth, making at least *some* money in *most* months.

At this stage of your business, the goal is to tend to that sprout and turn it into a stronger seedling. You want to narrow in on what actually works for you and your business in terms of the front-facing systems:

- Clarifying the clients you really want to serve
- Refining your point of view and message
- Establishing the ways you like to market and deliver, with a focus on achieving some repeatability or regularity in gaining new clients or revenue

The goal is to go from a spark of an idea to some consistent signal and increased momentum.

You develop roots in this stage by cultivating structures and rhythms to your week, month, and year. You're consistently getting in front of new people, expanding outside of your existing network, and working with people you didn't already know when you started. You're building out the foundations in every system in your business—marketing and sales, delivery, financials—developing light processes for how you deliver your craft or content.

You're embracing the long game. You're working on your business regularly and seeing some efforts pay off. You may not be achieving consistent revenue yet, but you have clients, and you're seeing the glimmers of results from your marketing and sales efforts.

Your goal at the Sprout stage is to define and develop your message, refine your offers, and create a marketing and sales strategy that will bring in regular work or revenue.

At this point, you might want to make all of the investments to grow revenue: spread yourself thin on marketing and sales, pay for operational help, and make big investments to grow faster. But seedlings and sprouts are delicate; growing too fast will outstrip their foundation. If you needlessly make those investments, it's like adding too much fertilizer—it can actually deplete you of the nutrients you need to grow sustainably. These investments put pressure on you to bring in more clients and revenue than your foundations might support in order to pay for that help.

"Bring on your first hire!"
"Invest in paid marketing!"
"Time for that podcast/course/etc."
"It's time to scale to groups or bring on team members to get out of the day-to-day!"

You avoid that pressure by embracing **radical focus on the foundational elements** in your business as you expand your client and services base, build your sales confidence, and incorporate rhythms and rituals to sustainably tend your business in the Sprout stage—to provide it with loving nourishment, sunlight, water and to give it light support and structure as it grows.

At this stage, think about tending your sprout:

- Continuing to increase your skills in delivering your service
- Expanding your network
- Deepening your sales skills and marketing systems (see Chapter 7)
- Clarifying your client base and your process to solve their challenges
- Constructing the basic infrastructure needed to build resilience
- Raising your prices commensurate with your skill set increases

As you get busier in this stage, you'll be developing the skills to manage client delivery, marketing, and sales, building up your capacity to manage all parts of your business system over the long term—taking on fewer business-building projects at once, lengthening timelines, and being intentional about attention.

Perils at This Stage

During the Sprout stage, you have to reach people outside of your immediate network, which can be scary! When you're being bombarded with scammy AI-generated cold pitches and "pitch-slapped" with every new connection you make on LinkedIn, you don't want to do that to people you meet. And there's always the pressure to bring in revenue and meet new clients, which makes us feel the tension between hunting for the sale and building longer-term connections.

The antidote? Cultivating real relationships and authentically expanding your network outside of your clients. Build relationships with referral partners, business collaborators, and friends—fellow travelers who come from different backgrounds and communities in your business ecosystem. Make real connections with people who genuinely care about you and want to help you succeed.

This stage also takes real work. Not that all of the other stages don't, but in the Seed stage, the process does feel a little freer—a little bit of "F around and find out." At the Sprout stage, there's more to manage and a lot more structure required to build momentum. You're trying to formulate a hypothesis about what works, meaning you're focused on delivering repeatable services, driving repeatable results, and not trying your hand at something new each month when something isn't working or you get bored.

And more money can come with more problems. When there's more money, there are more investments you can make. A $20,000 mastermind? You might have the money to pay for it, but as someone who once fell for one, let me tell you—most people do not get a return on that investment. Bringing on a virtual assistant (VA)? I also did this, but because I hadn't yet dialed in my regular marketing and sales activities, I was overpaying without seeing a return.

You're Ready for What's Next

You're regularly bringing in clients and revenue, even if things are not always as consistent or profitable as you'd like.

You've established the foundational systems of your business. You've defined your favorite marketing and sales activities, have a core offer you like to deliver, and are starting to implement a process around how you deliver it. You feel confident in your point of view—and your message is resonating with people you don't know personally, as you're starting to get inquiries and clients from people outside of your immediate network. You have your finances in a system (even just a spreadsheet or Google Sheet can work for now) and review them regularly.

STRENGTHEN

You've built the business fundamentals, growing stronger by the day. Your sprout has turned into a sapling. But you can't do it all anymore or you'll burn out. Depending on your business model (see Chapter 1) and the client base you serve, you're regularly making more than $5,000 a month—up to $15,000–$20,000. Until this stage, you were just trying to get traction. The goal is to figure out where to go from here now that you have it.

At this stage, your business is growing. You're facing a squeeze point: You're busier than ever with client work, marketing, and sales, and time is becoming your primary currency. You have enough data to see what works, but you feel like you're operating in semi-contained chaos most of the time.

Now is the time to take what's working and put more systems and structure around it to make running your business more effortless.

The goal of the Strengthen stage is to turn scattered revenue into predictable, profitable, and purposeful effort—to be more consistent and effective and receive more support.

This stage forces you to confront many decisions—covered in this book—about where to go from this point. Sheer effort, intentional network building, and even most beginning-a-business playbooks can get you here.

You're facing a lot of choices, especially regarding how you want to continue to grow from here. *(You know how frustrated you get when you're asked, "What do you want to be when you grow up?" This is* that *stage.)* Your decisions will inform the investments you make, the foundations you build, and how you allocate your time and money to deepen your roots so that you can continue to grow. They concern who you serve, your business model, the revenue you *really* need, and deliberate choices about visibility, impact, and responsibility.

These are difficult questions, and the remaining chapters in this book will address them. It can feel limiting to choose a certain path forward, to say "no" to potential areas of growth and things you *could* do if you had enough time/cash/energy/people … but you can't do it all.

You can't do everything once you start to get busier. The tendency is to try to grow in all directions and make all investments at the same time, which will keep you from growing in *any* direction. And the Casino isn't helping you decide—in fact, the influencers are telling you that you *can* do and have it all (because you can't hire them or buy their program if you don't plan to take on their chosen strategy).

"Rebrand!"
"Launch that signature course!"
"Write that book!"
"Build that team, hire that support!"

How do I know all this? Because my own business has been firmly in the Strengthen stage for a while, and I'm constantly bombarded with this advice.

First and foremost, this stage is about strengthening the foundational systems that support the business you want to build for the future, helping you attain the following:
- Even more definition on the clients you serve and their patterns
- More power and effectiveness in your chosen marketing approaches
- Deliberate and profitable design of your offer structure and business model, for now and for the next chapter
- Your right-sized team structure (if you want one at all), including team size and roles
- Your revenue and profit goals now that you're doing more than just trying to get business through the door

It's time to get specific with what you like and don't like about your business. You might hear this called "niching." But rather, this is firmly establishing your authority: your messaging, positioning, client and other stakeholder patterns, and signature process for how you deliver work or frame your content.

Perils at This Stage

This is the crossroads stage, and choosing certain paths closes off others. The cacophony of advice is growing even louder and requires more discernment and internal alignment. Taking all the advice you get won't work. It'll contradict itself; it'll be too much.

At this stage, you might have the money to invest in all of the paths forward. You may be able to pay the "first cost" of a course or strategy (aka buy it) but not the "second cost" (implementing it) or "third cost" (running that strategy over time). You have more money than time, which can lead to your attention fracturing.

This is also the stage where, for the first time, surface-level and beginner solutions don't apply to your business. At this point, you'll have to navigate more foundational decisions about your business to craft your next chapter. Doing so requires a more thoughtful sequence of your business-building efforts based on the foundation you've built and where you're headed.

Grow a team? Raise your prices? Launch a group, mastermind, or community? Run paid ads or hire out lead generation and sales prospecting? Implement automations or client-facing tools?

All of these different decisions will fundamentally change the type of business you are building.

The bulk of this book is dedicated to the Sprout and Strengthen stages of your business. These are the stages where foundational frameworks are necessary to know how to grow. And if you try to follow all of the advice out on the market—you'll burn out and crush your sapling.

You're Ready for What's Next

You have a predictable, profitable stream of clients. You can reasonably expect a certain amount of clients and revenue from your marketing, which you regularly put effort into. Your influence and authority are starting to grow, and your efforts are compounding. You are managing the metrics in your business, from marketing and sales conversion rates to the profitability of your individual offers. You've probably onboarded your first support person to help with operations. You are consistently balancing your time between executing client and/ or content delivery, managing the administration of your business, and building foundational systems for the future. You've built out systems and processes to manage tasks and projects, deliver services for clients / your content, and codify business operations tools. You're consistently paying yourself the salary you want, with a comfortable business profit.

SCALE OR SUSTAIN

You've got a strong business, one that can weather storms and has been through cycles of growth and cycles of rest.

You have consistent revenue coming in that covers your expenses, your salary, and your profit. Depending on your business model and client base, you're likely generating over $250,000 per year, or over $20,000 per month routinely. You've established predictable profit and firmed up the front end of your business: your point of view, what you stand for, how and what you deliver to whom, and your price points. (Note: If you're making a lot of revenue but are still focused on "How the hell do I get clients?" and not actually paying yourself a market wage, you're still in the Strengthen stage. We can't skip and rush stages without paying a cost later!)

You've got sufficient operational and financial infrastructure to support you at this stage: You're up to date on taxes and bookkeeping, you've documented your client delivery with core templates and tools, and you have 3–6 months of operational expenses in your bank savings account. If you haven't hired anyone yet, you're thinking about it (and have enough cash in the bank to cover the first few months of their salary).

You've reached a sustainable point in your business. You're focused less on establishing your presence and more on stabilizing what's been built so that it can weather seasons and storms.

And just when you thought you were done with decisions, you're faced with making even more of them about what's next. You're at the point where the vision, strategy, day-to-day, and numbers are too big for one person to handle. At this revenue point, so much goes into making a business run smoothly at the executive, operational, and management levels.

This is the stage of deciding if "Scale" is next for you. Isn't that the natural next step? Maybe not for everyone.

A lot of the shine may have worn off your business. You've probably been steadily working for years to get here, and you're tired. The level of work that got you here may not be sustainable for the rest of your career. You might even wake up every day wanting to burn it all down. It's a stage of confusion, and the default is always to grow—to dive back into work. But this is a call to take a step back, out of the Casino—back to your body, back to nature, back to your values about life—to determine the right next step for you.

Scale: Do I actually want to keep growing my revenue? This will often require changing who you serve or how you deliver, adding a team, or conducting broader-scale marketing (often requiring more money and expenses). You may want to make a larger impact, lead a larger team, become more well known, or make more money (though it doesn't always work out that way). You want to do more projects, reach more people, and become more established.

Sustain: Can I make this business rock solid at the level it's at? This means tuning out all of the advice to "scale"! Sustaining at this stage means decoupling from the narrative of constant, relentless growth and the conferred status that comes with big and growing numbers. You want a resilient business, using the systems you've built and the momentum you've generated to stabilize with less net new effort over time. Just like starting a flywheel is tougher than maintaining it, the Sustain stage is about how to be more effective and powerful, with an effort that is designed for the long term.

The entire cultural narrative we live in tells you that more is the answer. More followers, more clients, that next revenue ceiling—*no matter the cost to you or your bottom line*. And this may be the case for you. You might aim to step out of the day-to-day, translate your services to a creator or Agency model, or change your impact and responsibility level (which we'll talk about later) to grow.

But keep in mind that not all businesses *can* grow to $30,000+ months. You'll need a business with a process you can outsource to someone else, a service that you can turn into a leveraged offer (e.g., a course, training, or group), or a client base that supports that kind of revenue. And not every business wants to grow beyond being a soloist.

If you want to scale, this stage is all about building support:

- Documenting intellectual property and a methodology that others can help you deliver
- Implementing standard operating procedures, task and project management, and a clear team communication process
- Investing in team leadership and management skills for yourself: hiring, onboarding, delegating, and providing feedback
- Standardizing marketing and sales activities, consistently focused on ensuring your pipeline stays full and your team stays utilized
- Increasing your authority and expertise by stepping into more of a CEO role
- Setting clear goals, metrics, and projects so that every team member knows how their work contributes to revenue and company growth
- Confidently managing your financials (you might want a financial pro here, which we'll cover later in this book)

Scaling is more expensive than you think in terms of both time and money. Starting this journey exhausted and low on capital and energetic reserves is even harder. Scaling becomes more challenging when you're depleted. This is the stage where you're investing in people, systems, structures, and changing offers, so you need to build the foundation beforehand.

But what does it look like to sustain instead? And why might you choose that path?

Perhaps you need something new. Building this business, especially if you've done it quickly, might have taken over your life. You may be asking, "Who am I without the building? Who am I without the work?" Particularly when building your business may have been a dominant focus for years (it certainly was for me), what else in your life has fallen by the wayside in pursuit of this goal?

Sustaining happens at this level of revenue and complexity by cultivating resiliency and regeneration for the long term.

- Resilient client conversion: Building marketing and sales strategies that work for you when you aren't working. This isn't about evergreen funnels (though that might be a part of it). Mostly, this comes from establishing authority and influence with others, including on platforms, who can speak your name in rooms you aren't in.
- Profitable offers where you can enjoy your desired amount of rest and recovery: In the Sustain stage, you want to use that built-up authority and expertise to design offers or construct your financial forecast so that you aren't required to sit at your computer 40+ hours a week, fifty-two weeks a year.
- Right-sized team: While you might not want a team that can "scale," you'll want to thoughtfully design your team so that you can step into the work you most love to do but also have cross-training on the basic administrative duties of your business.

No matter which path you choose, you can't scale inefficient or ineffective processes or you'll just end up working more as the business grows. We want to build resilience, quality, and profitability.

Perils at This Stage

If you've gotten to this level, you've been working hard for years, addicted to the high of growth and success. The tendency is to rush to the next stage or revenue milestone, and the temptation is to add more. Yet everyone I've worked with, including myself, comes into this stage tired, needing to catch their breath—even if it only shows on the inside. The faster you run through these stages without pauses and breaks, the higher the tendency to burn bright—and burn out. This is not the time to barrel through to the next milestone but to plot your course.

Before making any decisions, take time to pause. You don't want to rush into the default without taking a break and lovingly, ferociously interrogating what you really want out of this business and your life. Many people inadvertently "scale" before they are ready (because who wants to turn down revenue!) and then end up trying to recover from bad or expensive hires later, when they're even more exhausted and operating with less cash.

Taking a break might just mean "don't add more" while deciding what to do next—to integrate and metabolize, clean up what you've built, and rebuild your emotional, financial, and energetic reserves. Like in strength training, your nervous system has to catch up with what you've built. If you can take a real break, do it!

This is the season for doing spring cleaning and preparing for family to come over. It's also the season for building anticipation and ensuring demand remains over supply consistently, not just for a blip.

You're Ready for What's Next

There's no next step here: Keep growing, scale, or stabilize, but you're always managing the ebbs and flows of a sustainable business.

You have defined a business model that diversifies your revenue and delivery to avoid founder burnout and build in resilience. You have deepened your thought leadership profile and are consistently appearing in front of new audiences. You've built your right-sized team that allows you to shift to your desired role in the business. You have a robust operating system to manage processes, tasks, and communications with your team members. You're thoughtful about how to steward your power to ensure the long-term health of your broader ecosystem (which we'll cover in Chapter 4).

You're playing the long game in business, with the model that's right for you.

But you're always aware of your business's vital signs and realize when they indicate something is shifting.

SUNSET

At this stage, you've built a thriving business. You may have hired a team, your expense level is likely based on a higher income, and you certainly have clients and a community. But … it's not as easy as it used to be. Maybe your programs are no longer filling up. Your core clients and customers have ended their engagements. The default solution is to fix the issues on the surface. But it might be deeper than that—you might be in the Sunset stage.

At this point, your business isn't working for you anymore. You may have moved past the content and become bored of the same questions and topics after years and years. You may not want to run the business you built because it comes with too much management overhead and marketing requirements. The market may have shifted, and you now need to pivot and adjust. Maybe a product isn't working for you or your students anymore, or a certain delivery model or a business line is no longer profitable. Or perhaps your life circumstances have simply shifted: You need more flexibility, you have different priorities, or you want to retire from full-time work at some point.

Sometimes you might just be tired after a long push, but other times, the existential dread becomes overwhelming.

We're always taught about how to go after more, run after growth, but rarely are we taught how to end or transition.

Transitions and endings are filled with the grief of letting go. Something you've worked hard to build (with the blood, sweat, and tears to prove it) no longer feels fully or partially aligned. The message no longer resonates with you, or the market says, "We're done." The transition could come along quickly (like the rapid collapse of cohort-based courses in 2022, once everyone was Zoom-ed out and the world reopened after COVID-19 vaccinations) or slowly (e.g., feeling niggling or increasing resentment and increased burnout over months).

But it's important to be intentional about the transition and care of the business: yourself, your team, your clients, and your community.

Most importantly, what do you need to heal?

With the concept of "wintering" coined by author Katherine May,[3] we don't just have bloom. We also have seasons of transition and healing. And archetypes reflected in nature and in other spiritual lineages can teach us so much about endings, healings, and transitions.[4] Just

---

3 Katherine May, *Wintering: The Power of Rest and Retreat in Difficult Times* (Riverhead Books, 2020).

4 The Rider–Waite–Smith tarot deck has many examples. The Death card doesn't signify an ending but a beginning. The Ten of Swords card looks so disheartening (ten swords in their back!), but there's a sun in the background. In the Eight of Cups image, the figure is leaving full cups behind in search of what's next—it's a hard choice, and there is a grief in letting go.

like trees don't always grow, neither do our businesses. Only cancer grows endlessly.

Sunset is the stage of honoring what you built and setting a clear intention for what's next. Whatever it will be, new seeds have been birthed from the mature business you built—you can go through the cycle again, should you choose to.

And now it's time to plan with intention. We do live in late-stage capitalism, where not working for an extended period of time has to be funded from somewhere else, if not the monthly operations of your business.

When there's a Sunset period, you'll need to account for rest and recovery time. If you choose to transition to a related business, you'll have inevitably planted some seeds for what's next, utilizing your existing network and business skills.

But growing a business or business model from Seed or Sprout takes time and money. In this stage, we prepare financially and energetically for the transition.

Create Your Transition Plan:

- Decide which parts of what you've built to retain and which to wind down—or jettison things completely
- Clarify your life's financial requirements and compare them to your existing financial position
- Establish how much time you need to step away for rest and recovery or establish a lower lift schedule

Transition Your Business:

- Solidify your team for this next chapter and either support them in finding their next steps or serve as a reference
- Provide a transition plan for your clients and community, including connecting them with trusted referrals
- Prune away expenses to reduce your revenue requirements

Communicate to Your Ecosystem:

- Share your plans with your broader ecosystem and communicate your boundaries, including posting schedules and response times

Secure Your Support:

- Build practices and relationships that will be generative and replenish your soul while also keeping you from rushing into something new while you're still in transition

Perils at This Stage

The perils of the Sunset stage include waiting too long to take a pause or prepare to make a transition. The longer you wait with a sense of dread, the shorter your cash runway gets and the more options you lose. Instead of holding on with your team members or marketing spend, reduce your expenses and give yourself breathing room. That breathing room will let you rest, recover, and cultivate your next step—your next seed for this current business or for something entirely new altogether. Know your financial numbers cold, interrogate them regularly, and make clear-eyed decisions about what needs to be done so that you have options. You don't want to be pushed into either extending a revenue stream you resent or having to formalize a Seed or Sprout business idea too early.

You're Ready for What's Next

You're ready for what's next once you've completed the cycle. You feel rested and recovered, and you're now energized and excited for the glimmers on the horizon—your next adventure. That feeling of excitement isn't tinged with panic or anxiety about not having a plan. It's like the first signs of spring appearing after a cycle of winter.

You feel inspired to go through the stages of business once again.

TENDING TO YOUR STAGE

You might have a business firmly in one stage, or you might have multiple businesses (see Chapter 1), each in their own stage. Just like when you have multiple business models, the way you tend to a Seed- or Sprout-stage business differs from the way you tend to a scaled company. For example, if you have a successful 1:1 business, with dialed-in messaging and marketing efforts, and you're trying to launch a creator-style business model, you'll have to go back to the beginning of this cycle.

The business foundations you established for a 1:1 Advisor model may change for a more leveraged offer that serves an earlier-stage client. That offer may fundamentally differ in terms of the client profile, messaging and positioning, delivery style, and marketing and sales processes—even if your overall authority and point of view remain the same. You'll still need to test and iterate as you build out a new business model and do the things that don't "scale," as this new part of your business goes through the Seed and Sprout stages, even if your core model is in the Scale or Sustain stage.

Additionally, even if you're experienced in business, avoid the temptation to skip stages.

For example, early in my journey, I suspected that I wanted to construct a creator-model business built around teaching groups.

But when I was in the Seed and Sprout stages, I didn't know exactly who I wanted to serve or how I was different from other alternatives on the market. I also didn't have enough authority and influence (not to mention audience size) to make that a viable business model. Adopting tactics of "scaled" businesses—hiring out my marketing, trying to launch a community, building courses, even writing this book—were substantially less effective because I hadn't built my foundational roots by knowing who exactly I was serving and sharpening my point of view.

Now, a few years (and a number of rewrites to this book) later, my business is in a very different stage (Strengthen, moving into Scale), and strategies that bombed a few years ago are working now.

SUMMARY

It's powerful to recognize and honor your current stage of business and the primary actions to take at each stage so that you plant deep roots and build stable foundations for future growth. Instead of rushing and paying the inevitable price, identify the markers of a solid foundation that move you from one stage to the next. Above all, ditch the concept of the ladder or linear growth and embrace the ebbs and flows that accompany the lifecycle of a business, including when you need to prune your business and return to an earlier stage or even sunset a part of it.

1. What stage of business is my core business model in?
2. Do I have other businesses or business models in different stages?
3. What stories or narratives emerge when I consider my current stage of business? Are those stories supporting my growth or hindering it?
4. What foundational steps have I missed or are underdeveloped for my stage of business?
5. Are any strategies I'm trying designed for a different stage of business?

If you want to assess your business stage, you can take the Rooted Lifecycle Quiz, located in the *Leaving the Casino* workbook or in the downloadable resources at deeperfoundations.com/casino

No matter what you do, your work will have ripple effects because changemaking work always does.

CHAPTER 3

What Impact Do You Want Your Business to Have?

EVERYTHING YOU DO HAS AN IMPACT. The work you do changes lives, and you being in business changes *your* life. The question isn't *"Will this change lives?"* It's about *how* it will change lives, *how* it will impact people. There's a belief that having "impact" means reaching as many people as possible, but this isn't true. Impact can be felt in a more intimate capacity, with a two-way depth of relationship between practitioner and client or customer. It's important to learn the differences between these impact models. There is no "bigger is better" when it comes to impact—there are only trade-offs and your personal values, capacities, and desires.

Impact can be reaching the masses: You might create a large-scale movement that impacts millions of people, yet you may not know those you touch personally or see your impact on them. I will write this book, and thousands of people I don't know may read it (though I'm pretty sure I'll never create change at the scale of Oprah).

But remember, you cannot have a human-to-human connection with someone you don't personally know. While an online influencer can change your life by inspiring you or giving you skills, they cannot hold space for the deeper, relational conversations you might need to help you navigate and integrate change. This can only be done on a smaller scale.

When considering impact in your business, you must look at the different types of impact you can have and how your company's character and design have to change to support that desire.

Do you want to create a **Broad-Impact** business model, reaching wide audiences and amplifying change on a grander scale, facilitating widespread transformation and making a significant difference in the lives of many—with, perhaps, less personal depth?

Or do you want to follow an **Intimate-Impact** business model, creating meaningful ripples in your chosen community and facilitating deep transformation and impact for a select group of people?

We're often taught that impact is large-scale and macro. Our society is geared for mass impact. The default is to design for a Broad-Impact business model—to reach as many people as possible. There are so many rewards for large follower counts, like badges and monetization thresholds on YouTube, blue or orange checks on social platforms, and the ability to bypass the gatekeepers to more mainstream or traditional publishing. Follower count is seen as a proxy for competence and influence.

Most of the strategies peddled by online influencers (who by design have a Broad-Impact model) are geared toward the macro. But you may very well be called to serve in the micro, with fulfillment in the quieter, yet equally powerful, work of Intimate-Impact models.

With a Broad-Impact model comes bigger deals, higher-profile invitations, and a flywheel that's easier to move once it's built. You can have your lexicon in the population and drive a movement. You have a chance to change culture. In theory, Broad-Impact business models are more profitable, though the operations required to reach a lot of people usually cost a lot of money to run.

But when you're operating with broad impact, you and your thoughts are on display at scale. You may not want your voice, image, and thoughts all over the internet. If you want to stay intimate and more private you can still have a thriving business without having to be in a parasocial relationship with thousands.

Your impact model changes how success is "measured" and how you receive validation. At scale, you get more likes, more external validation, more press and PR—but also more trolls, more "haters." You might gain more revenue and more customers but then feel pressured to keep producing to meet the algorithm and hire a team to keep you and your work in the public eye. It's not cheap to have employees help you post multiple times a day on short-form social media as you day-trade attention. And Broad-Impact entrepreneurs may also feel pressure to maintain visibility and to publish even when their energy is low.

In contrast, when you are reaching fewer people, there are fewer "markers" of praise, fewer likes and subscribes, but often more conversations—a visual, felt sense from a human being about how their life has changed, which doesn't come through a press mention or number of retweets. With an Intimate-Impact model, you experience the joy of meaningful relationships or witnessing direct transformation. There are often fewer moving pieces in the business, allowing you more flexibility and the ability to maneuver. But there's also emotional labor in grappling with the intensity of personal relationships.

"Impact" and the ripple effect you leave may not be related to the number of people you personally reach. Your impact might be defined through the well-being and harmony of your group, community, or family rather than individual achievement. Maybe impact for you is the ability to provide sponsorships or accessible spots in your program, to provide free offerings, or to fund the efforts of other creators in your world.

Impact might be defined less by how many people you work with and more by the health and depth of your business and personal relationships. For instance, it can be the effect on your family—the ability to be present at your children's games, to have the flexibility to care for relatives or participate in your local community.

When you design for an impact profile that's misaligned with how you work best, you may inadvertently design a business that requires you to interact with more people than you actually want to serve or be known by. You might work best in deep partnership, directly with individuals, but can end up designing lower-touch and higher-volume offers for "scale." These models require different marketing strategies and very different levels of visibility, particularly online.

Many entrepreneurs want to create impact on a broader scale, without realizing the work it requires to get there, and they may hate the journey.

We are often elusively looking for the tipping point where marketing becomes easier because there's a groundswell of influence while holding on to the sense of privacy that fame can obliterate. It's a delicate balancing act.

People tend to know where they fall, where they're naturally inclined to be. But we're never taught how to connect our natural tendencies to business models and design.

Kevin Kelly's[5] words here get to the heart of the question of impact: "To be a successful creator you don't need millions. You don't need millions of dollars or millions of customers, millions of clients or millions of fans. To make a living as a craftsperson, photographer, musician, designer, author, animator, app maker, entrepreneur, or inventor you need only thousands of true fans."

No matter what you do, your work will have ripple effects because changemaking work always does.

But the type—the shape, the contours—of impact you'll have? That is a decision you'll need to make.

THE BROAD-IMPACT MODEL

You may aspire to impact tens of thousands of people—or even more. You want to speak on big stages, have a podcast with a large following, publish a best-selling book. You want to create movements, shape culture, or amplify a big message far and wide.

Or you may not want to "work with" people at all. You love strategy, innovation, and crafting a vision more than you love hands-on delivery. You want to do research, think deeply on a topic, curate resources, and then communicate what you find through your content.

5 Kevin Kelly, "1,000 True Fans," last modified March 4, 2008, https://kk.org/thetechnium/1000-true-fans/.

You'll have to come to terms with the specific impact you're having on individuals. In the Broad-Impact model, you don't know the names of the people you're impacting. The relationship becomes a one-sided, parasocial relationship between you and your followers. The connection might be deep, like with the impact that your favorite music has on your life, but that won't be due to your individual work with someone.

Characteristics of the Broad-Impact Model

Example businesses:

- A podcaster with a million downloads
- A keynote speaker with ten books, a podcast, and a goal-setting community
- A productivity expert with three books, 300,000 followers on YouTube, and a community with thousands of members

Broad-Impact	
Focus Areas	• Building a large audience • Developing intellectual property (frameworks, systems, or thought leadership) • Scaling content and visibility to reach wide audiences
Your Role	• The face of the brand • The primary communicator of ideas • The thought leader and public figure
Business Model	• Creator-driven, often with low personal interaction • Scalable offers that can reach a large number of people simultaneously

Broad-Impact

Typical Offers	• Digital courses, books, subscriptions, and speaking engagements • Minimal or no high-touch consulting, unless positioned as a premium add-on • Research
Revenue Streams	• High-volume, lower-cost products (e.g., courses, memberships, or books) • Advertising/sponsorships • Licensing intellectual property (frameworks or content)
Marketing	• Scaled marketing strategies: content marketing, SEO, email marketing, and paid ads • Heavy use of social media and digital platforms to amplify the message
Calendar Focus	• Developing frameworks and assets (e.g., courses, books, or videos) • Managing a team to support content creation, marketing, and logistics
Impact Metrics	• Audience size and engagement (e.g., follower counts, downloads, and views) • Revenue generated from scalable products • Media mentions and cultural influence (e.g., shaping a movement or conversation)

Pros:

- **Scalability:** Once the systems, audience, and assets are in place, the business takes less startup effort to keep growing. The flywheel effect means that growth builds on itself over time, making things feel less effortful—eventually.

- **Metrics and Validation:** Our society rewards external markers of success—likes, followers, press mentions—and these can be motivating, concrete proof that your work is reaching people.
- **Revenue Potential:** Broad-Impact business models (mostly Creator-based models) have a higher revenue potential, as you're serving more people without increased pressures on your time.
- **Leveraging a Team:** Most Broad-Impact businesses require a strong team (across content production, business administration, and even some delivery of your materials or running of your community/course), which means that you don't have to do it all yourself. You can focus on the strategy, creativity, and vision while delegating the details.

Cons:

- **Pressure to Produce:** There's always the next book, the next course, the next campaign. You're not just creating for the joy of it—you're creating to keep the business moving, maintain your high profile, and sustain the expenses of your team. And you might feel constricted to only talking about the one thing you're famous for to "please the algorithm" and your current customers.
- **Visibility Fatigue:** Being in the spotlight can be exhausting. For those who value privacy or find criticism hard to handle, the constant exposure might feel like a heavy burden and tax your nervous system.
- **Addicted to Metrics:** The flip side of external metrics? You come to crave the book sales, the podcast downloads, the social media likes. It can be hard to disentangle yourself from the hard numbers in your business, even if your creativity or the market shifts.
- **Limited Personal Connection:** You might touch thousands of lives, but you won't know their names. The parasocial dynamic of a broad audience can feel hollow, and you might find that you've given all of your energy away to people that you don't know instead of investing in relationships that replenish your energy.[6]

---

6 Glennon Doyle, Amanda Doyle, and Abby Wambach, hosts, We Can Do Hard Things, episode 367, "Glennon's Dramatic Social Media Plan with Amelia Hruby," December 3, 2024, Audacy Inc., 59 min., 40sec., https://podcasts.apple.com/us/podcast/glennons-dramatic-social-media-plan-with-amelia-hruby/id1564530722?i=1000678999468.

- **High Upfront Investment:** It takes time, money, and energy to build your audience and assets, write that book, and become well known. "Overnight success" is never overnight—usually requiring tens of thousands of hours, lots of effort behind the scenes, and a healthy dose of network strength and luck to build an audience that can sustain the Broad-Impact model.

THE INTIMATE-IMPACT MODEL

Or … you may desire to impact a small number of people in a deep and transformative way, valuing personal connections and seeing the transformation you've sparked up close with an Intimate-Impact model. Your idea of "scale" may be to gather a community that can fit around a dinner table for a potent experience. You work best in deep relationships or with deep focus on your craft for an individual or organization.

Your output might not be scalable to tens of thousands or more, but it is wildly impactful for those you work with. You'll know their names and backstories. You might work alongside them in your business, or in theirs, for years. You'll see the evolution of your work in their lives, the ebbs and flows of individuals.

You may cultivate a community that forms bonds that you get to both steward and witness. You prefer to have lower visibility and cultivate a connected ecosystem within your sphere of control and community in the world. You want to do your work quietly, with flexibility, rather than cater to the visibility demands of being a public figure.

In the Intimate-Impact model, the impact comes less from their consumption and interaction with your content and more from their interactions with you personally. Not everyone has the energy or desire to sustain that level of engagement—holding space for an individual's journey or transformation requires a different style of energy management and nervous system regulation for you as a provider.

You don't even need a thousand true fans. You may require only 4–5 long-term client relationships and be connected to just a half-dozen colleagues or communities. An Intimate-Impact model may throttle your income on the top end, simply due to the low number of people aware of your work and the types of offers that serve you best. But you gain the ability to serve who you want to serve, make pivots, and have more flexibility because you aren't supporting a huge team and being thrust into the public eye.

A large audience may not know your message, but you're deeply impacting lives and are invested in the personal effects of your work. You're not just calling people to sit by your fire but actually having conversations with them there.

Characteristics of the Intimate-Impact Model

Example businesses:

- A copywriter serving 12–20 clients a year
- A life coach with ten clients on their roster, classes with twenty people in attendance, and a yearly coach training program with six students
- A podcast production agency with fifteen shows in production each month

Intimate-Impact	
Focus Areas	• Building deep, meaningful relationships • Facilitating personal transformation and lasting impact • Prioritizing quality over quantity in client interactions
Your Role	• Trusted guide, mentor, or service provider • Directly involved in client or customer outcomes • Often a behind-the-scenes leader rather than a public figure

Intimate-Impact

Business Model	• Delivery-based, with high-touch services • Offers designed to serve individuals or small groups • Premium pricing to support desired value or revenue
Typical Offers	• One-on-one coaching, consulting, or mentoring • Small group programs or workshops • Bespoke services, custom projects, or high-touch delivery models
Revenue Streams	• Premium pricing for personalized services • Limited volume of clients with high lifetime value • Potential for long-term client relationships or retainers
Marketing	• Referral driven, with strong emphasis on reputation and trust • Community building through word of mouth or local networks • Targeted advertising to aligned audiences, like collaborations or paid placements in a colleague's newsletter
Calendar Focus	• Client delivery and direct interaction • Building relationships with business ecosystem partners • Content creation, but to establish authority vs. gain a mass following

Intimate-Impact

Impact Metrics	• Sufficient owner's pay and business profit • Client transformation stories and testimonials • Deep connections and ongoing relationships with clients and community members

Pros:

- **Personal Fulfillment:** There's nothing quite like sitting across from someone and seeing the direct impact of your work on their life or business. It's deeply satisfying to know the names and stories of the people you're helping.
- **Lower Overhead:** Without a big team or complex systems to manage, you keep things simple. Fewer moving parts mean fewer logistical headaches and, overall, a higher percentage of profit in your business.
- **Human-Centered Marketing:** Relational marketing is about trust, word of mouth, and personal connections, which are an extension of the relationships you're already building through your work—not ads, algorithms, or high-volume campaigns.
- **Different Levels of Flexibility:** The smaller scale of your business allows for more flexibility, creative control, and time autonomy, allowing you to step off of the public-facing content calendar or to take on different creative projects.

Cons:

- **Relational Energy Demands:** High-touch work requires a different kind of emotional regulation as you manage project scopes, deadlines, and results while knowing that another human being is counting on you.
- **Income Ceiling:** Just like with all delivery-based businesses, there can be a natural cap on how much you can earn from delivering services and small group programs.

- **Ongoing Effort:** Unlike a Broad-Impact model, there's no "set it and forget it" automated marketing and delivery system. Relational marketing and delivery require constant, ongoing effort.
- **Different Validation Metrics:** With fewer external markers (e.g., likes or media coverage), it can feel harder to measure your progress—or celebrate it.

DECIDING WHAT IMPACT MODEL IS RIGHT FOR YOU

Most "celebrity" entrepreneurs have decided what model is right for them by nature of just being a brand figure. If they cultivated the Intimate-Impact model, they wouldn't be a celebrity entrepreneur, right?

So don't assume that's the only model for you.

Look at other models in your community—creators, group facilitators, course creators, service providers.

Just like we have hybrid business models, you might also have a hybrid impact model.

Amelia Hruby[7] runs a podcast production studio called Softer Sounds, serving at most twenty shows at a time. The studio prides itself on truly human podcast editing, listening to each show and editing directly in the audio, vs. transcript-based editing. They charge a premium for that service. But Amelia also runs a podcast called *Off the Grid*[8] about how to leave social media. *Off the Grid* reaches thousands of people and makes money with a paid community and a paid subscription for additional episodes.

Jay Clouse[9] has built a platform helping creators grow through observation, experimentation, and iteration, with 100,000 YouTube subscribers and about 25% of his revenue coming from brand sponsorships. But his main revenue driver? A community designed for expert creators, with an initial limit of 200 people in the community. He could have grown the community (and the revenue) by enrolling many

7 Amelia Hruby, https://www.softersounds.studio/.
8 Amelia Hruby, https://offthegrid.fun/.
9 Jay Clouse, https://creatorscience.com/.

more people—but then he wouldn't know everyone personally, and the value proposition for the community members would be diluted as well. The retention rate in his community is outstanding, providing a reliable level of revenue for his business.

Also consider that your model may change over time, both expanding the scale of impact but also contracting that scale.

Khe Hy,[10] a Wall Street banker-turned-creator, ran a well-known productivity course for a few years, growing his newsletter audience to 40,000+ people and enrolling hundreds of students. But after the COVID-19-fueled course bubble burst, he wanted to pivot, to talk about something else other than productivity and escape the pressure of having to market within an increasingly difficult environment. So he ditched his platform about productivity and now does intimate group coaching for exited founders and Wall Street executives. Shifting from a Broad-Impact model of courses to a high-touch coaching model has given him the flexibility to make money while he goes surfing every day and embraces his creativity, making videos about Wall Street for social media and learning to create apps using AI.

What if we worry about creating "enough" impact? To answer, I turn to one of my mentors: "I know when I'm sitting across from someone, and they're telling me about the influence that [this work] had on their life or their thinking or how they're thinking in other spaces that they're participating in, I trust they're telling me the truth. It feels really itty-bitty, but I don't think it's small. But I think our ideology around small and big and impact and influence and size and grandeur are completely out of whack. And so it's nice to point yourself back to the spaces that you also get the most out of. Where do you find the most fulfillment?"

Use the reflection questions at the end of the chapter to get curious about how different parts of you approach the question of impact. Listen to your head, your heart, and your body and nervous system as you reflect on the impact profile for your business. One early reader writes, "My ego wants the STADIUMS, but my heart wants to sit across from people and get to know their stories."

---

10 Khe Hy, "The $645,099 Business Pivot," *RadReads*, accessed March 9, 2023, https://www.khehy.com/pivot.

Instead of being caught in the duality of broad or intimate impact, embrace a blend of both or take intermediate steps of impact as you grow your business. When parts of you are in conflict, consider the other questions in this chapter, such as your stage of business, and read the upcoming chapters on responsibility. As in every chapter, your answer to the question of impact will change based on your season of life and business.

SUMMARY

Set aside the question of status and get curious about your desired impact profile. Recognize the trade-offs—both the opportunities and the challenges—of Broad-Impact vs. Intimate-Impact models. And also recognize that your desired impact may change based on the season of your life and business. As in many of these business dimensions, there is no binary: You might blend impact models as you design a business that operates on a visibility scale between the poles of the spectrum.

Reflection Questions

1. Do you want to personally know everyone in your orbit?
2. If you sat down with your desired community of impact, would you fill a house party or a stadium?
3. Close your eyes and imagine your work's ripple effect. Are you picturing specific faces and conversations or a large audience?
4. Are you interested in being a parasocial figure?
5. Is the work you want to do either so focused on craft and research that it's done alone or so focused on serving many humans at scale that it has to be curated into content? Or do you desire to work directly with individuals and organizations?
6. Do you have the tolerance for the Broad-Impact requirements of visibility and publicity from a nervous system perspective?
7. Do you have the desire for marketing and public speaking to cultivate a Broad-Impact audience? Are your marketing efforts more aligned with Intimate-Impact by default? Where can you adjust?
8. What measures of impact are most in alignment with your vision?

Responsibility in business isn't just about fulfilling contracts or legal obligations. It's about consciously deciding how you show up for your stakeholders—your clients, your team, your community, and yourself.

CHAPTER 4

What Responsibility Do You Want to Hold in Your Business?

WHEN YOU'RE IN BUSINESS, you inevitably impact others: You exchange dollars for services or content, lead teams, serve clients, and impact a community with your work. We're taught to look at success in business based on our revenue and profit goals. But rarely do we ask, what is the responsibility we want to hold? Responsibility is the commitment to act with care and integrity toward the people and systems we affect through our actions. It encompasses the promises we make—explicitly or implicitly—to ourselves, our clients, our teams, and our broader communities. Responsibility is about recognizing the impacts of our choices and striving to thoughtfully and ethically balance those impacts.

Responsibility in business isn't just about fulfilling contracts or legal obligations. It's about consciously deciding how you show up for your stakeholders—your clients, your team, your community, and yourself.

When we interrogate responsibility in our business, we ask about the duty that we have to others based on our word and our commitments and the trade-offs required when the needs of one stakeholder are at odds with those of another. While we're taught to continue growing— build the team, expand your audience, grow your revenue—we don't ask what responsibilities we must balance to support that growth and how different business structures change the type of responsibility we must carry and to whom.

When we evaluate responsibility and what we are prepared to balance and carry, we must look at the following four lenses: the self, the team, the clients, and the community.[11] This lens of responsibility has been adapted from Kelly Diels.

Responsibility in business is never static; it evolves alongside your business model, stage of growth, and life circumstances. Every choice you make—whether it involves scaling your offerings, setting your prices, hiring a team, or deciding how to serve your community—requires trade-offs. And these trade-offs don't just affect one stakeholder; they ripple across all areas of responsibility.

Just like in *Game of Thrones*, heavy is the head that wears the crown. By nature, a larger business creates more responsibility. If you have a team, you must lead them, setting clear goals and success metrics. And, of course, you must pay them, ensuring your sales and marketing systems are robust enough to keep your team utilized. If your team delivers on your behalf, you still have a responsibility to your clients to ensure that they are getting what's promised.

You also have a duty to your clients and community. Our clients rely on us to provide the service they've paid for at a fair value exchange. But the clarion call of "growth" can entice us to build an offer or take on a client roster that outpaces our capacity to provide that service. If we choose to pursue a Broad-Impact business model, do we have a responsibility to use our platform and audience to further collective goals? Again, as your profile grows larger and more people look at you as a mentor and role model, the spotlight grows larger on you and your work practices. Exploring responsibility helps us manage these sometimes conflicting needs with care.

And of course, we cannot carry all of these responsibilities for others and fail to adequately support ourselves. As Kelly Diels says, "If the

---

11 Kelly Diels, "The Self, The Client, The Community," last modified August 15, 2023, https://kellydiels.com/the-self-the-client-the-community/.

feminist in the business isn't thriving, it's not a feminist business."[12] We have a duty to ourselves to build a business with which we can support ourselves (and our teams) without running roughshod over our own energetic, physical, mental, and financial needs. If you're working long hours and still not earning enough, your balance is off in your pricing, customer base, or offer structure.

All of these responsibility questions assume you're not consciously exploiting the stakeholders other than yourself. If you're reading this book, you're probably aware of the many ways that even "ethical" or liberatory businesses exploit their teams, clients, and community for their own wealth gain:

- Payment amounts or plans that stretch clients financially or encourage going into debt to afford their services, punitive payment plans, loopholes used to avoid giving promised refunds, and nondisclosure and nondisparagement clauses.
- Teams underpaid or saddled with a laundry list of responsibilities that far exceed the hours they're contracted to work while the business owner celebrates their "freedom" (and then uses their "success" as a reason to charge clients more money).
- Literal nondelivery of services as outlined in marketing materials— for instance, the creator or coach may not be involved in delivery, leaving clients to work with underqualified (and underpaid) "success coaches."
- Manipulative marketing practices, and the overuse of the "weapons of influence" outlined by Robert Cialdini, like selective testimonials, urgency, and reciprocity.[13]
- Using terms like "trauma-informed" without proper training or certification, failing to define clear boundaries about who they're equipped to serve, or operating outside of their scope of practice.

Traditional late-stage capitalism business is designed with one lens in mind: to create the maximum value for shareholders—either those who own the company or those who invest in the company through the

---

12 Kelly Diels, *We Are the Culture Makers*, online course, 2022.

13 Robert B. Cialdini, *Influence: The Psychology of Persuasion* (Harper Business, 2006), 2.

stock market—at the expense of everything else, including employees, customers, and the environment. We see big companies hire cheap overseas labor or price gouge to juice profits. And those practices trickle downstream: overpriced "masterminds," service providers who just don't deliver, business owners who hire VAs and expect them to do the job of three highly paid marketing managers. In this case, the balance is tilted away from the clients, team, and community.

In a world often driven by profit and extraction, embracing responsibility means questioning traditional norms and designing businesses that prioritize people and values over exploitation.

But even operating within ethical values, the question of responsibility still looms large. Different business models, structures, and growth stages simply require different types of responsibilities. And similar to the other chapters about impact, business structure, and stages of growth, there's no right or wrong level of responsibility. Choosing a business model that has less responsibility to a team or community isn't inherently better or worse; it's simply embracing what you have the capacity to carry. What is problematic is letting down one or more of these stakeholders because you listened to the Entrepreneurial Casino's advice and built a business that was unaligned with what you're really prepared for.

You might not be ready or equipped to hold more responsibility in some areas. You don't want the duty of managing a team and you dream of a work schedule where you can take months off in between projects—both of these choices shift more responsibility back to yourself. While running group programs and community offerings can be more financially lucrative, you might not want to navigate interpersonal conflict between members or lock yourself into a business offering you might tire of before long. Maybe you don't desire to be seen by lots of people on social media. You can still have a thriving business, recognizing the responsibility you actually want to carry.

But responsibility can be a gift. When you show up for your clients and community over the long term, your business gains momentum, and you become a trusted voice, unlocking doors to rooms you're not already in. Clients treated with care and integrity are more likely to return, refer others, and advocate for your business. Embracing the responsibility of leadership by building a team also means that you can grow a larger business while also creating an environment of mutual respect and partnership—and, often, better outcomes. Embracing the responsibility for a community can turn your business into a movement that leaves a legacy and generational wealth that you can distribute to others.

In each segment of this chapter, we'll look at what it means to be in balance and then examine how decisions about our responsibilities can impact each of these stakeholders.

THE FOUR AREAS OF RESPONSIBILITY

Responsibility to the Self

When we are considering the "self," we are considering our own needs: our financial viability, creative autonomy, time flexibility, energetic capacity, and ability to shoulder the other responsibilities in our business. (Of course, we have to define what "enough" looks like for the self, which we cover in depth in Chapter 5.)

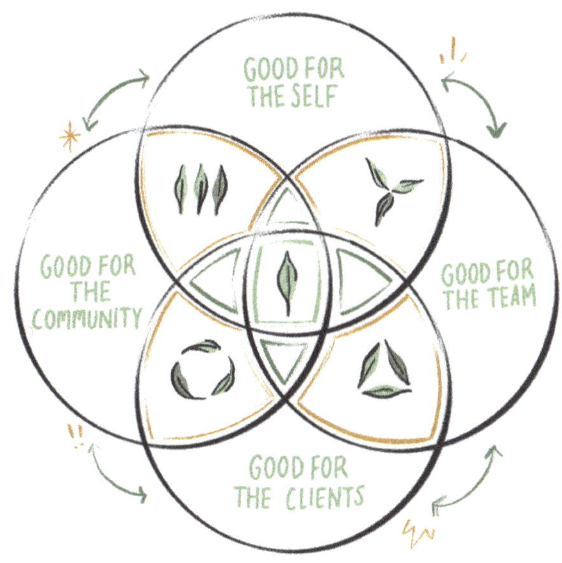

When the self is in balance, you're financially secure, creatively fulfilled, and able to lead your business sustainably without compromising your health or relationships.

Balanced:

- Your business generates enough revenue to cover your needs, pay yourself and your team fairly, and reinvest for growth without overworking yourself.
- You've set time and energetic boundaries that honor your commitments to your customers and team, and your schedule reflects your values and capacity.

- You monitor and protect your mental and physical energy, allowing for sustainable leadership and client delivery without risking burnout.
- You're pricing your services in a way that reflects their value while also meeting the financial needs of your business.
- You have sufficient creative freedom and autonomy based on your business structure and stage.

Responsibility to the Team

Certain business and impact models require us to take up the responsibility of leading teams—you can't be an Agency without a team! Other business models do not require this responsibility; you can be a sustainable Craftsman or Advisor with a small or nonexistent team.

So when we're considering what is good for the "team," we're considering whether we want to build a team at all—and, if so, whether we're prepared for hiring, training, compensating, and leading that team. We're balancing our need for control with the team members' desire for autonomy, our desire for freedom with their desire for clear direction and management, and our avoidance of emotional conversations with the responsibility of communicating to them with clarity and kindness.

If we choose to hire a team, we need to strive for balance: well-compensated members who understand their role, feel supported, and work within an environment that fosters creativity, loyalty, and a sense of shared purpose.

Balanced:
- You pay team members fairly, with wages and benefits that reflect their contributions and sustain their well-being.
- Each team member has a well-defined role, with realistic responsibilities, timelines, and support for success.
- There's a balance between autonomy and oversight, with regular check-ins to ensure alignment without micromanagement.
- Team members have manageable workloads that account for their contracted hours, avoiding burnout or overextension.
- Communication is open, respectful, and consistent, fostering a culture of trust and shared goals.

- You provide opportunities for growth and development, ensuring your team members feel valued and empowered in their roles.

Getting this right creates a team that is fairly compensated, knows exactly what's expected of them, and feels both supported and empowered. A balanced approach to team management fosters loyalty, collaboration, and a shared sense of purpose. By building the capabilities for clear communication, equitable pay, and reasonable workloads, you build a team that thrives—and, in turn, helps your business flourish.

Exponential Responsibility of Leadership

Your responsibility level grows exponentially when the number of people you bring on rises.

Hiring one person, like a VA? That's one line of communication.

Hiring four people, such as two marketing contractors, a community manager, and your VA? Now you're talking nine lines of communication, particularly if these individuals need to communicate with each other.

Hiring full teams, including team leaders? You'll need to lead through others, including developing their leadership skills and determining how you'll manage the department when you aren't the one having the direct conversations.

As you can see, your responsibility level certainly does not grow linearly.

Responsibility to the Clients

We got into business to help people! But even in this sense, we want to balance our responsibility to our clients.

We must consider exactly who and how we serve: our pricing, delivery and offer structures, and client communication processes. We could try and serve everyone but end up not making enough money because we're charging too little. We could accommodate all client scheduling requests but run ourselves or our teams ragged. At the same time, we must avoid underdelivering or underserving our clients in the pursuit of "scale" or revenue goals.

While certain business models, like long-term delivery-based relationships, might look easier from a marketing perspective, we end up carrying a lot of responsibility by working with those clients at a high level of depth and a high investment level. Compare that to the level of client responsibility that comes from delivering a $25 course—often an impulse buy that's substantially more transactional, with much less duty to the client and responsibility for their results.

If you build a business model of a community, membership / subscription, or retainer for the "recurring revenue," you have a long-term responsibility to your clients to provide that service through yourself or others, even if you need to step away from the business at some point. If you don't want the long-term responsibility, you might structure your business around impactful bootcamps or intensives instead. But for this to be sustainable over the long term, the responsibility you carry for your clients should match your desires.

Balanced:

- You carry a client or customer load that allows you to meet or even exceed your promises and expectations within your stated working hours.
- If you're a practitioner, you are transparent about your scope of practice and who is a fit—and not a fit—for your program.
- A majority of your clients see results because you've structured your services to meet their needs, with transparency about who is delivering and the quality level of the service.

- Pricing is fair for the value provided, and you have ways to serve those who can't pay standard rates should you choose to do so. Payment plans account for churn and fees, including your administrative time, but avoid significant differences from the pay-in-full price.
- Clients leave satisfied, often returning and referring others to your work.
- Communication with clients and/or customers is clear and regular, with communicated boundaries appropriate for both parties.
- Refund policies or "opt-out" program policies are stated clearly and provided without an unreasonable amount of effort.

Balance related to client service is uniquely personal. My own personal capacity for handling communication outside of "set" working hours will not be the same as yours based on our varying health, age, and personal circumstances. You may choose to have different program pricing, cancellation, or refund policies, again depending on your own goals for your business. Determining the number of clients and customers you can serve in a given offer is yet again personal: One person might be able to support twenty in a small group, and another might want to limit that same program to five people because of how they like to work and what works best for them.

Responsibility to the Community or Collective

As you grow your business, your influence extends beyond your clients and team. You become a mentor, a role model, and a steward of resources and power, whether intentionally or not. And others are watching and taking cues from how you operate. This responsibility to the collective includes the broader community you impact through your decisions, from your accessibility practices to the voices you amplify.

Balancing your responsibility to the collective means aligning your business practices with your values while acknowledging the limits of your capacity. Championing practices to balance collective responsibility can come with a short-term cost to your personal wealth, particularly if you are in a higher position of power based on your gender, sexual orientation, or educational background. But again, as with all areas, we need to balance our need to support ourselves and our teams with our duty to the community. This concept is about using your influence in ways that reflect equity, integrity, and intentionality.

Balanced:
- You incorporate tiered pricing, scholarships, or discounts for underserved communities while still maintaining the financial health of your business.
- You use your platform to highlight underrecognized[14] voices, sharing resources and opportunities that go beyond your own business. You advocate for diversity in panels, events, and collaborations, refusing opportunities that don't reflect equitable representation.
- You are transparent about who you're equipped to serve and provide referrals for those who fall outside your expertise.
- You steward the groups you lead or your public platforms with clear norms, expectations, and active facilitation to address harm when it arises.
- You go beyond mentoring by actively sponsoring others—advocating for them, recommending them for opportunities, or funding their work. You hire those within your communities, going beyond capitalism to foster a gift and reciprocal economy.
- You tend to your nervous system, balancing visibility with self-care and ensuring you can sustain your leadership role over time.

While these four lenses—self, team, clients, and community—help us evaluate where our responsibilities lie, they don't exist in isolation. Each decision you make about growing your business creates trade-offs that ripple across all four areas. Balancing these responsibilities requires recognizing the tensions between choices like scalability and depth, accessibility and profitability, and short- and long-term focus.

When we explore different business decisions, we must understand how the responsibility shifts across multiple stakeholders and what we're prepared to carry.

---

14 N. Chloé Nwangwu, "Why We Should Stop Saying 'Underrepresented,'" *Harvard Business Review*, last modified April 24, 2023, https://hbr.org/2023/04/why-we-should-stop-saying-underrepresented.

HOW RESPONSIBILITY INFORMS BUSINESS DECISIONS

The following sections provide an overview of how a given business might structure its model differently, even for the same title or service area, based on the lenses of responsibility.

Here are three axes to consider:

- **Breadth Based vs. Depth Based:** How changing the impact model shifts the responsibility for a therapist operating as a sole practitioner vs. an Edu-Tainer.
- **Accessible Pricing vs. Premium Pricing:** How changing your pricing and offer structure changes the responsibility profile for a business consultant.
- **Short Term vs. Long Term:** How changing the duration of your offers changes the commitments for digital writing education businesses.

Breadth vs. Depth

Just as outlined in the chapter on impact, building a Broad-Impact business is fundamentally different from building an Intimate-Impact business, as each has its own unique responsibilities and opportunities. Consider the different responsibilities of two therapists, one who runs a depth-based business (a private practice) and the other that runs a breadth-based business (a media arm and course/community platform).

A **depth-based business**, like a therapist's private practice, often runs with a small team or no team at all, so the practitioner ends up wearing many of the hats. While this setup offers the therapist flexibility and autonomy to design their work around their energy and needs, it might also mean managing billing or client admin during off-hours. This style of business works with fewer but higher-paying clients, creating space for transformative relationships—but, of course, there's the responsibility to consistently meet with clients to fund the business. There's often pressure to offer more accessible services in a way that's financially sustainable. However, because the therapist's practice is built through referrals, they don't need to maintain a public-facing platform and deal with that type of marketing. Instead, they can focus on their craft, showing up fully for their clients while managing their own energy.

A **breadth-based business**, like that of a therapist-turned-Edu-Tainer, brings an increased profit potential but also an increased level of responsibilities with that scale. This therapist no longer does private practice, but instead operates as an author, podcaster, and course and community creator. With a larger team, including a podcast manager, programs coordinator, and marketing specialist, the Edu-Tainer can offload a lot of the day-to-day tasks and spend more time in their "zone of genius." But with a larger team comes a heavier leadership responsibility: Ensuring the team is aligned, meeting goals, and feeling supported falls squarely on the business owner's shoulders. While there are no clients, it sometimes feels like there are what with the publication deadlines and financial commitments tied to book contracts and sponsorship agreements. While their programs are accessibly priced to serve lots of people, they also require constant interaction and fresh content to keep everyone engaged. And with a larger platform comes a larger spotlight, which can bring pressure to navigate sensitive topics or steer clear of divisive issues altogether. But ultimately, the Edu-Tainer has built a business that can run beyond their direct, daily involvement—which might be your dream.

Breadth-based businesses can be transformative at a societal level, highly profitable, and operate with a lot of freedom, but they require strong team and community leadership to avoid mismanaging team members or missing customer expectations. Meanwhile, depth-based businesses have personal connection and schedule freedom but may require a higher level of ongoing work to maintain financial stability.

Accessibility vs. Profitability

Another choice concerns pricing for accessibility vs. profitability. In this case, we'll look at two different business consultancies that work with expertise-based business owners.

Provider One, who focuses on **accessible pricing**, primarily works in groups, such as in workshop settings or over community calls. Their work is intentionally priced to serve as many people as possible, which often means they cater to earlier-stage entrepreneurs, those selling lower-priced products or services, or those who prioritize accessibility themselves. While the lower price point allows Provider One to serve a wider audience, they have the responsibility to bring in a higher volume of clients to make the business viable, which means using higher-volume marketing strategies. They must also manage the complexity of running a community, including the technology and logistics, and they have to hire an assistant who helps keep everything moving. While they sometimes wish they could pay their assistant more or spend less time marketing, they love creating a space that's accessible and supportive for those who might not otherwise have access to this kind of work.

Provider Two, who has a substantially **higher-priced service,** exclusively works in a 1:1 capacity. Their clients expect—and pay for—significant transformation, personal attention, and measurable results, which have their own level of responsibility. Every client engagement requires full attention, expertise, and customization, which can be both challenging and deeply rewarding. To attract and serve this level of client, Provider Two has spent years building their public body of work, refining their frameworks, and cultivating relationships with peers and industry leaders. While this type of pricing allows the provider to work with a smaller client roster, it also means that their price point is out of the investment range of many potential clients. So to serve their broader community, they've created other ways to share their expertise, such as offering a free podcast or newsletter as a way to give back to their broader community and continue making their knowledge available.

Accessible pricing fosters community growth and inclusivity but can stretch your resources thin, affecting your team and your own well-being. Meanwhile, premium pricing ensures sustainability for yourself and your team but may limit how your work impacts a broader audience.

Short Term vs. Long Term

The duration of your offers changes your responsibility levels as well. Let's evaluate two styles of digital writing education businesses—short-term vs. long-term offers.

The short-term educator runs short cohort-style programs, working with 20–100 people over six focused weeks. This model offers flexibility: After the cohort ends, the educator has some space to step back, pursue other projects, or simply recharge. But that flexibility comes with responsibility. Short programs require consistent marketing between cohorts to keep the pipeline full, which can feel relentless. Students get short-term results and a short-feedback loop but require a tightly structured curriculum that delivers those fast results. And because the educator's relationship with clients is brief, there's less responsibility for long-term outcomes, which also means missing out on the deeper connections and transformations that come with time. This model can also lead to fluctuating revenue, adding a responsibility for cash flow management. And because of this model's cyclical nature, the team may consist of temporary help rather than long-term partners, limiting the business's operational foundations.

The long-term educator runs a year-long group program with fewer participants. The longer timeline means less frequent marketing pushes but requires a carefully considered sales process to ensure the right people join. Over twelve months, the educator has to keep participants engaged, which means designing not just a curriculum but a full experience: milestones, community interactions, and ongoing support. The educator must lead the program for the full year and include prescheduled plans for vacations, breaks, or a backup plan if they are out of the office for any reason. There's also a higher level of responsibility for long-term results—clients expect to see real progress, which can feel demanding. On the flip side, the predictability of long-term revenue makes it easier to plan ahead, build systems, and hire a team to support the program. With the right infrastructure, this model can reduce launching fatigue and create steadier operations.

Though both have different embedded forms of responsibility, the short-term educator gets to enjoy the freedom of breaks and quick-turnaround results, while the long-term educator has the stability of consistent relationships *and* consistent revenue. The question isn't which option is better—it's what kind of responsibility you're ready to carry and what rhythm works for your business and your life.

A BUSINESS IN BALANCE

As we grow our business, it becomes quite difficult to balance each of these areas equally at all times. Certain business models, like the Craftsman, require different trade-offs: We have to limit the amount of accessible offerings we provide because of how our business model is structured. And other models, such as the Teacher, might lead to taking on more students than we can thoughtfully serve and support. We might feel pressured to bring on a team member at the Strengthen stage of business even though we can't pay the rates we would otherwise want to, or we may find ourselves dropping the ball with clients as an Advisor before we've put in strong processes and structures.

It's easy to get out of balance in the areas of self, team, clients, and community because running a business often feels like juggling competing priorities. Pressure to meet financial targets, grow quickly, or satisfy everyone's expectations can lead us to overextend ourselves, neglect certain stakeholders, or default to habits that reflect larger societal systems like capitalism or patriarchy. For example, we might prioritize revenue at the expense of our health (self), underpay our team to control costs (team), overpromise results to clients (clients), or ignore our broader impact on equity and inclusion (community). These imbalances aren't always intentional—they often stem from unconscious norms or reactive decision-making.

As businesses grow, responsibilities don't just increase—they shift. Models that seem more profitable, like breadth-based enterprises or high-priced offers, often place greater demands on leadership, systems, and delivery. Short-term models may look flexible, but they require more frequent marketing and fast results, while long-term models demand consistent effort to meet promises. By examining these shifts through the four lenses of self, team, clients, and community, you can design a business that aligns with your capacity and values while navigating trade-offs with intention.

Responsibility in business isn't just about what you can handle—it's about what you *want* to handle. The decisions you make about your business model, pricing, and structure shape not only your day-to-day operations but also your long-term experience as a business owner.

Some responsibilities might be aligned for you, like deep and long-term work for clients or mentoring a team. Others might feel heavy, like constant marketing or managing a large community. And vice versa—you may thrive on building a movement and stewarding a community or find that you love the public nature of marketing and don't want the responsibility of long-term individual client work.

SUMMARY

The key to achieving balance is to design a business that aligns with your capacity, values, and vision. You may want to build a business with more responsibilities to other stakeholders, including your clients, your team, and your community. Or you may be in a season where you'd like less responsibilities and to honor the business model requirements that decision drives. Some practices are truly out of balance and exploit stakeholders, but when you're in balance, decisions about shifting responsibilities become much more nuanced. Responsibilities in your business exist in the context of the responsibilities in the rest of your life. What's right for you in this season?

Reflection Questions 

1. What responsibilities am I excited to carry because they reflect what I care most about?
2. Where do I need to set boundaries to protect my energy and focus?
3. How do my choices in one area ripple across the other areas?
4. Am I carrying responsibilities that no longer serve me or my business?
5. How do my pricing and offers impact my ability to sustainably serve clients?
6. If I have a team, am I providing fair pay, clear expectations, and a supportive environment?
7. What responsibility do I have to my community, and how does that show up in my business?
8. As my business grows, what new responsibilities will I need to take on or delegate?
9. What does a balanced business look like for me in this season of life?

Responsibility in business isn't just about what you can handle—it's about what you want to handle.

What happens when the pursuit of "more" conflicts with what you actually want for your life? What happens when you lose sight of your own values, desires, and definition of success?

CHAPTER 5

What Is Enough?

THIS IS PERHAPS THE MOST IMPORTANT question you'll answer in your business journey. In a world where we're constantly sold the dream of having it all—money, freedom, creative agency, flexibility, autonomy, and stability—it's no wonder we find ourselves caught in an endless cycle of striving. The problem? These goals don't just come with trade-offs; they often contradict each other.

A business built for time freedom may not be very financially lucrative. A systematized, predictable business might lose its creative novelty. The image you're sold—a wildly profitable business that offers unlimited flexibility, creative freedom, and low responsibility—is unattainable for most.

And think about the people selling you this dream. Do they actually have it all, or are they sacrificing essential elements of sustainability? Are they deliberately hiding the costs and trade-offs behind their success? Or, worse, are they exploiting their teams and communities to sustain the illusion?

We live in late-stage capitalism, where "more" is celebrated at every level. More power, more wealth, more status—it's an underlying defense against society's problems. But what happens when the pursuit of "more" conflicts with what you actually want for your life? What happens when you lose sight of your own values, desires, and definition of success? That pursuit will likely bring you into conflict with your real desires—and with the other Big Questions raised in the first four chapters.

Without defining what enoughness means to you, you may chase a vision of success that isn't yours. The endless pursuit of growth can lead to resentment, burnout, and a business you no longer recognize—or no longer want.

The stakes of not answering this question are high. If you don't define what's enough for you, you create a hole that will never be filled. A growing, gnawing resentment about what could be possible because you haven't really gotten clear on what role this business plays in your life. It is so easy to get seduced by societal stories of success and never stop striving for more instead of asking what we really need and defining what is enough for us. This insatiability leads to constant dissatisfaction, no matter your business revenue or influence. Not deciding what's enough for you leaves you vulnerable to external definitions of success, especially in the entrepreneurial world, where highlight reels and overnight success stories dominate the narrative.

Author Luke Burgis, exploring philosopher René Girard's work, explains the concept of mimetic desire—the idea that our wants are shaped by those around us: "Each of us is surrounded by people who generate, shape, and manipulate our desires at every turn. The consequences of mimetic desire are startling. Because people learn to want what other people want, they are easily drawn into rivalries and conflict. But mimetic desire does not have to be in control. We are free to choose. And those who understand mimetic desire have a tremendous advantage over those who don't—they can use it for good or for ill."[15]

The questions we end up caught in are endless: Are you living up to the promise of what others appear to have done? Are you a good enough business owner? Are you simply good enough?

If you haven't established the business you want to run, you will always be comparing yourself to others and wondering, *"Am I the problem? Is it me?"*

When you don't define what enough means to you, you risk exploiting others—your team, your clients, even your community. Scarcity breeds shortcuts, and shortcuts often come at someone else's expense.

---

15 Luke Burgis, *Wanting: The Power of Mimetic Desire in Everyday Life* (St. Martin's Press, 2021).

This chapter is here to guide you through defining enoughness for yourself. We'll explore the Enoughness Framework—a way to understand the four dimensions of enoughness in your business: money, time, flexibility, and creative freedom. You'll discover how to set your own bounds, optimize intentionally, and create a business that works *for you.*

THE ENOUGHNESS FRAMEWORK

We live in a world where "enough" feels like a radical concept.

Capitalism thrives on scarcity. Its engine runs on the fear that there is never enough and the promise that you can always have more if you just work harder, buy more, or optimize your life. It teaches us to hoard instead of share, to compete instead of collaborate. And the consequences are seen everywhere—depleted natural resources, labor exploitation, crumbling care systems, and environmental crises that threaten the future of humanity itself. Many entrepreneurs reading this book might not yet know how they will pay their rent next month, and we have no societal safety net in case that happens.

The depletion of the commons—the shared resources and social structures that sustain us—is one of the clearest examples of what happens when we pursue more without boundaries.[16] From the Western

---

16 Kate Raworth, *Doughnut Economics: Seven Ways to Think Like a 21st-Century Economist* (Chelsea Green Publishing, 2017).

United States's disappearing water tables to the destabilization of ecosystems that once regulated Earth's climate, the costs of relentless growth and consumption are all around us. Yet our society continues to preach growth at all costs, leading to widespread harm not only to the environment but also to the social fabric of our communities. We see this mirrored in the business world: extractive pricing to vulnerable populations, selling a service and failing to deliver it, and even stealing others' intellectual property in the pursuit of profit.

Scarcity isn't just a sociological concept. It's a mindset deeply wired into our nervous system. Early experiences with financial instability, social comparison, or pressure to achieve shape how we perceive enoughness. We can feel the pressure to overwork, overproduce, or chase growth *not* because our business requires it but because we fear falling behind others or failing to meet external criteria of success.

- **Survival mode:** "If I don't take every opportunity, I'll lose momentum, and my business will fail."
- **Hustle conditioning:** "If I'm not busy, I'm not valuable."
- **Comparison anxiety:** "They're charging more, posting more, doing more—so I must not be doing enough."

If scarcity fuels consumer capitalism, "abundance" often becomes its spiritual mirror. Self-help and entrepreneurial influencers preach a message of infinite abundance: "The world is full of possibilities! There's enough for everyone!" This worldview may sound optimistic, but it often feeds the same hunger as scarcity, leaving us feeling inadequate if we're not swimming in wealth, time, and opportunity. For many business owners, more revenue, more clients, and more visibility actually create *more* stress, not less, as seen in the other chapters around impact and responsibility.

Both scarcity and abundance mindsets assume that nothing is ever enough—that more is always the answer.

As my colleague Kate Holly proposes in her podcast *The Space Beyond Scarce*,[17] the opposite of scarcity isn't abundance—it's sufficiency.

---

17 Kate Holly, The Space Beyond Scarce, episode 1, "Episode 1: Welcome to The Space Beyond Scarce," October 12, 2021, 59 min., 31 sec., https://podcasts.apple.com/us/podcast/episode-1-welcome-to-the-space-beyond-scarce/id1588805241?i=1000539088134.

While scarcity and abundance both focus on endless striving, sufficiency invites us to pause, reflect, and ask, "*What is enough for me?*"

In her book *The Serviceberry*[18] and its accompanying talks, Robin Wall Kimmerer speaks about sufficiency as a kind of balance or homeostasis—a place where we recognize what is enough for us, personally and collectively. She writes about the dangers of always striving for more. In her words, sufficiency isn't about scarcity or abundance; it's about contentment, justice, and balance.

Kimmerer's concept of enoughness challenges the relentless hunger of a consumer-driven system. She reminds us that sufficiency is not just about meeting our own needs—it's also about creating abundance for others. "When we have enough," she says, "that also means all the abundance that is left over, we can share."[19] This redistribution is vital for both our communities and the natural world. Earth has long shown us how ecosystems thrive when excess is shared, from the serviceberry trees that provide fruit for animals to the intricate fungal networks that nourish forests.

The serviceberry thrives in ecosystems where its fruit nourishes not only itself but also birds, animals, and insects. The same applies to forest root systems, where older trees share nutrients and water through their underground networks, ensuring weaker or younger trees thrive alongside them. These ecosystems model sufficiency, showing us that unchecked growth and resource hoarding are not sustainable. As Kimmerer says, the only thing in nature that grows without boundaries is cancer.

In this context, defining enoughness isn't just about your business. It's about resisting the narratives that pull us into infinite striving. It's about aligning with values like justice, reciprocity, and sustainability. When we ground ourselves in enoughness, we take a stand against a system that asks us to exploit, extract, and consume without end.

The Enoughness Framework offers a lens to evaluate sufficiency in your business across four dimensions: money, time, flexibility, and

---

18 Robin Wall Kimmerer, *The Serviceberry: An Economy of Abundance* (Zando, 2024).

19 Dan Harris, host, *10% Happier with Dan Harris*, episode 861, "The Antidote to Not-Enoughness | Robin Wall Kimmerer," November 13, 2024, 1 hr., 9 min., https://open.spotify.com/episode/49Qiac2ZdlxVzFrnk7vlhO.

creative autonomy. Each of these dimensions represents a key area where we're often tempted to overreach—or where societal norms push us to want to optimize without question.

But enoughness isn't about finding a perfect balance or checking boxes in each category. It's about understanding your personal thresholds—what's too much, what's too little, and what feels just right. We have to learn to recognize and navigate the **Zone of Enoughness**—a dynamic space where your needs are met, your values are honored, and your business is sustainable for both you and the world around you.

WHAT IS ENOUGH MONEY?

Money is often the starting point for understanding enoughness. It's essential not only for survival but also for creating stability, safety, and opportunities for growth. It would be disingenuous to not talk about what we need to personally thrive, to protect our futures, and to pass down wealth (if possible) to our children. However, defining enough money isn't about accumulating as much as possible; it's about meeting your real needs in the context of your life and values.

In the United States, the lack of a social safety net—no guaranteed healthcare, childcare, or retirement—means we bear the burden of providing for these necessities ourselves. Honoring your financial enoughness begins with understanding these needs, without guilt or shame, and aligning your business to meet them.

What does money mean to you? What does it represent?

Our beliefs about money can tell us a lot about how we feel about ourselves, others, and life. How money was treated in our homes growing up plays a profound role in shaping our internal stories around safety, security, and connection, in addition to cultural narratives of responsibility, success, and citizenship.

Particularly in the entrepreneurial world, money is associated not only with safety and security but also with status and achievement, trotted out as social proof by influencers who use income-claim marketing. The "six-figure" creators, the "seven-figure mentors," the "billion-dollar" creators—wouldn't you buy from someone who had proven to be successful instead of someone with a smaller business? Of course, business revenue is not necessarily indicative of the results you'll get if you invest with these influencers. Interrogating our relationship with money also requires questioning our stories about success and status.

I encourage you to reflect on your relationship with money and how it impacts your enoughness stories: what you may hope money does for you materially and emotionally and how you wish it would transform your life. Narratives about money are some of the most deeply embedded stories we must reckon with—otherwise, we risk acting on beliefs we'd rather revise.

Reviewing Your Numbers

This section focuses mostly on the more concrete requirements about money and how to understand your needs from a more numerical perspective. To understand your broader relationship with money in your life, I suggest learning from voices I've enjoyed, such as Ramit Sethi (*I Will Teach You to Be Rich*),[20] Bari Tessler (*The Art of Money*),[21] and Morgan Housel (*The Psychology of Money*).[22]

Start by understanding what your business needs to provide for you to feel secure. This process begins with calculating your **Survive Number**, the baseline amount your business must generate to cover the essentials: food, housing, utilities, childcare, elder care, and insurance. Think of this as the minimum threshold for living without constant financial anxiety. Generally speaking, your business needs to generate revenue that's twice your Survive Number to cover business expenses and taxes (see Chapter 1).

From there, layer in your **Sustain Number**, which includes what makes life feel sustainable and supportive: occasional travel, dining out, household help, or even a class or experience that enriches your life.

Finally, consider your **Strengthen** and **Serve Numbers**, which represent long-term financial health and the ability to redistribute resources. These might include retirement savings, investment accounts, contributions to

---

20 Ramit Sethi, *I Will Teach You to Be Rich*, 2nd ed. (Workman Publishing, 2019).

21 Bari Tessler, *The Art of Money: A Life-Changing Guide to Financial Happiness* (Parallax Press, 2016).

22 Morgan Housel, *The Psychology of Money: Timeless Lessons on Wealth, Greed, and Happiness* (Harriman House, 2020).

big life goals like education or home buying, and philanthropic giving or angel investing.

How do these numbers feel to you? Wildly larger than you can possibly conceptualize earning in revenue? Or within the realm of possibility?

Pursuing more money than is enough for you comes with trade-offs, as you would expect: a different client roster, a larger team size, more work hours, or a higher level of required marketing and sales. You might feel constrained in the other dimensions of enoughness, like time and creative freedom, feeling pressured to publish content more frequently than you want or take on clients you otherwise would say no to.

Again, our societal narratives tell us we have to accumulate more and more and *more* to be protected. Bill Perkins's book *Die with Zero*[23] challenges us to think critically about how we use our money in each season of life. The goal, according to Perkins, isn't to hoard wealth for a hypothetical future or to passively let it accumulate. Instead, it's to intentionally invest in experiences, relationships, and goals that enrich our lives now while ensuring we have enough for later.

This perspective pushes us to ask, "What does it mean to have enough money to live a full, present life?"

WHAT IS ENOUGH TIME?

How should we think about the amount of time our work will take up in our lives?

Time is another essential lens of enoughness, one shaped by a few dominant entrepreneurial narratives. Of course, there's the "hustle culture" entrepreneur narrative, where if we outwork our competition, we will emerge victorious. But beyond external pressures, many of us tie our sense of identity and merit to how much we work—whether it's proving our value through long hours, chasing achievement as a form of self-worth, or responding to the urgency that capitalism conditions us to feel. On the higher end of the range, how do we anchor the top of

---

23 Bill Perkins, *Die with Zero: Getting All You Can from Your Money and Your Life* (Mariner Books, 2021).

our workload, ensuring that our ambitions don't pull us past the point of sustainability?

On the other side—that of working less—we also see a few different narratives. The entrepreneurial bros promise that you can hack your way to less work and more profit. Other voices, like Kate Northrup (*Do Less*),[24] frame rest as a counterbalance to hustle culture, urging us to reclaim time from the grind. Meanwhile, activists like Tricia Hersey (*Rest Is Resistance*)[25] challenge the entire premise, arguing that rest isn't something to optimize or balance against work but an inherent part of how we move through life.

While these narratives challenge us to work less (and defining our upper limits is crucial), working as little as possible might not be the goal for you. What if the craft, the creation, the client relationship, or the act of building something meaningful is part of what sustains you? What if having commitments on the calendar keeps you engaged in the work?

Designing a business where you're completely removed from that work could be counterproductive—or even counter to the joy that inspired you to start in the first place. If you're a graphic designer who loves creating, would building an agency to take over design work actually be fulfilling? If you're a coach who thrives on client connection, would stepping away from delivery align with your values? Do you thrive with a largely empty calendar or a slightly fuller one with more external rhythms to it? The real question isn't just *how little* you can work but what level of work keeps you engaged, connected, and anchored while providing space for rest, creativity, and care.

My personal relationship with status and worth isn't tied to money: It's tied to time and achievement. I can look at money with a dispassionate lens, as something that funds my life. But the enoughness dimension that challenges me most is *time*. I've always measured myself through effort and achievement. I was the kid chasing perfect grades, and I'm now the adult chasing milestones. As an entrepreneur, I have the drive and the passion to work every day, and I'm rewarded for overworking. My

---

24 Kate Northrup, *Do Less: A Revolutionary Approach to Time and Energy Management for Ambitious Women* (Hay House, 2019).

25 Tricia Hersey, *Rest Is Resistance: A Manifesto* (Little, Brown Spark, 2022).

business grows faster, I receive external accolades, and I spend more time doing the things that I'm best at.

But if I'm not careful, work becomes everything. I spent much of my twenties and thirties prioritizing achievement over everything else. Relationships, health, rest—those were secondary to performance. Enoughness, for me, means reckoning with my stories about success, achievement, and worth. It means investing in the parts of life that happen outside of business. And it means setting upper bounds on how much I work, not because I don't love it but because I want to build a full, meaningful life alongside it.

As Oliver Burkeman reminds us in *Four Thousand Weeks: Time Management for Mortals*,[26] our time is startlingly finite. The goal isn't to cram in as much as possible or work as little as possible—it's to spend our time intentionally, focusing on what truly matters. Every "yes" is also a "no" to something else, and defining what's sufficient for you means deciding how your time spent aligns with your values and priorities.

Some questions to consider include the following:
- What impacts how much time you want to commit to your business?
- Are you juggling childcare, elder care, or other familial obligations?
- Do you need more margin in your calendar to accommodate fluctuating energy levels or chronic health conditions?
- Do you dream of sabbaticals, shorter workdays, or a travel-heavy lifestyle?
- How much time do you need to work to stay engaged?
- Are you prioritizing fast growth in your business at an early stage?

WHAT IS ENOUGH FLEXIBILITY?

Flexibility is often a core promise of entrepreneurship—the freedom to set your own schedule, work from anywhere, and shape your calendar around your life. But true flexibility is about more than just control over your schedule and working location. It's about creating a structure that adapts to your unique needs and capacities.

---

26 Oliver Burkeman, *Four Thousand Weeks: Time Management for Mortals* (Farrar, Straus and Giroux, 2021).

This may take some reflection and acceptance. There's nothing wrong with you if you can't fit yourself into the work styles or schedules sold to you as "most productive" or desirable for success—and trying to do so might be costing you time and energy.

Susan Boles, fractional CFO/COO, calls her work style a "potato-or-tornado":[27] "I am either going at 150 percent or I am going at zero. There is no in between. I don't have a consistent, steady effort kind of vibe. I am all in or I am sitting on the couch doing nothing. So I really had to think about how I structure offers that lean into that. Because every time I try and fight that, to let me do a consistent effort every day, I get so frustrated and exhausted because I don't really have the ability to sit at a steady 50%."

For many entrepreneurs, the need for flexibility isn't just a preference—it's a necessity. Living with chronic health conditions, managing neurodivergence, meeting caregiving needs, or living in a different location means that business models with lots of live delivery time or fixed schedules may not work.

True flexibility allows you to:

- Work during your most productive hours or at a pace that aligns with your energy levels
- Create asynchronous workflows that reduce the pressure of constant meetings or rigid deadlines
- Adapt your business model to prioritize remote work, seasonal schedules, or extended breaks

However, a business designed for ultimate flexibility often requires trade-offs, such as opting for fewer clients or less work during certain periods of the year. Creating systems and processes that allow for flexibility—like more self-guided procedures—or delegating responsibilities takes significant upfront effort. Maintaining flexibility might mean saying no to projects or clients that require too much of your time or impose on that flexibility.

---

27 Jessica Lackey and Meg Casebolt, hosts, Aggressively Human, episode 14, "14. Calm Business," featuring Susan Boles, February 20, 2025, 53 min., 39 sec., https:// aggressivelyhuman.substack.com/p/14-calm-business.

In some cases, growing your business might change your flexibility and what's required of you to maintain it. For example, if you have a team and, therefore, day-to-day flexibility, but you want to take a sabbatical, you need a plan for who is making sales, creating content, or doing client delivery so that your team still gets paid. Alternatively, if you're a soloist who still does all delivery, you get to craft your own schedule as long as you prepare for that with your finances.

Some questions to consider include the following:

- How predictable is your energy within a day and/or a week?
- How predictable is your schedule within a day, week, or month considering other responsibilities?
- How aligned are you with your clients' schedules or time zones?
- How many meetings can you have in a day before you lose focus or can't recover?
- What's your relationship with deadlines? Do you do your best thinking on a deadline, or do you need lots of time?
- Do you prefer to work in bursts with accompanying rest, or do you prefer a more stable level of effort?
- How much do you enjoy building and operating with systems vs. having the freedom and flexibility to deliver as you are called to do?

WHAT IS ENOUGH CREATIVE AUTONOMY?

Unlike flexibility, which often addresses how and when you work, creative autonomy is about *what* you work on and *how* you express yourself through your business. For expertise-based entrepreneurs, this is often one of the most personal and challenging aspects of the enoughness framework.

At its core, creative autonomy is about choosing work that energizes and excites you rather than feeling trapped by routines, expectations, or external demands. It's about working with clients who spark your passion, not just those who can pay your invoices. It's about preserving the space to explore new ideas, experiment, and grow creatively, even if that doesn't always lead you down the most financially attractive path.

While creative autonomy may sound like an obvious goal (isn't that why we got into business?), there are trade-offs. *Shocking, I know.*

Creators who gain traction in one topic often feel pressured to continue talking about what they've become known for, making it difficult to pivot or diversify. For example, you may have built a following by making content about productivity tips, but now you want to sell products related to creative writing or slow living—making that transition can feel both daunting and financially risky. In the online world, platforms and audiences reward consistency and predictability.

Creative autonomy also often means turning down lucrative opportunities that don't feel right for your vision, which can come at a financial cost.

Additionally, if you choose to grow your team, you need to consider adding structures and responsibilities. Incorporating processes that provide a stable operational rhythm in the business for your team (and for your customers) may lead to less spontaneity for you. However, if you remain a solo expert, you can choose to be more creative and experiment, knowing there's just you to support.

Some questions to consider include the following:

- How much novelty do you need? Are you what authors Russell Nohelty and Monica Leonelle[28] call a "Grassland" or "Forest"—with the ability to be laser focused on a single topic or intertwining worlds for years—or a "Desert" or "Tundra," always searching for the next new market or next new launch?
- How much business stability do you have in your finances and client roster?
- Are you in the season of planting something new, or are you in the season of completing the harvest for something you've been working on for a while? These are times where you might want much more creative freedom since you're in the dreaming or ending zone, not sure of what's next.

---

28 Russell Nohelty and Monica Leonelle, *The Author Ecosystems* (Russell Nohelty, forthcoming 2025).

NAVIGATING THE ZONE OF ENOUGHNESS

You're in the Zone of Enoughness when you've defined what's enough—and what's too much—for each factor. If one factor is truly undernourished or overstretched, then it limits your ability to feel settled across your business as a whole.

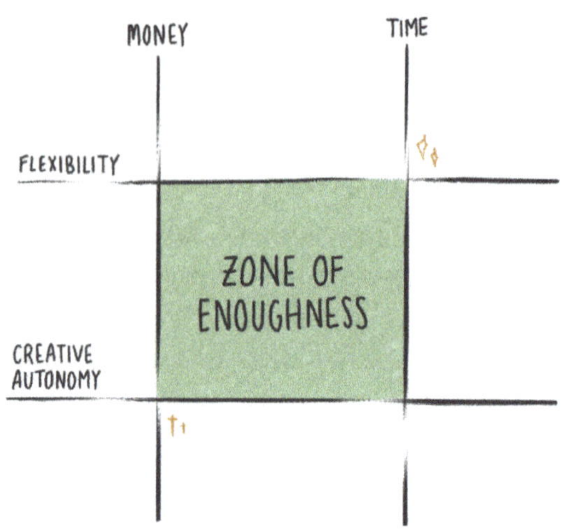

For you, that may mean working a fifteen-hour workweek with high-end accounting customers but then capping your revenue and saying no to fun projects that would fill your creative cup.

For others, that may mean working over forty hours a week coaching clients, making time to create lots of content (like this book), and working hard for growth—but that'll mean your calendar gets filled with colored blocks of meetings and not a whole lot of white space. *(In case you missed it, this is my life right now.)*

But the choice really is yours.

The Zone of Enoughness isn't static. It's a fluid space that shifts with your seasons of life, business goals, and personal priorities. The key is understanding that trade-offs are inevitable—and that those trade-offs should align with your values, not with societal pressures.

For example:

- **Money:** Pursuing more revenue might mean sacrificing time with loved ones or creative freedom in your work. What level of income feels sufficient to meet your needs and goals without compromising what matters most to you?
- **Time:** Aiming for a lighter work schedule might limit the types of clients or projects you can take on. Conversely, working more hours to grow your business might come at the cost of rest or relationships.

What are the minimum and maximum amounts of hours you want to work?

- **Flexibility:** The freedom to work from anywhere or on a flexible schedule might require scaling back on offerings that demand in-person delivery or synchronous schedules. What level of flexibility do you require?
- **Creative Autonomy:** Maintaining total autonomy over the projects you take on might mean turning down lucrative work that doesn't align with your vision. What amount of creative freedom is nonnegotiable?

Every move you make within the Zone of Enoughness requires effort, and every trade-off comes with consequences. The goal isn't to eliminate trade-offs but to navigate them intentionally, asking: *What am I willing to give up to maintain balance? Where am I compromising, and is it worth it?*

Factors Influencing the Zone of Enoughness

Navigating the Zone of Enoughness is deeply personal. It requires balancing the realities of your life with your business aspirations. Understanding these factors allows you to design a business that works for you instead of being dictated by circumstances or cultural scripts.

Caregiving Responsibilities

For those managing care responsibilities—whether for children, aging parents, partners, or even extended family members—your time, energy, and focus are often split. The "sandwich generation" finds themselves balancing the demands of child-rearing and elder care in a society that provides few support systems for either. These responsibilities may require shorter workdays, flexible schedules, or even periods of stepping back from growth-focused efforts. For instance, if picking your child up from school every day is nonnegotiable, you may need to design your business model to fit around that commitment.

Health Conditions and Neurodivergence

Living with chronic health conditions, different abilities, or neurodivergence introduces unique demands that significantly shape how you engage with your business. Health fluctuations might require flexibility in your schedule or the ability to take frequent breaks. Neurodivergence may mean creating workflows that reduce cognitive overload, leaning into your strengths, or eliminating environments that trigger burnout. If you have limited energy, what work lights you up the most? If traditional schedules don't work for you, how can you design a business that honors your rhythms?

Your Relationship with Leisure and Travel

What does leisure look like in your life? Some entrepreneurs dream of taking extended sabbaticals, spending afternoons in creative flow, or working just four days a week to create more space for hobbies and relationships. Others thrive on balancing focused work with short bursts of travel or taking entire summers off. Personally, if I never have to show up anywhere at 8 a.m. in the morning, I'm happy.

Your vision for leisure and travel directly influences the structure of your business. For instance, if frequent travel is a priority, you may need to prioritize a model that offers location independence or relies less on synchronous calls. If rest is central to your values, building systems to ensure you can step away for extended periods becomes essential.

Your Season of Life and Business

Enoughness shifts over time. Think of it on macro and micro levels: the big-picture vision for your business and the immediate priorities of the current season. The macro helps you stay grounded in your long-term goals; the micro helps you adapt to present realities.

Early in your business journey, you may need to put in more hours and effort to establish stability and meet your baseline financial needs. You might take on more projects or clients that aren't a perfect fit as you build up your reputation. This might mean prioritizing income over flexibility, time freedom, and autonomy. However, as your business grows and becomes more established, you may find opportunities to shift your focus. Perhaps you begin emphasizing creative freedom or stepping back to reclaim more personal time.

Your personal life season also plays a role. Are you a new parent seeking more time with your family? Are you supporting aging relatives and need to scale back on commitments? Are you in a period of exploration, focusing on creative projects that may not be financially lucrative? Or are you preparing for long-term goals like retirement that require more financial focus now? Each season brings different priorities, and the Zone of Enoughness adapts accordingly.

Enoughness isn't a one-time decision. It's a practice—a framework you revisit and refine as your circumstances, goals, and values evolve.

Ultimately, enoughness is about making active choices instead of being swept along by default scripts. It's about pausing to ask: Am I still aligned with my values? Is my business still working for me? Have I crossed into a space of "too much" or "not enough"?

Defining enoughness is an act of resistance. It's a refusal to play by the rules of a system that profits from our dissatisfaction. And it's an invitation to step into a new way of being—one where your business serves your life, your values, and the greater good.

SUMMARY

The Enoughness Framework gives you the tools to understand your thresholds for money, time, flexibility, and creative autonomy, allowing you to break free of societal norms and scripts. Considering enoughness as a Zone of Enoughness helps you navigate trade-offs between these factors with intentionality. Enoughness shifts over time, inviting you to revisit and refine your definition of it as you and your business evolve.

Reflection Questions

Money:
- What revenue level meets my essential needs (survive), provides stability and reinvestment (sustain), and allows for more creative risk and freedom (serve)?
- Am I making financial decisions based on what I actually need or based on external expectations of success?
- Where do I feel scarcity or excess in my financial goals, and what would true enoughness in this dimension look like for me?

Time:
- How does my schedule reflect my priorities, not just in work but concerning my broader life and responsibilities?
- What level of time commitment keeps me engaged in my work, and what level of time commitment makes me feel overextended?
- Am I making space for rest, deep work, and personal needs?

Flexibility:
- How much structure do I need in my schedule to feel grounded, and where do I need more flexibility?
- What work rhythms feel most sustainable to me—consistency, project sprints, seasonal waves, or something else?
- What external responsibilities (e.g., family or community commitments) shape my availability, and am I acknowledging them in how I construct my business?

Autonomy:
- If I had full creative control without financial pressure, how would my work shift?
- What projects, clients, or creative outlets feel most nourishing right now?
- What type of work makes me feel powerful and energized? What drains me?

Balance:

- What's currently overgrown in my business—taking up too much space, energy, or resources? What's undernourished?
- Am I in a season of planting new seeds (exploring), tending sprouts (strengthening traction), or deepening roots (solidifying foundations)?
- What do I need most in this season—financial stability, expansion, creative exploration, more spaciousness, or something else?
- Where am I making decisions for the business I want in the future vs. the one I have right now?
- How do my business responsibilities fit within my life responsibilities, and what needs to shift to create balance?

YOUR VISION MATTERS

There's no single "right" way to build a business, no matter what the Entrepreneurial Casino tells you. Each choice you make comes with trade-offs—some visible, others hidden beneath the surface. Your business model, the stage of growth you're in, the impact you want to have, your sense of responsibility, and your definition of enoughness all shape the unique contours of your business. These foundational questions ground your decisions, allowing you to create a business that aligns with your values and serves your vision.

But as we've explored, these decisions don't exist in a vacuum. They're made within a larger system—a society that feeds us default scripts about success, growth, and achievement. We're constantly bombarded with messages telling us what a "real" business looks like, how we should define impact, and why more is always better. The Casino is built to make you believe there's a guaranteed, step-by-step formula for success—one that leads to big things if you follow it and failure if you don't. It's easy to get swept up in these narratives, chasing someone else's version of success rather than crafting your own.

This is why your business vision matters so much. Think of it as your lighthouse—a steady, guiding light that helps you navigate through the noise, calling you back to what's true and meaningful for you. It reminds you to step off the conveyor belt of societal expectations and onto your unique path.

The Big Questions we've asked in this part of the book aren't just about your business—they're also about reclaiming your discernment. They help you recognize the forces pulling you toward default decisions and equip you to make choices that are aligned, intentional, and yours. They give you the clarity to evaluate the advice you encounter and decide what, and who, deserves your attention.

As we move into Part II, it's time to take this reflection and put it into action. You're going to leave the Entrepreneurial Casino—the seductive, high-stakes game of promises and quick fixes. The Casino thrives on convincing you that someone else holds the key to your success, but you've started to see through the facade. You've explored the deeper truths that shape your business, and now we'll turn our attention to the practical decisions that define it.

In the chapters ahead, we'll look at the core areas where the noise is loudest—pricing, marketing, time management, hiring, and offer design. For each area, we'll uncover the tropes you've been sold, the price of the game, and the foundations you must put in place to make decisions that work for you.

The Casino wants you to keep playing, but you're ready to step away. Let's leave it behind and build something real.

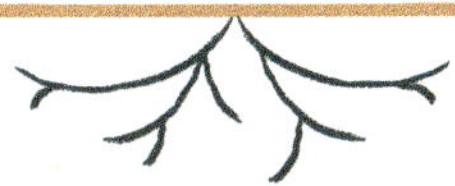

There's no single "right" way to build a business, no matter what the Entrepreneurial Casino tells you.

THE BIG DECISIONS

Your Strategic Business Foundations

There's no one right way to build a business, and no one—not even the Casino—can tell you exactly what to do. Part II will teach you the foundational frameworks to navigate every Big Decision in your business (like pricing, hiring, marketing, and more) based on what's right for *you*.

DECISIONS AWAIT YOU at every turn in business—decisions about pricing, marketing, hiring, offer design, and time management. These aren't just tactical questions; they're inflection points where the direction of your business can shift dramatically. And at each juncture, doubt creeps in. What's the "right" choice? Which path feels secure? How can you know you're not making a mistake?

We must face the Big Decisions.
And the Casino is there for you!

At every decision point, you've been offered solutions wrapped in certainty: blueprints, roadmaps, and "secrets" that promise to solve your problems and deliver everything you want. These offerings feel tantalizing because they tap into real struggles—pricing, marketing, hiring, time management, and offer design are genuinely hard. And when you're facing these challenges, who wouldn't want a simple answer?

But here's the thing: Most of these promises are illusions. The roadmaps and "proven paths" they sell rarely account for the complexities of your unique business or the trade-offs required to grow sustainably. Even when their advice addresses a real pain point—a tough decision, an area of struggle—it often oversimplifies the solution, leaving you feeling gaslit when it doesn't work or feeling like there's something wrong with *you*. Worse, it pulls you further into their system, convincing you to buy yet another course, join another mastermind, or hire yet another coach.

You're not crazy to feel disillusioned. You're not imagining that the solutions sold to you are incomplete or that they ignore the nuance of your business. And you're not alone in recognizing that these quick fixes often come at a cost—to your time, your energy, your wallet, and sometimes even your integrity.

The advice peddled by the Entrepreneurial Casino isn't entirely false. In fact, its power lies in its partial truths. The snappy advice we encounter— "Charge your worth," "Delegate everything," "Create passive income"— addresses real challenges in running a business. The problem is it simplifies complex issues into catchy slogans, glossing over the deeper work required to make thoughtful, aligned decisions. The cost of following this advice blindly is high: burnout, resentment, and a business that doesn't feel like yours.

The advice sold to you is designed to bypass your analysis, make you feel like you're falling behind, and convince you to spend more. So how do you stop chasing the illusion of a perfect path and start making decisions that work for you?

The answer lies in reclaiming your agency. You don't need another guru, blueprint, or silver bullet. What you need are *foundations*: the approaches, frameworks, and questions that will help you make decisions that reflect your values, goals, and unique business needs. These are the roots of your sustainable business.

Your business is deeply personal. It's a reflection of your unique gifts, your priorities, and the life you want to lead. One-size-fits-all advice doesn't apply here. To make the Big Decisions that truly serve you, you need to filter every decision through your values and vision, the Big Questions we raised in Part I. You need to see the foundational questions and trade-offs clearly so that you can navigate them on your terms.

CHAPTER BREAKDOWN

This next section of the book is about helping you navigate these Big Decisions that shape the core of your business. I'm not here to hand you a checklist or a step-by-step manual. Instead, we'll dig into the tropes you've been sold, uncover the truths they're based on, and reveal the price you'll pay if you follow them without question. Most importantly, we'll replace that snappy advice with frameworks for decision-making rooted in your own analysis, values, and goals.

Every decision comes with trade-offs. The question isn't "What's the right choice?" It's "What's the right choice *for me*?"

The Big Decisions we'll discuss in the upcoming chapters include:

- **Pricing:** Why pricing advice often focuses on confidence instead of strategy and how to approach pricing from a lens of value, sufficiency, and ecosystem support.
- **Marketing:** Breaking down the myths of constant visibility and viral growth and focusing on sustainable strategies that align with your business model.

- **Time Management and Efficiency**: Examining the pressure to automate everything and work as little as possible and helping you design a rhythm of work that fits your life.
- **Hiring**: Addressing the trope of "build a team to scale" and exploring what it means to hire intentionally and lead with clarity.
- **Resiliency**: Setting aside the promise of passive income and designing offers, delivery structures, and marketing approaches that balance profitability, creative freedom, and client value at a sustainable pace for the long term.

HOW TO READ THIS PART

You may be coming into this book facing all of these Big Decisions simultaneously, but more than likely, you'll face these decisions over time as you grow your business. Some you'll face earlier, such as pricing and marketing. Others you may encounter later, such as hiring and resilient business design. I encourage you to read the chapters that resonate with you now, even if that means reading out of order or not finishing the entire book in one sitting. Complete the reflection exercises as they become relevant to your business.

This guide isn't a step-by-step playbook—it's a map of the landscape. When you're tempted to listen to snappy, sensational advice as you face business crossroads, pull out this book and revisit these foundational principles, along with your vision and values. This guide won't tell you exactly what to do, but it will help you navigate the decisions ahead with clarity and confidence. Guided by your internal compass and the landscape map, you can leave the Casino behind and start building a business that's sustainable, aligned with your desires, and deeply rooted in your values.

Let's get started.

Your business is deeply personal. It's a reflection of your unique gifts, your priorities, and the life you want to lead.

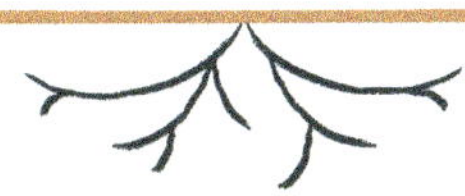

Money is rarely just about numbers. Money is tied to narratives we've absorbed from childhood, past experiences, and societal norms.

CHAPTER 6

Pricing—The High-Ticket Hustle

TO STAY IN BUSINESS, you need pricing that supports profitability and sustainability—so that you can make what you need without overworking. But if you're like most business owners, you probably worry about what to charge, and you've likely ended up setting your prices based on what "felt fair" or what you thought the market could bear.

And then you walked into the Casino.

You pass by poker tables, where low bets offer low payouts that barely feel worth the effort to play the game. Further in, the high-ticket tables call to you, promising big payouts—but only if you are willing to pay the price to play.

In the flashy world of online business advice, the **Pricing Game** promises a big win: the allure of high payouts and financial freedom. It's tempting to sit down at the table and play along. But no matter what you're selling—whether it's one-on-one work, a course, or even a product like a book—you will be inundated with the same pricing advice: "Double your prices!" "Charge your worth!"

In the Casino, everyone wants to be a millionaire, rich AF. "You're leaving money on the table," calls out the dealer at the high-ticket table if you aren't charging sky-high prices and playing their game.

"Make your offer high ticket!"

"High prices = high commitment!"

"If they can't afford it, they're not your ideal client!"

"Your price is your vibe. Raise it!"

"Why have ten clients paying $5K when you can have one paying $50K?"

"Your pricing is a mirror of your limiting beliefs!"

The house rule for pricing is clear: Charge as much as you can.

This advice is loudly proclaimed by influencers who encourage your spending by showcasing their own skyrocketing incomes: "I'm rich and you can be too!" Their wealth seems like proof their strategies work … but remember, the house always wins. They are charging you high prices and then turning around and using their income levels to prove they are successful to justify those prices.

A host of online influencers are charging exploitative amounts of money to show you how to raise your prices, often by changing your mindset around money. These businesses sell an image that your investment makes possible—because they're successful once you've paid them an exorbitant amount of money for "being in their proximity." Some of these programs encourage their clients to take on substantial debt, to borrow money from family, to sell belongings to pay for a program that will likely *never* give them a return on their investment. Or they promote mystery offers that are never delivered or get no results, with any negative comments about the program being deleted or removed by the program's legal team.

And if you struggle to take any of their advice and still have no idea what you should be charging, you'll learn that "it's all about having confidence in your rates—just say a number that feels good!" If you've ever felt like you're guessing at your prices, you're not alone. Pricing isn't just a number—it's tied to our stories, our market, and our capacity.

It's easy to fall into the chair and play the game. After all, if you're not financially sustainable, what other decisions matter? You won't have the cash flow to bring on a team, to build effective systems and client delivery processes, or to strengthen your marketing—because you'll constantly be in survival mode.

The truth is, when starting out, you probably *are* undercharging and overworking!

Market pressure often pushes us to keep our prices low because we're constantly measuring ourselves against what others charge and how they position their offers. When your industry feels saturated with other businesses, global competitors, or even no-cost AI agents, it's tempting to lower your prices to stay competitive in the market. Why would a client pay you $100 an hour when they can hire someone overseas for $7 or just hand it over to an AI model for a cheap subscription? This pressure isn't just external—it seeps into your confidence and decisions, making it harder to set a price that feels sustainable and reflective of your value.

Our culture **systematically undervalues care, creativity, and relational labor.** Professions like teaching, caregiving, and art-making—the ones that prioritize human connection and transformation—are often poorly compensated, and these patterns show up in how we price our services. When society has signaled that certain types of work aren't valued, it's easy to internalize those messages and hesitate to charge appropriately for your expertise. The issue isn't just what clients think your work is worth— it's the broader narrative that has shaped how we see ourselves and our contributions. Pricing your work fairly can feel like an uphill battle against deeply ingrained beliefs about *who* deserves to be paid and *what* deserves to be paid for.

Finally, **money is rarely just about numbers.** Money is tied to narratives we've absorbed from childhood, past experiences, and societal norms. Maybe you grew up in a household where talking about money was taboo, so asking for higher rates now feels uncomfortable or even shameful. Or perhaps you've internalized the idea that wealth is inherently selfish or greedy, making it hard to reconcile charging premium prices with your values. On the other side of the spectrum, you might feel pressure to raise your prices to "prove" your worth or success, even if that doesn't align with your expertise or audience. These emotional layers create a tug-of-war in our pricing decisions, which makes the Casino pricing strategies that offer "easy" solutions so appealing.

Each of these factors—market pressure, societal undervaluation, and our relationship with money—shapes how we approach pricing, often without our realizing it. When we play the Pricing Game, we're reacting to these forces instead of intentionally designing a strategy that matches our business values and vision.

Making more for what we do sounds great. These simplistic tropes give us permission to both raise our prices and make more money—but simply charging the most you can comes with a price. This advice is given without consideration for the market you serve, the true value or return on investment of what you're offering, and what you actually need to build a strong, sustainable business.

I've seen too many people raise their prices substantially at the advice of their well-intentioned business mentor, only to see their sales plummet. Yes, it might be your "money mindset" holding you back, but it also might be the market you work with. When you dramatically change your pricing, you might be **out of sync with your existing client base and their perceived value, your network, or your demonstrated expertise.** Your pricing might end up out of integrity with your skills, process, or client results. If you work with newer entrepreneurs or a population that legitimately can't afford or won't get a return on investment with your new pricing, you may struggle to sell at those new prices.

There is also a significant price in the form of stress—*a misalignment in your nervous system* because you don't believe your work is worth that much. This can often lead to overdelivering to justify your prices. I have fallen guilty of this, internally negotiating against myself when it comes to my prices or feeling pressure to deliver out-of-scope items or be more responsive to clients when I've raised my rates.

Instead of vacillating between undercharging (and overworking) and pricing based on these arbitrary soundbites (potentially losing sales in the process), we need to first ground ourselves in our money needs, money stories, and pricing philosophies and principles by doing the following:

- Understanding the revenue we truly need (because "more" is not a goal)
- Evaluating pricing from a number of lenses that incorporate feedback about our market, our expertise, and our offer structures
- Developing a path to bridge the gap between the prices we're currently charging and what we need to charge
- Identifying the ways we can build accessibility into our work without risking our sustainability

This chapter will help you craft a pricing strategy rooted in clarity, confidence, and sustainability rather than gamble on arbitrary price hikes or undercharge out of fear.

LEAVING THE PRICING TABLE

How, then, do we figure out what we should really be charging without exploiting people and while funding our life and work? How do you create a pricing approach that makes sense for your business and can adapt to your changing needs over time? Instead of following the simplistic guidance to "double your prices," you'll want to answer these questions:

1. Do you actually need to raise your prices?

2. If so, then by how much?

3. How does that align with who you want to serve?

4. And if you have the power to raise your prices … should you?

Rather than struggle with your values as you charge ever-higher rates that your core clients can't pay, first understand the foundations of pricing and how to anchor your pricing around your real needs, a realistic value exchange, and your market.

We'll first look at the purpose of money in your business before evaluating five different ways to look at pricing. Next, we'll discuss your pricing currency and the portfolio of pricing. Finally, we'll cover what to do should these prices not line up with your target client.

After reviewing these philosophies, you may decide that you should "double your prices." Or you might see that you need to increase your prices by three or four times what you're charging. You may even realize that you need to change the market you serve *in order to* increase your prices.

Alternatively, perhaps you'll see that *instead* of increasing your prices, you actually need to streamline your business expenses or design a business model that allows you to serve or reach more people in less time.

You may decide to temporarily decrease your personal expenses to have the flexibility you need as you pursue your passions and creative dreams or to get a part-time job to maintain the creative freedom you want in your business. Don't put pressure on your craft or service to fully pay your bills at the start.

Or maybe you'll see that you have an opportunity to give back and charge less in some areas because *you have enough* and are not optimizing for increased revenue.

Know the Goal

Our business needs to cover not just our take-home pay but also the costs typically covered by employers—taxes, health insurance, and other benefits. As an entrepreneur, your pricing must account for these operational expenses while also providing financial stability and reflecting the personalized value you bring. Before you even start with pricing your services, go back to Part I and determine the answer to this foundational question: How much money does your business need to make for you based on the role it plays in your life?

- Are you in a survive, sustain, or strengthen and serve mode?
- Are you intending to support yourself with full-time wages for this work?
- Are you hoping to turn this business into a scalable asset that generates profit beyond what you can pay yourself?
- Is this a passion project, where you'd like to cover your costs and earn some money to make the effort worthwhile?
- Do you have another source of income, like a working partner or a part-time job?
- Will you need to cover health insurance or retirement savings from your income?
- If you had to choose, would you optimize for more profit, more time or location flexibility, more creative control, or less responsibility?

When I launched my business, I was making a $200,000 salary from my corporate role, which I knew would be challenging to replace. And even now, a few years in? I'm making more than that in revenue but taking home a lot less, thanks to taxes, business expenses, and investments in support to help me grow the business. But I planned for this. In the years heading into my business, I cut expenses from my life to drop my take-home needs in half.

My husband and I got married and combined households. We decided on a smaller home than we could have chosen if I had kept my corporate salary. We dramatically cut lifestyle expenses during my first few years of building the business to relieve the pressure of having to make that same sort of salary quickly. Thanks to my time spent in the corporate mirage, I'd already saved up a substantial amount for retirement and could ramp down my savings rate.

In my own business, I'm not optimizing for increased revenue. I know what I need to bring in from my business to fund my life, which is my goal. And knowing that "enough" number for you is the first real step.

Once you know what you want to pay yourself, you can thoughtfully design your business—and your pricing—to align with your real goal, not some arbitrary revenue number.

The Five Approaches to Pricing

When most business owners start pricing their products or services, they do one of two things:

1. They take the prior salary they were earning, divide it by the number of their working hours, and voila! There's their hourly rate.
2. They look around at the other businesses in their immediate vicinity (locally or where they hang out online) and charge a similar price. If you're on a platform like Upwork or Fiverr or in a coach training program, you'll set similar prices to what you see others setting.

Both of these approaches have a few flaws that almost always lead to undercharging.

The salary-based calculation usually ***overestimates*** the amount of time you're able to spend on client work or on your business in general and ***underestimates*** the amount of money you'll spend on taxes and running your business.

And comparing your rates to what else is on the market means you're competing on price instead of pricing based on who you serve, the problem you solve, the value you create, and your business model.

But by reviewing your pricing across multiple lenses, you eliminate the biases from any one approach to ensure you're pricing appropriately for the value you're providing to your chosen market.

This chapter reviews five approaches to pricing:

- **Hourly-Based Pricing:** Pricing based on time spent, most common with delivery-based business models
- **Audience-Based Pricing:** Pricing based on how many people you can reach or enroll, most common with creator-based business models or delivery models that involve a one-time purchase
- **Value-Based Pricing:** Pricing based on the result or transformation your offer creates
- **Market-Based Pricing:** Pricing based on what others in your space are charging
- **Justice-Based Pricing:** Pricing with access, equity, and sustainability in mind

This pricing list might look intimidating, but we'll walk through everything so that you can decide how to weigh these different considerations in your own unique pricing approach. Once you've examined your pricing through these five approaches, you can make shifts to help you achieve your desired total revenue level.

HOURLY-BASED PRICING

In Hourly-Based Pricing, you are aligning your pricing to meet your desired take-home pay based on your working capacity and the time spent to deliver your offer or service. This model is primarily designed for pricing delivery-based services, not creator-based offerings like courses or group programs.

In this approach, you are calculating the hourly rate you must charge to meet your needs and multiplying that rate by the number of hours it takes you to deliver an offer. This is often the floor for your pricing because charging less than this price—assuming the offer stays the same—means you'll be taking home less than you want.

But how is this approach different from just dividing your desired pay from your total working hours?

You'll work fewer hours than you think. As the business owner, you have to factor time off, sick pay, and vacations into the hours you have available for working, as well as consider the impact of chronic illness, care responsibilities, or other constraints on your availability. Also consider the energy it takes to run your business because being "on" in your business is more energetically taxing than other comparable working time.

I don't know about your last job, but a lot of my "forty hours" was spent disengaged in meetings, chatting with coworkers over coffee, or just processing the emails. So. Many. Emails.

I can only put in about six or so real hours into my business a day at most, not accounting for lunch, coffee, and walkies with my dog.

Working hours do not equal delivery hours. You won't be delivering to your clients during the full hours you're working because you will need to dedicate time to marketing, sales, and all of the admin required to run your business. Even "live" session hours require pre- and post-session preparation and administration time that you might not have considered.

In Chapter 8, we'll take a more in-depth look at the time split in your business. At least 20%–30% of your working hours will be spent doing marketing, sales, or business admin, even if you wish you could just do the work you love to do! There's a reason why doing the same work as a contract coach or a subcontract freelancer or consultant doesn't pay the same hourly rate as what they charge their clients—the business owner takes on the risks and costs of business development and operations.

Your revenue does not equal your take-home pay. You'll have expenses as part of running your business and even more if you have hire employees or contractors to deliver services, as we covered in Chapter 1.

And unlike what you might hear on social media from "tax hacking" accounts, when you earn money, you have to pay taxes on that money! If you're making more than you're spending on business expenses, you'll owe taxes on that money. (And when you want to buy a car or a house, you'll need proof that you have a profitable business that regularly pays you. This is why it's bad advice to spend everything you make just to avoid paying taxes.)

Unless you are set up as an employee of your business and paying taxes on each paycheck, money that you pull out of your business to pay yourself or to pay for personal expenses is taxed, and you need to set aside money to cover that future bill.

Base Hourly Rate

A safe rule of thumb for soloists? You'll have to generate up to **twice as much** revenue as you need to pay yourself, with delivery time making up only **about 50%** of the hours you are able to work.

To bring home $60,000 working a "forty-hour workweek," you'll probably need revenue of at least $100,000–$120,000 and to deliver client work within roughly twenty hours a week.

To make $100,000 in twenty hours of client work a week, you'll need to charge at least $100–$120 per hour if you're delivering a service in a 1:1 capacity.

This is a rough rule of thumb. You might not choose to work as much, or you may keep your business expenses very lean so that you can take home more profit with less revenue. You may work as a Craftsman with a few long-term clients, where you spend more than twenty hours a week doing delivery and less time on admin and marketing. So if you need to make $100,000 annually and can spend thirty hours a week delivering for 1–2 long-term clients—in what is essentially a part-time job—you could make your target revenue charging ~$75 per hour.

If you run an Agency model with a team, you'll determine your firm's base hourly capacity by factoring in contractor rates and building in an additional margin to account for periods of underutilization along with a profit margin for you as the business owner. That's your firm's hourly base rate for services.

Pricing a Specific Offer

To price a specific offer, you'll multiply that base hourly rate by the hours you spend preparing or delivering the offer. For instance, a brand designer may spend fifty hours working on a brand, including design and preparation time. Multiplied by $100 per hour, the capacity-based price for that offer is $5,000. If that brand designer can sell and deliver one brand per month, they will make $60,000 per year.

You may look at the rate or pricing for that offer and say, "There's no way I can charge that kind of money." Or, depending on your market, you might say, "That's too low for us to be considered as an option compared to other firms." We'll address the question of how to bridge gaps in your pricing—from what you are charging to what you may need to charge—later in this chapter.

AUDIENCE-BASED PRICING

If you're running a creator-based business—selling courses, memberships, or group programs—you can't price based on hours worked. Instead, your pricing needs to reflect the revenue you want to generate *and* the 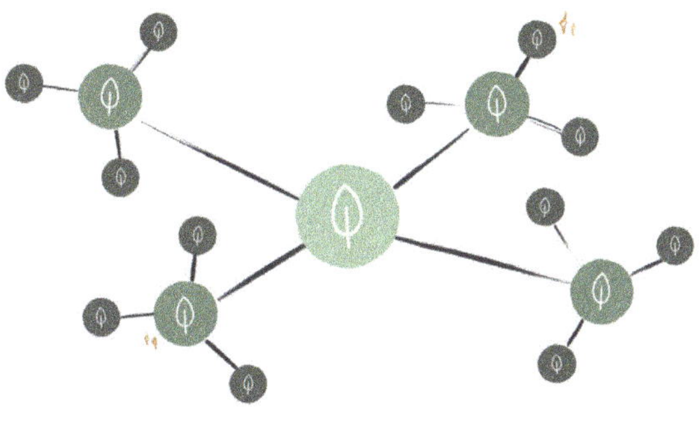 number of people you can realistically enroll based on the size of your audience. This also applies to time-bound service offerings like intensives or VIP days.

When developing your pricing, you must consider
- the number of people you can realistically enroll
- the level of effort required to deliver the offer
- the total revenue goal you want to achieve for that offer

For example, if your goal is to earn $5,000/month from a creator-model offer:
- Enrolling 5 people? You need a $1,000/month offer.
- Enrolling 50 people? You need a $100/month offer.

Know Your Audience Capacity

Common business wisdom states that only 3% of individuals are ready to "buy now."

- To enroll 5 people, you need at least 200 potential buyers in your audience or ecosystem.
- To enroll 50, you need at least 2,000.

This is where one-time delivery-model offers can run into trouble. If you want to sell one short-term project, intensive, or VIP day per month, each to a new client, that's twelve clients annually—meaning you need to maintain steady access each year to a few hundred qualified potential clients or to cultivate strong referral systems.

The audience size challenge also applies to low-cost memberships. If your audience is small, you may only get 5–20 signups. Is that enough to meet your revenue needs? If not, you either need to raise the price, change your offer, or grow your audience.

If your pricing approach for a given offer relies on more than 5%–10% of your audience converting, it may not be sustainable.

Align Price to Effort and Offer Style

- A high-touch group advisory service with ten seats at $1,000/month requires deeper involvement but fewer sales and would be feasible to enroll with less than a thousand subscribers.
- A lower-touch community at $100/month requires a high audience size but lower ongoing delivery efforts.

Audience-Based Pricing isn't just about target revenue—it's about aligning the audience size and expected enrollment rate to the offer structure, price, and promise.

VALUE-BASED PRICING

We've all heard the story about the plumber who charges a hefty amount to fix the toilet. You're not paying for the five minutes it took to tighten the bolt—you're paying for the experience required to know where to look and avoiding the cost of repairing a destructive home leak.

While hourly or audience pricing is a good starting point to set your pricing range, you're ultimately not charging for the hours worked or the number of modules in your course.

The price you can charge isn't related to the hours you're actively delivering; it's directly related to the value of the transformation.

When you construct your pricing from an hourly perspective, working efficiently and gaining expertise effectively reduces your price. And as you get more skilled in your business, you'll be able to deliver that transformation faster, which is an incredibly valuable proposition for your client! Why should they pay for you to spend months working together if you can address their issue in a week? And why should you make less if you're delivering the same value proposition more efficiently for you?

If I'm an accountant, and I bill you by the hour, when I get faster I make less money. Even though as the client, you got results faster! This is the same for other service providers: if as a business consultant, I can get you the same results (or sometimes, better and/or faster results) through a combination of live calls, asynchronous materials, and community support instead of weekly calls, then why would I charge less money for that result?

It can be easy for us to devalue what comes naturally to us, because it's easy and enjoyable, but Value-Based Pricing helps us to anchor on the value from the client's perspective.

Ideally, you're solving an expensive problem with a solution that's easy to deliver.

Quoting author Jonathan Stark, "When I use the term expensive problem, what I mean is that someone is having a problem that they would like to spend a lot of money on to solve right now. An expensive *solution* is something that costs the seller a lot of time or money to deliver. But this has nothing to do with the value to the buyer. The fact that a solution is expensive to deliver *does not* mean that there are buyers who have a problem that is *expensive* enough to them to justify paying what the seller would need to charge to make a profit."[29]

Components of Value and Risk

So, let's look at the *value* we're delivering to our clients:

- How much value are you delivering from a time, financial, or emotional perspective?
- How much time will you save them, or what impact will you create that wouldn't otherwise be possible?
- What is the opportunity cost of not investing in you to solve their problem or help them achieve their desire? How much is this impacting their health, wealth, and worth?
- What are the costs of other solutions they could choose to achieve their desired result?
- What aspects of your offer increase the value to your clients (e.g., speed, having it done without their involvement, or providing an easy way to book)?

We can also reduce the *risk* to our clients, which increases the value proposition. Clients are investing not only their money in our service or product but also their time, energy, and attention. So, decreasing risk can increase the perceived value, even at the same price point:

- Have a clear process with proven results
- Have different levels of access or flexibility in how you schedule
- Change the payment structure (e.g., a payment for just Phase 1 of a project until you know the full scope or monthly payments vs. an upfront payment)
- Be paid in equity and/or profit, which transfers the risk from the client to you but has the potential for a big payday later

---

29 Jonathan Stark, "What Is an Expensive Problem?" *Jonathan Stark Daily*, February 16, 2021, https://jonathanstark.com/daily/20210216-1602-what-is-an-expensive-problem.

- Have an "out clause" (e.g., after a purchase, the client has thirty days to "love it or leave it"—just as long as the "leave it" is actually an option and not just a manipulative sales tactic)
- Include a guarantee (e.g., if the client does the activity and doesn't get results, you'll keep working with them until they do or refund their money—this should *also* not be a manipulative sales tactic)

These factors can make your offer a "no-brainer" and increase its value to your target clients.

Price the Client, Not the Job

We also want to evaluate the value of what we do in relation to the market we serve. The same deliverable or the same amount of time spent on two different projects could deliver very different value and should be priced commensurate with that value. As author Blair Enns says, we should price the client, not the job.[30]

Designing a five-page website for a brand-new entrepreneur who doesn't have a client base yet? That will deliver some impact but probably won't deliver the same financial value because the base revenue just isn't in place yet.

But designing that same five-page website for an established brand with demonstrated website traffic? That website could deliver over millions of dollars in incremental revenue. The value capture is much larger here than for the smaller entrepreneur. It might take you the same amount of time and the same level of skill to create those five pages, but the value you generate—and therefore capture—differs greatly between those scenarios.

Even if you don't work with business owners or organizations who will make a direct return on their investment, these principles still apply. The busy executive looking for a bespoke health coach will likely prioritize time over money vs. a twenty-something who wants to *save* money. The same goes for being a financial advisor to high-net-worth individuals vs. working with those who are setting up a budget for the

---

30 Blair Enns, *Pricing Creativity: A Guide to Profit Beyond the Billable Hour* (RockBench Publishing Corp, 2018), 37.

first time. We might spend the same amount of time and bring the same amount of expertise, but the value and impact of our services might be felt differently by the different markets.

MARKET-BASED PRICING

Market-Based Pricing is an art and a science. With a little research, you can often find out what your peers and mentors are charging. And based on your Zone of Enoughness, you can do the math to determine whether you need to charge that amount of money for a given offer. But Market-Based Pricing is influenced by many factors:

- **Positioning:** Are you positioned in the right market? Executive coaches can charge more than therapists for the same hour. A content subscription can be positioned at the same cost as a latte or marketed as a masterclass subscription with high access to experts at five times the price. Communities can be priced at $5/month or $1,000/month depending on your market and value proposition.
- **Target Client:** Are you actually serving the same market? Business coaches who serve new entrepreneurs probably will charge less than business coaches serving multimillion-dollar CEOs.
- **Brand Authority:** Do you have a proven track record of success, recognized by testimonials, a proven process, publications / press releases, and a public body of work?
- **Type of Work:** Strategic work is often valued higher than more execution-based, ongoing work. How much do you talk about strategy vs. relying on more transactional work?

JUSTICE-BASED PRICING

As you grow in your business, you may decide that your pricing decisions need to serve a broader purpose because the prices the other four approaches yield are simply out of reach for the population you want to serve.

This approach is considered Justice-Based Pricing. You're changing your pricing, offer structure, funding structure, or even business model to support this community.

Below, we'll discuss three approaches to embedding more accessibility into your business as a whole—without sacrificing your own ability to make the money you need for your Zone of Enoughness.

Changing Your Pricing Structure

One option is tiered or sliding scale pricing, where you offer different pricing tiers for the same service. Popularized by Alexis J. Cunningfolk at Worts and Cunning, the three levels are a standard tier to cover the cost, a reduced rate, and a higher rate that subsidizes the lower rate.[31]

You may choose to give scholarships or discounts, funded by the standard rate most of your clients are paying.

If you find that a majority of your clients need to take advantage of the discounted rates, though, you may have a business model or structure problem: You might be serving a market that can't afford to pay for the offers as they are set up, or you don't yet have the strong value proposition required to command the higher rate.

Adapting Your Offer Structure

As an entrepreneur with a limited number of live hours, 1:1 work does come at a premium and needs to be charged in line with that for your own sustainability.

But that may mean you need to change your offer structure if the price you'd charge for individual services is outside of the range of your

---

31 Worts & Cunning Apothecary, "Sliding Scale - Worts & Cunning Apothecary: Intersectional Herbalism + Magickal Arts," last modified August 11, 2015, https://www.wortsandcunning. com/sliding-scale.

desired clients: Offer more groups, community support, or blended asynchronous and hybrid offers. You might move toward a "done with you" offer instead of a "done for you" offer.

Changing Your Funding Structure or Business Model

As Trudi Lebrón says in *The Antiracist Business Book*, sometimes your client is different from the community you serve.[32]

You might choose to work primarily with corporate organizations doing high-priced consulting or training and offer free classes to the community you want to serve. You could partner with grant organizations or even bring on corporate sponsors who can financially fund your work with your clients in exchange for visibility. Explore grants, especially if your work supports underserved communities or noncommercial causes.

Crowdfunding can be an effective way to raise funds for specific projects while building community engagement. Maybe you make money through sponsorships or subscriptions to a podcast or newsletter instead of making money directly from services. (Remember, this changes your business model!)

Ultimately, some businesses may need to be structured as nonprofits or work with a fiscal sponsor to take advantage of these opportunities or to simply be reduced to a side hustle / creative endeavor.

EVALUATING ACROSS THE APPROACHES

When you run your business through each of the five pricing approaches—Hourly, Audience, Value, Market, and Justice—you may come up with five different price points. That's the point.

Each lens gives you a different way to understand what's sustainable and what's possible based on your audience, goals, and values.

Let's say you're a marketing strategist creating content and copy for solo business owners without a marketing team:

---

32 Trudi Lebrón, *The Antiracist Business Book: An Equity Centered Approach to Work, Wealth, and Leadership* (Row House Publishing, 2022).

- **Hourly:** Based on your time and hourly base rate, you'd need to charge $2,000/month per client to meet your income goals.
- **Audience:** You only want 5–10 clients at a time and aim to make $10,000/month, so you land at the same $2,000/month rate—and that fits your audience size.
- **Value:** Your clients are newer and may only make an additional $4,000/month from your work. If you capture 25% of that value, your rate would be closer to $1,000/month.
- **Market:** Other providers in your niche are charging $750/month for similar services.
- **Justice:** You want to keep working with early-stage soloists, but taking on too many clients burns you out and limits your ability to teach the free classes you love. You may need a split model: free resources for newer folks, while your client services shift toward more established businesses.

Hourly Pricing	Audience Pricing	Value Pricing	Market Pricing	Justice Pricing
$2,000 per month	$2,000 per month	$1,000 per month	$750 per month	$2,000 per month for full services Free classes

A clear gap exists between what this market is willing to pay and what you need to charge based on the time and effort required to deliver the service. Here are a few ways you could bridge that gap:

- You might **pivot your client base** toward more established soloists or small businesses with the resources to invest at your current rates.
- You might **de-scope your offer**—reducing done-for-you deliverables and shifting toward a recurring strategy-intensive model, where clients implement the blueprint themselves with light guidance.

- You might **adjust your business model entirely**, moving into a hybrid Teacher approach—offering templates, swipe files, and low-lift strategy sessions through a membership or group program. That shift would reduce delivery time but would require a **larger audience** to sustain your revenue goals.
- Or, if you're deeply committed to serving newer business owners, you may keep a lower-priced offer but add on **higher-tier services or alternate revenue streams** to subsidize the impact work you want to keep doing.

Now, let's look at a different example: selling a self-guided, twelve-module course on content and social media trends geared toward new business owners. You want to make $4,000/month from the course, or $48,000/year.

- **Hourly:** Not relevant—this model isn't tied to your time.
- **Audience:** You have 1,000 people on your email list now and expect to grow by 500 per year. With a ~3% conversion rate, you might sell thirty seats up front and fifteen annually, putting your sustainable price point closer to $3,000.
- **Value:** For newer business owners, $3,000 may feel steep for a self-paced course. A more realistic value-aligned price might be $1,000.
- **Market:** Similar courses sell for $1,500 but are backed by big-name influencers with larger followings.
- **Justice:** You want to offer a sliding scale, so you may anchor your public price at $3,500 and offer discounted rates to increase access.

Hourly Pricing	Audience Pricing	Value Pricing	Market Pricing	Justice Pricing
N/A	$3,000	$1,000	$1,500	$3,500 with sliding scale options

In this case, your audience size, offer structure, and pricing goals are out of sync. To address this issue, you have a few options:

- Shift your **positioning** and the **course content** to attract more experienced buyers who can better use and value the course.
- Change the **offer structure** to a higher-touch cohort model, with live Q&A calls and community support.
- Keep the lower-priced course and add a **premium tier** or companion service to increase the total revenue.
- Revise your revenue expectations and align your business model more closely with your current audience size and energy. Maybe the total revenue for the course makes half of what you had planned, aligning with the market pricing, and you add on more services to meet your business's revenue goals.

The takeaway? Pricing isn't just about picking a number. When you look across all five lenses, you can discover what needs to shift—your audience, your offer, your expectations, or your business model—to create a more aligned and sustainable strategy.

Meanwhile, online business influencers might tell you the problem is your "money mindset" and convince you to invest with them to get more comfortable with charging rates through the moon. The thing is, though, sometimes it's not about the money mindset. Sometimes it's the reality of market rates and your value proposition.

CLOSING THE GAP WITH INTENTION

When you start to close the gap between what you're currently charging and what you need to charge, the actions you take span the strategic, the emotional, and the tactical.

- **Strategic:** Strengthening your value proposition, changing your target market, or restructuring your offers
- **Emotional:** Confronting your narratives about value, money, worth, productivity, and identity and how they impact your pricing
- **Tactical:** Communicating pricing shifts to your client base, including how to transition clients who are at one rate or structure while enrolling new clients at a different rate

Strengthening Your Value Proposition

When you're starting out, you're honing your skills, establishing your reputation, and building up that social proof. You're legitimately getting better at what you do, even if you were doing this work for a long time in your prior professional career.

It's important to consider all of the types of currency you're being paid in: time, attention, energy, trust, and, of course, money. To work with you, even at a "free" or low price, a client would need to clear their schedule, show up for the work, and process whatever is provided. Any offer has an opportunity cost in time because the customer could have been doing something else or working with another service provider.

You'll want to get as much practice as possible so that you can start seeing patterns and deepening your expertise—which allows you to command a higher rate. If your prices are too high for you to consistently get sales, that counterintuitively prevents you from getting in the repetition required to deepen your expertise and achieve the portfolio of results that give potential clients more confidence in your work. Over time, once you increase your skill at delivering your work and become known for what you do, that pricing currency can shift.

So while you *could* try to charge what your more experienced mentors and peers are charging, it's important to really be honest with yourself as to where your skill levels are. You can increase your pricing over time to be more in line with your market as you increase your skills, get more clarity on who you serve, build your processes, and deliver value and transformation with certainty. You'll eventually shift the ratio of payment currency from more qualitative factors to that hard-earned cash.

Changing Who You're Aiming to Work with and Targeting New Markets

When your current target clients aren't able or willing to pay what you need to charge, the solution may not be about lowering your prices or changing your offer. Instead, it might be time to shift who you're targeting altogether, which often means targeting larger clients or clients with a higher level of problem awareness. For example, solving a business-critical problem for a company with a large budget has more impact—and justifies higher prices—than solving the same problem for a smaller company.

You can also aim for higher-maturity clients who already understand the value of your services and are willing to invest in expertise rather than shopping for the lowest price. This shift may require changes to your positioning, networking strategy, and messaging. Move into a new network with intention, building off of your existing clients and business ecosystem over time.

Changing the Structure or Scope of Your Offer

If your hourly-based pricing doesn't match your value- or market-based number, you may instead decide to streamline or restructure your offer:

- Fewer rounds of revision
- Less pre- + post-session notes
- Productized templates as a starting point
- Video resources instead of live instruction
- Async communications
- Hybrid or group models

Or you may find that you need to overhaul your offer in a different way.

For example, accountants that charge by the hour at tax time are often overwhelmed and overloaded during that time, cramming in as many clients as possible to make their revenue for the year.

However, accountants who shift to a subscription-style CFO package provide value all year long by answering IRS letters, helping prepare tax forecasts, and creating investment and tax savings strategies before tax time. They still have busy periods, but the ebbs and flows of time and money are blunted by spreading the cost and revenue out over the year.

The clients benefit from having access to expertise throughout the year: There's more value provided in your being an expert to help them plan (not just prepare taxes). Moreover, the clients have a steady expense they can anticipate, and they avoid a huge expense at tax time as well. That's a win–win in changing your business structure for the right client.

Healing Your Money Stories and Nervous System Regulation

No amount of strategic pricing, offer redesign, or market positioning will work if, deep down, you're not comfortable receiving more. Money is more than a number on a balance sheet; it's deeply tied to our identity, past experiences, and nervous system regulation. Many entrepreneurs underprice themselves because of unresolved money narratives, fear of rejection, or nervous system dysregulation, all of which make the idea of charging more feel threatening.

Rewriting these beliefs involves recognizing that charging appropriately reflects the value you create, not your worth as a person. Nervous system regulation also plays a role: Pricing anxiety can trigger a stress response, making it feel unsafe to ask for more. Practicing grounding exercises, implementing gradual price increases, building resilience around rejection, and incorporating gratitude can help expand your capacity to receive. When priced appropriately, your work delivers real, measurable value—and the client benefits just as much as you do.

The goal isn't to overcharge; it's to charge a price that reflects the transformation you create.

Transitioning to New Rates or Structures

Raising your prices is more than just updating a number. It involves a shift in how you position your work, communicate value, and manage client relationships. Once you've aligned your new pricing with your offer structure, the next step is implementation. This process can be complex, especially if you have long-standing clients at legacy rates, but a thoughtful transition can help you maintain client trust while ensuring your business remains sustainable.

This process could be an entire book in itself, but here are some ideas to start:

1. **Assess Your Existing Clients and Approach to Legacy Pricing:** Review your current client base and identify who is most underpriced relative to your new rates or who isn't a fit for your future offers. You don't have to take a one-size-fits-all approach. Some clients may get a gradual increase over time, others may be kept at their current rate as a strategic choice, and some may no longer fit your new structure at

all. Decide now who gets what to avoid making case-by-case decisions under pressure later.

2. **Roll Out New Pricing to New Clients First:** Start applying the new rates to incoming clients before adjusting existing ones. This approach validates your pricing, allows for adjustments if needed, and builds your confidence before you implement the shift across the board.

3. **Communicate the Change Clearly and Give a Simple "Because":** Give clients enough time to adjust to the new pricing. A simple, direct email outlining the change and when it takes effect is sufficient. Whether the new rates result from an increase in demand, expanded expertise, or rising costs, a clear but brief explanation smooths the transition.

4. **Offer a Transition Incentive (If It Makes Sense):** Some clients may be more willing to commit if they can lock in a lower rate for a limited time before an increase takes effect. This gives them time to adjust while still honoring your new pricing.

5. **Bundle in Added Value:** A price increase can feel like an upgrade rather than just a cost bump if you adjust the service slightly, whether via a streamlined process, an extra touchpoint, or clearer deliverables.

6. **Refine How You Present Pricing Publicly:** If you're still fine-tuning your positioning, avoid locking yourself into fixed public pricing. Use ranges, implement "starting at" pricing, or keep high-touch services off your website entirely to provide flexibility as you introduce new rates to potential clients.

7. **Expect Some Attrition—And Welcome It:** Not everyone will continue at the new rate, and that's okay. Raising prices creates space for the right clients—those who fully value your expertise and are aligned with your evolving business.

HARVEST PRICING

To conclude this pricing chapter, I offer a different analogy and approach. Instead of trying to have "one signature offer" and making each offer in your business maximize your pricing and profit, you might approach your offers and pricing as a portfolio—or as a harvest that can provide a nourishing meal for yourself, your teams, and your clients and community.

In her book *Braiding Sweetgrass*, biologist and indigenous scholar Robin Wall Kimmerer shares the story of the Indigenous Three Sisters planting tradition,[33] in which corn, beans, and squash are planted together:

> *For millennia, from Mexico to Montana, women have mounded up the earth and laid these three seeds in the ground, all in the same square foot of soil. When the colonists on the Massachusetts shore first saw Indigenous gardens, they inferred that the savages did not know how to farm. To their minds, a garden meant straight rows of single species, not a three-dimensional sprawl of abundance. And yet they ate their fill and asked for more, and more again.*

Corn sprouts first and grows quickly. Then the beans rise, using the stalks of the corn to grow and taking advantage of the light and height provided by the corn. Pumpkins and squash grow slowly but provide much-needed shade and ground cover. And while it seems like the beans are taking a free ride on the corn and squash, their roots provide nitrogen to the soil, acting as a fertilizer.

These three plants grow more food together than they do separately. They provide defense against single-species insects and disease. Yet each plant serves a different purpose.

Think of your business as a garden of intertwined plants. When we consider the elements of our business, particularly with pricing, we often think "every element has to make money, has to be profitable."

We've been schooled by the mass-market teacher/trainer businesses to have a single offer, with a single funnel, all geared to your "million-dollar scalable offer"—which, after reading Kimmerer's book, sounds a lot like industrial farming. Sure, it might make you more money and harvest out of the gate—but it may also deplete the soil's nutrients, rely on external fertilizer (like ads) and pesticides (like nondisparagement clauses), and be more susceptible to disease (like algorithm changes).

---

33 Robin Wall Kimmerer, *Braiding Sweetgrass: Indigenous Wisdom, Scientific Knowledge, and the Teachings of Plants* (Milkweed Editions, 2015), 128–141.

So let's instead look at the elements of our business like a garden, where the sum is more than the parts.

Purpose in What You Plant

As you plant your business garden, it's the time to consider the purpose of each aspect of your business.

Some services, especially high-touch 1:1 or done-for-you services, are designed to be profitable. This is the corn, providing the **structure and financial stability** needed to fund the rest of your garden. (Side note: When I say "1:1" I don't necessarily mean 1:1 coaching. This can include marketing / legal / financial retainer work, leadership training and facilitation for a company, work through a larger agency, or B2B consulting—or even having a job that's unrelated to your business but provides stability to a creative practice.)

Other services, like building group programs or communities, might allow you to reach more people. This is **the slower-growth arm of your business,** like the squash, because gathering people takes a larger audience and a consistent message delivered over time. But the act of gathering people might be your preferred way to work long term and can be a good approach to build deeper relationships with your community. These group programs might be priced lower to feed into 1:1 work or to build a larger ecosystem you work with at a different level of access.

And some portion of your business garden might be explicitly planted to **give back to or support a community,** where the purpose is accessible learning, providing signal-boosting for smaller businesses, or gathering people at cost. For example, a podcast might cost you money to produce and may take a long time to generate clients; a community workshop or retreat might never yield revenue depending on how it's priced. But in the meantime, you are providing guidance to individuals who might not be in a position to work with you while also deepening relationships with potential clients. And these programs might fill your soul's cup, providing nutrients to your soil, just like the beans.

The Portfolio Approach to Pricing

So now that you see the different purposes of the parts of your business garden, it's important to maintain the right balance.

As your business grows, you may find that the purpose of each aspect of your business shifts. Maybe the squash—the slower-growing group or community program—takes the primary financial position, while 1:1 work keeps your hands busy creating new curricula or providing ballast to smooth out launch cycles.

Just like over-indexing on growing beans without the support of corn would leave beans "an unruly tangle on the ground, vulnerable to bean-hungry predators,"[34] we need an appropriate balance in our portfolio.

- Do you have at least one core service or funding stream that's appropriately priced for you to make a sustainable income with your audience or network size? (This may not be a part of your business but can include corporate sponsors, a part-time job, or a partner's income.)
- Can you release the need for any "slow growth" offers to make you money out of the gates until your audience size is larger?
- Do you have a portion of your business that fills your soul's cup, that allows you to express your callings or your dharma?
- Are you deciding very clearly up front what amount of time, energy, and money you have for accessible offerings?

An example of a portfolio in your business might be doing high-end B2B consulting with companies on topics like DEI but then offering regular low- or no-cost workshops and classes to educate and work with individuals who otherwise wouldn't be able to access the services.

This principle is important to me. I'm committed to having a reasonably priced group offering and free classes in my business geared toward emerging entrepreneurs because I have the stability of a recurring, higher-priced advisory service with more established expertise-based businesses.

---

34 Robin Wall Kimmerer, *Braiding Sweetgrass: Indigenous Wisdom, Scientific Knowledge, and the Teachings of Plants* (Milkweed Editions, 2015), 132.

SUMMARY

As we now know, pricing isn't just a number you pull out of thin air, nor is it simply about spreadsheets. Pricing is a decision you make grounded in your own values and in the value you provide to your customer. I encourage you to consider your pricing across multiple approaches and assess where you stand. If your pricing is out of alignment across one of the five approaches, multiple avenues can help you bridge that gap, and no answer is the right one. But you can move forward with intention—with a clear action plan to thoughtfully design pricing that matches your offer design, market, authority, and values and business vision.

1. If I deliver services, what is my average hourly rate based on my desired revenue level and working hours?
2. How many customers might I expect for an offer based on my audience size and growth rate?
3. What is the pricing for each approach for my primary offer or service, and how do the rates compare to each other? What am I observing about the alignment and what that means for my business pricing?
4. How can I improve the perceived value of my services? How can I reduce the risk of my services?
5. Do I need to change my target market or offer structure to more closely match my desired pricing?
6. Have I incorporated strategies to address those who may not be able to afford my primary services if this is important to my business and personal strategy?
7. What offers serve as my "corn," "squash," and "beans," and do I have a mix commensurate with the total harvest I need from my business?

You can find the "5 Pricing Approaches" template to help you compare your prices across approaches in the *Leaving the Casino* workbook or in the downloadable resources at deeperfoundations.com/casino

It's important to consider all of the types of currency you're being paid in: time, attention, energy, trust, and, of course, money.

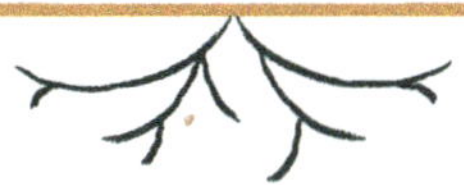

Marketing isn't just about algorithms, funnels, or churning out endless content—it's about connecting with the right people in a way that feels authentic to your values and sustainable for your business.

CHAPTER 7

Marketing—The Followers and Funnels Fallacy

AFTER LEAVING THE PRICING GAME, where you've aligned your rates to sustain your business and yourself, another question looms large: **How do I get more clients and customers?** For many small business owners, the answer to this question starts simply—your first clients likely come through your immediate network or via word of mouth. But as you grow, and as your client base moves beyond your personal connections, the challenge of marketing begins to feel more urgent.

Then you stumble upon the Entrepreneurial Casino's slot machines—shiny, enticing, and seemingly simple to play. All you have to do is keep feeding the machine and pulling the lever. The influencers assure you that if you just keep at it, you'll hit the "777" of viral success, with followers and clients flooding in.

"Turn on that marketing funnel!"

"Post daily on social media!"

"Grow your audience—the gold is in your list!"

"You're one piece of viral content away from success!"

"If you're not everywhere, you're nowhere!"

"The more you post or email, the more you sell!"

The rules of the Marketing Game are clear: Amass as many followers as possible, grow a massive email list, and broadcast relentlessly. It's a numbers game, and the bigger your reach, the bigger the reward.

When you look for advice from the Casino on growing your business, you're likely to see the same tactics being promoted over and over again:

- Automated DMs from cold outreach you didn't ask for: *"I guess you're not serious about [benefit]?"*
- Outsourced solutions to lead generation: *"If I could guarantee adding 30 new leads/month to your business, would you say yes?"*
- Funnels and timers: *"This offer expires in 23 minutes and 47 seconds—don't miss out!"*
- The daily social media grind: *"You just need to show up every day. Post 3 reels, 1 carousel, 5 stories, and go live twice a week. It's that simple!"*
- Focusing on followers and reach: *"Here's my secret to get you to 100k followers fast."*
- Literal shiny objects: *"This new AI-powered tool will 10x your content strategy overnight!"*

It's all splash and dazzle without any real substance.

The coaches, courses, and gurus selling these marketing methods promise that their strategies will generate endless leads and skyrocket your sales. Just implement that twice-a-day content calendar, film that automated webinar, and write that email sequence to sell your digital course, and you'll be set. *It works for them!*

The secret to their success? Most of these influencers got in the game early and built up followers and influence when the market was less saturated, customers less discerning, and platforms much less "pay-to-play." Their marketing approach works because they fuel it with so many expenses: webinar and funnel software, a content creation team, sales assistants and appointment setters, and paid ads.

And when you struggle to do those same tasks as a soloist or small team, who swoops in to help you implement these strategies? Those influencers, who make their money by teaching you to market like they do. They make money while you burn cash at the altar of Meta and Alphabet ads and funnel software subscriptions.

The reasons sales, marketing, and visibility are hard are structural, not personal. You are not a failure, whether you play their game and it doesn't work or you choose not to play at all. So much of what we've been taught about marketing is based on a framework of manipulation, conformity, and being the product. So why do we keep playing?

We're swimming in a world of **manipulative marketing promising easy results**. The allure of quick results is hard to resist, particularly if you didn't get into business to be a marketer—you got into business to do the work you love, serve your clients, and have more autonomy about how you work.

Funnels, ads, and automation promise a steady stream of clients with minimal effort, often using psychological triggers like scarcity, urgency, and authority to get customers to buy, as identified by Robert Cialdini.[35] These tactics prey on the fear of missing out or being left behind, making you feel like the only way to grow is to use these methods. These influencers may nudge you toward practices that compromise your values and alienate your audience, such as fake scarcity or overly aggressive follow-ups.[36] Many of the "codified" best practice marketing and launch approaches that have been around for decades rely on these tactics and don't provide any alternatives.

Social media and content platforms dangle the promise of growth: **a scalable way to reach beyond your personal network**. They promise that with one post or reel a day, you can avoid having to traipse around town at networking events or hop on endless Zoom coffee chats that eat up your calendar. You can expand your reach from behind your laptop or in the comfort of your yoga pants, on your own time and schedule, with automated emails and social media posts that can reach thousands.

Particularly if your time is limited for any number of reasons, like family commitments, health circumstances, or a full-time job, social media and broadcast platforms seemingly let you spread your message without holding individual conversations. And that approach was quite effective early on, when the platforms were trying to build their own

---

35 Robert B. Cialdini, *Influence: The Psychology of Persuasion* (Harper Business, 2006), 2.
36 Maggie Patterson and Michelle Mazur, *Duped: The Dark Side of Online Business*, podcast, accessed March 25, 2025, https://duped.online/.

user base, relying on the product (that's us) making content and grabbing attention to monetize with ads.

But the platforms have since degraded, become ensh*ttified.[37] They're designed to exploit your labor, with small businesses finding themselves trapped in the grind of posting, emailing, and engaging just to stay visible, even when it feels like the algorithm is working against them. And your consumers might actually have stepped away from those platforms after seeing the harm they can cause to their mental health and attention span. Do you really want to spend your time becoming an expert in day-trading attention?

The promise of automated, behind-the-scenes marketing methods can feel like a lifeline for women and other underrecognized[38] groups, **offering them a way to grow their businesses without constantly being in the public eye.** For many, visibility in marketing isn't just challenging—it's risky. Showing up online often means facing scrutiny, biases, and even harassment, making the act of "taking up space" feel exhausting. And even when you do show up, systemic inequities mean the same efforts don't always yield equal results—requiring you to work harder to earn authority and trust. The cost of overexposure is real: Trolls, doxxing, and the emotional toll of constant judgment can push even the most resilient business owner to retreat, making the allure of a less visible, automated solution all the more tempting.

The appeal of these more automated, more scalable, and less relational marketing approaches is clear—but the price you pay is high.

If you grow through frequent content marketing, you might pay *thousands of dollars a month* on a podcast production team, a YouTube team, and a social media team, not including the cost of *your* time recording the podcast, filming the videos, and creating the content. There's also the time cost to create and monitor all of the funnels: coming up with lead magnets and freebies, writing all of the funnel emails, setting up the automations, and monitoring ad and funnel results. And I'm not

---

37 Cory Doctorow, "The 'Enshittification' of TikTok," *WIRED*, last modified January 23, 2023, https://www.wired.com/story/tiktok-platforms-cory-doctorow/.

38 N. Chloé Nwangwu, "Why We Should Stop Saying 'Underrepresented,'" *Harvard Business Review*, last modified April 24, 2023, https://hbr.org/2023/04/why-we-should-stop-saying-underrepresented.

quoting unrealistic numbers; I personally pay a few thousand dollars a month for various content marketing contractors, charging prices that I know are fair (based on the pricing chapter).

If you grow through paid traffic, ad managers run thousands a month, and you'll shell out thousands of dollars for the ads themselves because the algorithm can't run well if there's not enough data. Without clear messaging, a strong sales process, and a validated offer suite, you can burn through cash in a hurry (and give it to the ultimate winners of this game, the platforms).

The price of playing the game isn't just in cash and time. The constant grind to keep up—posting, engaging, tweaking things—can lead to *an addictive focus on numbers and clicks*. Over time, this obsession can erode your confidence, compromise your values, and leave you wondering whether your business is even aligned with who you are.

You understand that without a steady pipeline of clients, you'll struggle to stay in business. But while these scalable methods might suit certain business models, many small business owners don't need massive traffic or high-volume funnels. Instead, you can build a sustainable flow of customers by aligning your marketing efforts with your specific business model and relationship style.

Just like with pricing, you can step away from the slot machines and design a marketing approach that fits your business model, values, and capacity.

Marketing isn't just about algorithms, funnels, or churning out endless content—it's about connecting with the right people in a way that feels authentic to your values and sustainable for your business. This takes doing the following:

- Understanding the core "jobs" marketing needs to do for your business based on your business model and business goals
- Mapping the stages of the marketing journey and addressing the ones you may be avoiding or neglecting
- Going beyond the typical "marketing channels" to demonstrate a more diversified, holistic approach to marketing
- Creating your specific marketing approach so that every effort supports your objectives without wasting time or resources

Instead of falling into the traps of the "followers and funnels" game, this chapter will help you build a marketing strategy rooted in clarity, alignment, and meaningful connection—designed to support your business goals and resonate with the people you serve.

LEAVING THE MARKETING TABLE

Your marketing methods should be curated for your business model and customer segment, designed for how you like to interact with people in your ecosystem and how you like to create, and ultimately concentrated in the fewest activities that accomplish the goal.

Let's break that down a bit:

1. **Your Business Model**: A marketing system designed to "attract" tens of thousands of leads and convert thousands each year to a low-priced course? That requires a very different strategy than the marketing and sales approaches appropriate to bring in a handful of clients each year for six-figure consulting engagements.

2. **Fewer Activities**: Spreading yourself thin with too many activities means you can't get good at any one of them. Becoming a world-class speaker, a seasoned network builder, a writer, or an entertaining YouTuber? Each avenue requires different skills, and the norms of each platform and the qualities required to succeed vary.

3. **Choose What You and Your Customers Like**: If you hate dancing in reels on social media or if your customers don't read a weekly newsletter? Don't do it. But understand the role that those activities serve in your marketing approach and ensure you have another activity that does the same job.

As with so many of the business aspects discussed in this book, you have to understand the *purpose* of a marketing tactic first before knowing whether it makes sense for your business. Ultimately, these activities worked for *someone*—otherwise they wouldn't be taught! But the wrong tactic, even done well, might waste your time, money, and energy. Instead of trying every marketing tactic under the sun, build a marketing and sales approach—dare I say, system—designed for your style of business.

When we look to do focused, intentional marketing activities, we operate with power: clear messages delivered with effective rhythms that build momentum over time.

We leave the Marketing Game by understanding the foundational jobs to be done in marketing and how to choose the right activities for your business based on your business model, personality, and stage of business.

We'll first review the four stages of the buying journey before showcasing the different activities or tactics you can use at each stage and how to choose between them (because you can't do it all, especially not as a soloist). We'll then learn how to help these activities compound over time. After reviewing these philosophies, you may ditch the funnel or decide that a scaled marketing approach is right for you after all.

DESIGN THE SYSTEM FOR THE GOAL

The first step is understanding the purpose of your marketing and sales efforts. The system you design is dependent on a few factors, which you can come back to later after reading this chapter.

- How many customers do you need? Do you need one or two long-term clients each year or twenty course purchasers per month?
- Is your service a one-time purchase or a recurring purchase (e.g., a subscription, membership, or retainer)?
- How do customers buy? (Fortune 1000 C-suite executives don't "click to buy" from an email newsletter or find their next service provider by spending a lot of time perusing LinkedIn posts.)
- Where do your customers pay attention?
- Who is involved in the sale? Are you working with complex organizations with multiple stakeholders or with a consumer who can buy off of a single social media post?
- What's the timeline from awareness to conversion? One customer might make a $100 impulse purchase, while another might need to budget for months to save for a four- or five-figure investment even if they know they want to work with you.

Answering these questions helps you understand the purpose of your marketing and sales efforts, quantify the number of people you need to reach, and choose activities suited to your buyers and their approaches.

THE BUYING JOURNEY

No matter the number of clients you need to reach, there are four general stages of marketing and sales. Of course, I *could* tell you that this is a unique framework—but in fact it's a conglomeration of almost every marketing and sales approach on the planet:

- **Connection:** Meet and get exposed to new people, sparking curiosity.
- **Consideration:** Build trust and increase their readiness to make a change—and decide whether your solution is the right fit.
- **Conversion:** Guide them to make a decision and confidently choose you.
- **Champion:** Deliver results that turn clients into repeat customers and advocates.

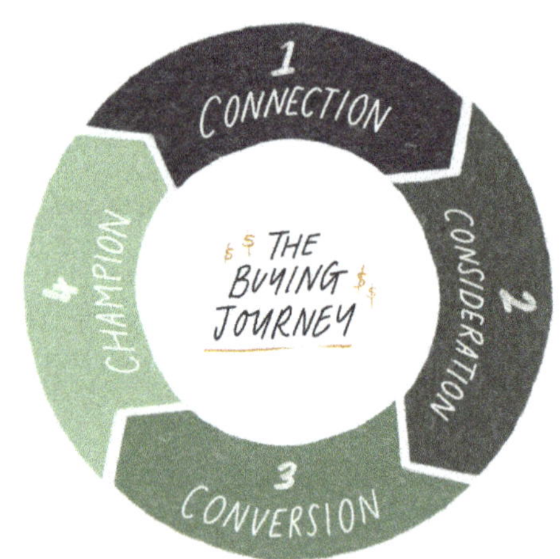

Stage 1: Connection—Meet New People

In this stage, you are connecting to new people, and they are curious to learn more about you and what you do! Activities here can include the following:

- Personal outreach: Joining communities and having virtual Zoom calls; having someone refer you
- Collaborations and guest appearances: A newsletter swap with a business bestie; connecting with a mutual friend on social media; speaking at conferences or on podcasts
- SEO: Having a powerful search presence on Google or using paid ads

At this stage, you're most likely showing up through borrowed audiences or leaning into channels that naturally drive more discovery, like YouTube (where the algorithm surfaces your content to new people). For anyone just starting out, I always recommend leveraging more established audiences rather than trying to brainstorm how to stand out in the sea of content.

Michelle Warner calls the spectrum relationship marketing vs. traffic marketing.[39] I clarify a middle ground called "collaboration marketing"—using 1:1 relationships to gain exposure to shared audiences. Go where your people are already congregating!

At this stage, you're also not just trying to connect directly with **potential clients!** You're building relationships with **collaborators** and **connectors,** the people who will provide you with opportunities for visibility or directly connect you with clients. Seeing you speak on stages, hearing you on a podcast, being referred by a trusted friend, or seeing hundreds of five-star reviews will do more to build trust among prospective clients and make an easier sale than almost any copywriting or sales strategy will. Also, you don't have to cold pitch to make connections with potential clients. However, unsolicited outreach—preferably to "room temperature" connections who are adjacent to your network and not cold contacts who wouldn't

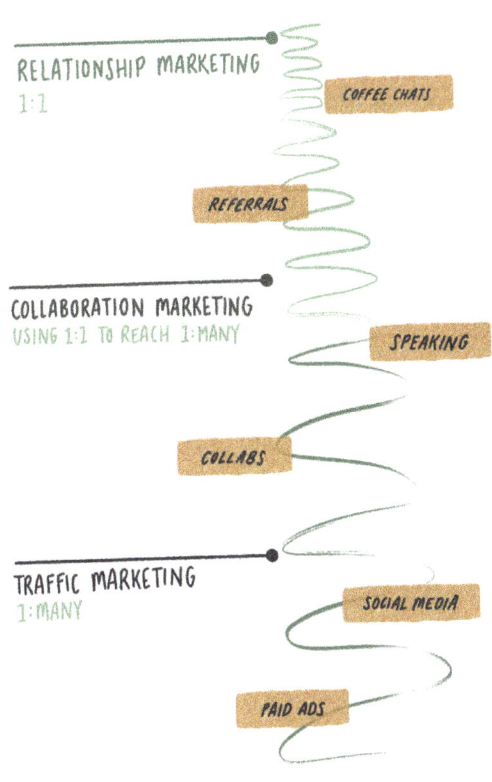

---

39 Michelle Warner, Sequence over Strategy, "How to Get More Clients with Relationship Marketing," accessed April 25, 2024, https://www.themichellewarner.com/blog/sos001.

recognize your name—is a good way to accelerate the initial process of getting your first clients.

In the Connection stage, you're actively starting relationships with people in your business ecosystem who either need what you offer or can connect you with opportunities for visibility that you might not otherwise have access to.

In other frameworks, you might hear this first stage called "Attract," "Grow (your audience)," "Awareness," or "Discovery." I don't use these terms, especially "Attract," which always brings up an image of posting on social media and just hoping you're manifesting or "magnetizing" your clients to you through your energy. That might have worked when the social media landscape was less saturated and less pay-to-play, but I encourage you to take a much more proactive approach to making connections. You might not even need an email list or an "audience" based on what and how you sell.

Particularly when you're running a relationship-based business, you probably don't have enough of an audience built up to let the algorithms really work for you or to rely on more passive activities that assume people will hear about you and then seek you out.

Stage 2: Consideration—Deepening Trust and Increasing Readiness

In this stage, you're building trust and deepening relationships within your ecosystem, including potential customers. You're helping them understand how to know when they need a change and why your particular approach helps them move beyond their status quo and increasing their readiness to make a change.

Change can be scary! And to buy your solution, people first need to be ready to make this particular change now, with a sufficient investment of time and money.

While some people you connect with may be immediately active buyers who only reach out to you once they have an urgent and important problem that you solve, many people you connect with don't fit that mold.

In your audience:[40]

- About 3% are "active buyers": Their need aligns with what you're offering, and they actively reach out.
- Another 7% intend to change: They have a need and would be interested in working with you to solve their problem, but they aren't actively pursuing options.
- 30% have a need but aren't ready to act: They are learning about what you do and see that you solve a problem they might have, but they lack the time, budget, readiness, or urgency to solve the problem right now.
- 30% don't have a need: They may like what they read from you or otherwise want to stay connected, but they won't be a purchaser.
- 30% aren't interested in your company at all: Hopefully, you don't have too many of these people in your world or on your newsletter lists, but who doesn't subscribe to some of the online biz gurus just to see what they say?

You have three goals in Stage 2: to build relationships, build trust, and build real education about the problem you solve or the opportunity you help clients reach so that you're the obvious choice to hire when they need you. You are showcasing your values and what makes you stand out.

We can also use this stage of marketing to shorten that time frame by helping clients gain quick wins or ethically increasing the urgency of their problems via illustrating what's possible, making the symptoms of the issue and their solutions clear, and reducing the risk to get started.

In this stage, you're mostly shifting your methods from channels you're borrowing (e.g., guest posting to other people's audiences) to channels you own, with more relationship-building strategies, like a newsletter, a podcast, or live classes and calls.

And personal outreach, which works to build connections, is a fantastic way to deepen relationships! Don't forget about the power of

---

40 Jeremy Johal, "The 3% Rule: Engage Customers Before They Need Your Services," accessed February 24, 2024, https://stickybranding.com/blog/3-rule-engage-customers-before-they-need-your-services.

a text, call, or mailed dinner party invitation as a way to stand out and forge relationships.

You're increasing your "time under talking": You want people to spend more time with you and understand your philosophies, approaches, and values. This is why social media (consumed in fleeting, bite-size moments) is less effective than spending thirty minutes with you each week on a podcast.

Potential clients might linger in this stage for years:

- They might have other areas in their lives or businesses that are demanding their attention first.
- They might try other approaches to untangle the same problem you solve.
- They might not have the budget or time to work with you.

But, ultimately, you are in the back of their minds when they are finally ready to make a change and looking for a solution.

Stage 3: Conversion—From Interest to Investment

In this stage, you are inviting a potential client into an active sales process and converting them into a customer. They've moved from "interested in making a change" to "made an investment" with you.

This movement could be a proactive personal invitation:

- A shoulder tap, where you're reaching back out to someone who had indicated interest at some point
- A "handraiser" email, where you're inviting people to raise their hands (digitally, through an email response) if they are interested in learning more about how you can help
- A launch sequence or an invitation to a waitlist for an upcoming offer

These invitations and offers interrupt people's day-to-day rhythms, making it more likely that they'll now choose to start the change process. We forget that everyone is inundated with noise and competing priorities. Our to-do lists contain an overwhelming number of items dealing with work, life, and family care. When someone reaches out to me personally and says, "You indicated interest in this, are you ready to get started? I can make it easy for you!" the default response on my end is relief. They have taken one of the things on my plate and helped me solve it.

People may also move to the sales process by booking a discovery call through your website, clicking a sales link in an email, or joining an offer after hearing about it on your podcast. These are more passive forms of invitation, but you must make it clear how potential clients can work with you across all of your marketing channels.

Once they've indicated interest, they are moving toward an active sales process.

When it comes to converting interested people to buying what you're selling, there is one maxim I think we should all remember: Sell like you serve.

Sales isn't just about copywriting and launch emails. It's about guiding your clients through the purchasing decision in a format that matches how you serve. If you're selling high-touch, high-value, or highly customized services? You'll probably want a high-touch, high-trust sales process.

If you're selling low-touch, standardized products or services? You'll want a low-touch, scaled sales process. Scaled sales processes aren't inherently low trust, but you do lose the ability to address concerns, mitigate risk, and increase value perception through conversations, relying instead on copywriting and brand positioning.

All sales processes go through four steps, discussed below.

Step 1: Discovery and Qualification: In this stage, you're discovering what the client is looking to accomplish, why now is the time to solve that problem, who the decision-makers are, and what else they've tried so far. Before moving too far along in the sales process, establish whether your potential clients are qualified for the offer—whether they have the budget, the authority, the need, the time, and the readiness to work with you at this stage. You may find that potential people who are interested aren't actually a fit for your offer because they aren't ready and won't get the full return from their investment. It's great to help people appropriately navigate to the solutions that best fit their needs and avoid being hired for a wrong-fit client. They might have interest but not intent to buy at this point.

Step 2: Value Awareness and Risk Management: Throughout the sales process, you're uncovering the value and scope of your services for the client and understanding the tension. You're uncovering the problem they have and illustrating why it's causing them pain or highlighting their desire and the opportunity to fulfill it. What is the value of solving this problem? What's getting in the way of rectifying this issue or addressing this opportunity?

Step 3: Confirming Scope, Timing, and Investment: You're finalizing the scope, timing, and investment that align with the client's needs and their agreed investment in this step. With standardized offers, these factors are clear up front. With more customized offers, more complex stakeholder maps, or where the investment is linked to the value, this dialogue is often handled in a series of conversations in which you cocreate the final outcome alongside the client—perhaps even coaching your primary contact to sell this proposal within their organization to their stakeholders!

Step 4: Finalizing and Onboarding: This step is about payment, contract, and onboarding. In this process, even when the client has said "yes" verbally, you're still their partner in the sales process until the work begins. The procedure of signing your contract or statement of work, paying your invoice, and getting started is an important part of the sales process and should be tailored to your audience. Big corporations are not going to pay with a credit card through the same systems that a consumer or solo entrepreneur would use. And a smooth onboarding process demonstrates safety for the client and assures them they've made a great decision.

If you have a *more complex sales process*, these four stages are often done in conversation, cocreating the scope of work in conjunction with your potential client. A complex sales process occurs when you serve larger organizations, have multiple stakeholders or decision-makers, and/ or have variably priced and scoped projects.

If you have a *simpler sales process*, such as selling a product or standardized program directly to the end consumer, this process can be done with low or no dialogue. You might instead have a sales page, a cart, and an onboarding email sequence. The long-form sales page is designed to qualify and address value and risk through copy and assets

instead of a conversation. The launch sequence aims to talk to customers'
pain points, tensions, dreams, and problems. This more asynchronous
strategy tends to work best when the offer is standardized, the value
is relatively straightforward, and the offer is scaled and needs to serve
at volume.

Stage 4: Champion—From Clients or Colleagues to Repeat Buyers, Referrals, and Raving Fans

Once you've started working with a client, the journey continues but
in a different way. You want to turn those clients into raving fans who
are excited to renew with you, engage in recurring work, or refer you to
their friends. While some marketing is all about the sale, where the client
is ignored or dismissed once you have their credit card info, our clients
can become the most powerful resource in our business.

This is how sales and marketing turns into a flywheel—a true
cycle that gains momentum over time—instead of a one-way funnel
that requires new eyeballs being churned and burned through a
marketing sequence.

Earn the Referral: If your customers don't have a great experience with
you, they won't refer you! The client's experience once they've paid is just
as important as the sales experience. We can make sure our customers
have clear expectations regarding their results by providing transparent
processes, clear timelines, and standardized communications.

Repeat Business: A client with a great experience is much more likely
to buy from you again than a new client. They get the value of having
someone who already knows them and their context, and you get to be
of service without having to get up to speed fast in a new client's context.
It's important to understand the customer's lifetime journey in moving
toward their goals and have an offer that matches them at each stage.
Your offers might be structured like an ongoing subscription or retainer,
you may have additional offers once the initial work is complete, or you
might check in with clients each year to help them maintain the changes
they've made.

Plant the Seeds: Our clients and colleagues are busy and might not
remember to talk about you or send business your way! But we can help
plant the seeds for future referrals and connections. Send thoughtful gifts

to referral partners or offer to make introductions or collaborations. We can use Cialdini's[41] reciprocity principle in our favor by being generous with our network, which will bring more opportunities back to us.

Celebration: Who doesn't love being seen? Sending a personalized birthday card, taking a client out to lunch or coffee when you're in their city, extending an invitation to a party you throw for your clients each year—these are all simple ways to show people they aren't just a transaction in your checking account.

The fortune is *always* in the follow-up, in consistently planting, tending, and harvesting those seeds of relationships over time.

Once you build the systems needed to maintain a list of clients, referral partners, and advocates and start implementing processes to reach out to them on a regular basis, the momentum begins to build for a steady stream of inbound requests for client work or visibility opportunities.

MARKETING BEYOND SOCIAL MEDIA

So now that we know the stages of marketing and the numbers we need to fill our client or customer roster, we can choose the right method at each stage of marketing for our business models.

As growing business owners, we might see only one way to "market": social media and broadcast-style email marketing.

Why is that the only approach we see?

Because the people teaching business building through courses have to scale, as their business model doesn't work if they only enroll a handful of new clients each month.

But what they did to start or grow is actually not how they scaled or what they do now. Not only is their business model different, but also the tactics they used probably don't work anymore for newcomers (thank you, market saturation).

When we consider marketing and sales as a system, like a flywheel, we can choose different activities based on what we've already built and how quickly we need results.

---

41 Robert B. Cialdini, *Influence: The Psychology of Persuasion* (Harper Business, 2006), 2.

Depending on where your business stands, you might need rapid results to fill your client roster—or you might be ready to build a reputation that effortlessly attracts clients over time. The trick is knowing when to focus on immediacy and when to invest in long-term strategies.

These different models range in power and in immediacy.[42] Outreach will have the most immediate impact on your sales results but is limited in its power. Discovery, especially once you've built a body of work that establishes your authority, has immense power but takes years to develop.

What does your business need right now?

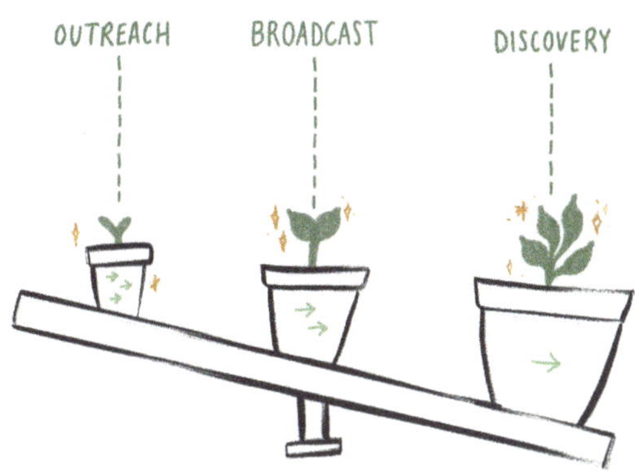

Outreach: Results Through Relationships

Outreach is an oft-neglected approach in marketing and sales. We might not even think we're "marketing" if we aren't publishing an email newsletter or posting on a social media account. But you may not need any of that to achieve your goals, especially early on in your business journey.

In a world where we want to reach "volume at scale" through mass marketing approaches (like we see many celebrity entrepreneurs do), the easiest way to get started—and actually get more results early on—is to build relationships through reaching out to connect with people.

In a world where everyone is busy, being proactive is the best way to break through the noise.

Outreach isn't just a way to meet new people, like joining communities and going to networking events. Outreach is a powerful approach at each stage of the customer journey: extending a Zoom or phone call invitation to someone who attended an event you hosted, mailing

---

42 Blair Enns, *The Four Conversations: A New Model for Selling Expertise* (Gegen Press, 2024), 30.

newsletter subscribers an invite to join your program or retreat, or meeting up with colleagues and clients when you travel to their city.

I once took a trip to Europe and met up with a former client in every city I visited. Those relationships are now substantially stronger because I reached out, and a few used that visit as a prompt to spotlight me to their friends.

You can reach out via sending DMs or texts, organizing a dinner at an in-person conference, sending snail mail, or starting a voice memo chat.

Outreach might be aimed at your ideal clients—or it may be aimed at referral partners, collaborators, and advocates who can powerfully introduce you to new customers.

One of the biggest ways I grew my client roster? I took a client out to lunch when she was in my city. She invited me onto her podcast and then to contribute to a course for her community, and now referrals from that network make up a large portion of my client base. And I'm one of *her* biggest advocates: inviting her onto my own podcast, referring everyone I meet to her community, and championing her work. But this all started with a real relationship.

Outreach can feel intimidating to introverts. And this approach might seem like it takes too much time. Doesn't just posting on social media seem more efficient? Why do you have to spend so much energy talking to people?

But outreach has so many benefits, even for those who don't like "networking," don't want to be "salesy," or are introverts.

Outreach reduces the latency between you talking about your work and getting a response. It increases the time you're in conversation with a particular human, deepening that relationship, so you don't have to be quite so visible to everyone, particularly trolls on social media.

And outreach doesn't have to occur through conversation! A thoughtful text, card, or email can do wonders to strengthen your relationship with others, and your reach won't be penalized by an algorithm when you don't show up multiple days in a row. You can batch these outreaches based on your capacity.

It's not about meeting *more people*—it's about truly building relationships with the *right people*. At the beginning, this may mean planting more relationship seeds without knowing which ones will be the most fertile. But cultivating a tight-knit circle of colleagues and trusted clients can fuel your business without the exhausting dance of content and generic conversations.

Building outreach doesn't mean simply going from "people who have inquired to work with you" and zooming across the spectrum to "cold pitching strangers." Instead, send a "room temperature" email to people who might not have talked to you but might recognize your name or know you have connections or mutual interests in common. Simply strike up a conversation and be curious about *them* first.

Importantly, in at least some of your outreaches, make an ask—and make it specific. Do the heavy lifting for the person you're reaching out to and make it easier for them to respond. For example, ask for a specific introduction to someone or to collaborate on a project or visibility event. Request feedback on a specific offer or idea. Ask if they have fifteen minutes next week instead of saying, "Let me know if I can be helpful at some undefined time in the future." In some cases, you might even ask whether they'd like to know more about what you're doing (aka soft intro to sales).

Outreach is the smallest flywheel. It's easy to quickly start up and increase the activity level when you need it.

Need an influx of clients? Set up free connection calls or reach out to 5–10 people in your network every day. You can rapidly build up your ecosystem and find yourself in direct conversation with individuals who might need your work or know someone who does.

Busy with client work? Turn the activity down to maintenance level, staying top of mind and adding value in a personal way with a handful of special touches each week or month.

The peril of relying on social media or email marketing is that people have to be in your audience or subscribed to your newsletter to see what you post! So instead of posting to the void, focus on reaching out and building relationships first. Then, more people will start to see you on the broadcast-based channels.

Outreach is your starting point—the quickest way to build relationships and generate results when you need them most. While it does require consistent effort to maintain, as it's a "lighter" flywheel, it can be systematized over time.

But as you gain traction and strengthen your network, it may be time to expand your approach, amplify your message, reach more people, and start creating a lasting presence.

Broadcast: Scale Your Visibility

Broadcast marketing is what we often think of as simply marketing: showing up where the clients are already consuming your content or hearing your message.

While outreach is about planting seeds one by one, broadcast marketing is the season of larger-scale irrigation.

This might involve popping up in their social media feed, podcast player, YouTube algorithm, or inbox. It could be arriving as a guest presenter in a community they're a part of or being featured in an ad in your colleague's newsletter. You might show up in their mailbox with a direct mail campaign or as a sign on a community events board.

Broadcast marketing is designed to reach more people: You put something out once, and multiple people see it, on their own time and in a leveraged way. This style of marketing is harder to get started than outreach, no matter what the gurus tell you. But there are a few different ways you can approach it.

You can build your **own channels**: social media, hosted events, a newsletter, a podcast, or free communities. While this can be a strong way to deepen relationships with the people who already know you, if potential clients aren't on your email list, no amount of conversion copywriting is going to get them to buy from you! Unlike in the early days of social media, the algorithms are not helping small accounts grow by showing your work to more people. You're probably going to have to proactively go find your people in the places or communities in which they are already congregating.

You can show up on **borrowed channels**: Be a guest on other people's podcasts, host workshops in other people's communities, be a keynote speaker at conferences, or be a preferred partner on their favorite marketplace. Particularly when you're starting out, it's substantially easier to go to where other people already are instead of hoping they come to you!

Of course, the best way to borrow channels is *through building relationships*, which again requires that upfront time and effort first. People aren't going to want to put you and your content in front of their audiences if they don't know you and your work—which means you'll still need outreach and ecosystem building as a core part of your marketing strategy.

You can participate in **paid channels**: ads, sponsorships, or other paid placements. But this approach should be reserved for validated offers with validated messaging first; otherwise, you'll burn cash.

Ultimately, broadcast style requires your marketing to be good enough, with a sufficiently clear message, to cut through the noise. No one is going to pay attention to your generic Instagram post about a holiday— but in an outreach-based conversation with you, the person on the other end of the line is actually listening to you.

Compared to outreach, which requires consistent proactive effort, **broadcast-style marketing is a heavier flywheel that can create momentum** and hold it longer once you get the flywheel moving:

- That social media post can be reposted again.
- That newsletter can be turned into a blog and sent out again.
- That podcast can be consumed long after you recorded it.
- You can host a workshop for multiple people and then post it on your website for others to see.
- The same email can be read by 100 people or by 1,000 people without increased effort on your part.

But remember, broadcast-style marketing still requires consistent output. As this content is often ephemeral—it pops onto your feed and then is gone—this effort doesn't really compound over time unless specifically designed for that purpose. Broadcast marketing gets your message out to many people at once, but it's still tied to the effort you put in.

To truly create a marketing engine that works while you sleep, you need to build discovery-based assets—resources and systems that let clients find you, learn about your work, and take action without you needing to lift a finger.

Discovery: The Long Game of Authority

Discovery marketing is the ultimate long game. It's where your expertise, reputation, and visibility combine to create opportunities that come to you. Clients seek you out, referrals flow in, and your existing work speaks on your behalf—all without you needing to actively do broadcast or outreach marketing every day. But building this level of discoverability requires long-term investment in content and assets over time.

Building discovery assets isn't a quick fix—it's a deliberate process of creating resources that consistently showcase your expertise and attract your ideal clients. They might search for a term you rank for through SEO or hear about you from a friend. Perhaps they search for you and see your multiple five-star reviews on Google or Yelp, or they stumble onto a YouTube video about you while searching for something else. They might even read a book you write, like this one! *(P.S. Recommend this book to a friend if you're enjoying it!)*

And through a robust approach that covers all of the stages of the buyer journey, potential clients can learn more about you, how you work, and whether you're a fit for their needs without having a conversation with you first or seeing a piece of your content in their social media feed. They might find you through a search and then see videos outlining your approach online, read case studies, and then book a call or buy your intro course. These assets build trust before you ever even talk with them, making sales smoother and reducing the need for constant outreach.

Of course, you're thinking, "Yes! I want all the people to come to my website and decide to work with me." (Maybe you really *can* make sales while you sleep!)

But discovery is the heaviest flywheel because it requires substantial assets to be built first and time for the flywheel to start generating results.

When I need a window repaired, I'm not joining a window repair company's email list or following them on social media. I'm not even talking to the owner. I'm asking a friend for a referral and then going to their recommendation's Google page and looking at the reviews. And maybe this is just me, but I don't hire the company with only two reviews or the one that shows up at the bottom of the search results.

But when that window repair company I chose started and didn't have any five-star reviews? I bet you they hustled to get the word out—through building partnerships with contractors and community management properties, door-to-door knocking campaigns, and direct mail. (How do I know? Because as a homeowner I now get all the knocks on my door.)

I know plenty of business owners who don't post at all on social media or have a podcast: They have pieces that rank on search, essays or case studies that get shared through personal networks, and books that appear on Amazon. And once you find them, you can consume all the content and information you want, all on your own time, until you're ready to work with them, thanks to the journey set out that works on their behalf.

Discovery is about scalability but not in the high-volume sense of traditional broadcast marketing. Instead, it's about creating depth— providing enough value and insight that potential clients feel confident in reaching out to you. It takes heavier lifting up front, but the payoff is a system that works for you indefinitely.

But building these assets in your business may take a while, and discovery is investing in the long game.

It may take months for a piece to rank on SEO …

… many videos to find one that hits with the algorithm …

… years to build a strong referral network …

… hundreds of jobs to get tens of five-star reviews …

… time and expertise to write a signature essay or micro-course that gets shared and gains traction.

But once you have those assets? They continue to work on your behalf, even when you aren't working. We just don't want to start there, as we don't have enough expertise and likely need clients more immediately.

The beauty of discovery is that it compounds over time. A single well-written article or a compelling client success story can generate leads for years, creating a sustainable foundation for your business. But discovery doesn't replace outreach or broadcast—it builds on them. By integrating all three approaches, you can create a marketing ecosystem that balances immediacy with power, serving both your short-term needs and long-term vision.

MAPPING YOUR METHODS TO YOUR BUSINESS MODEL

Now that we know the buying cycle and the types of activities comprising it, we can select the appropriate activities for your particular system design.

If you're making money from your business through a creator-based business model with a course or community vs. a 1:1 service, you may need to enroll 100 people per year. The conversion expected here is much lower because it's not a relational service, where you're having real sales conversations.

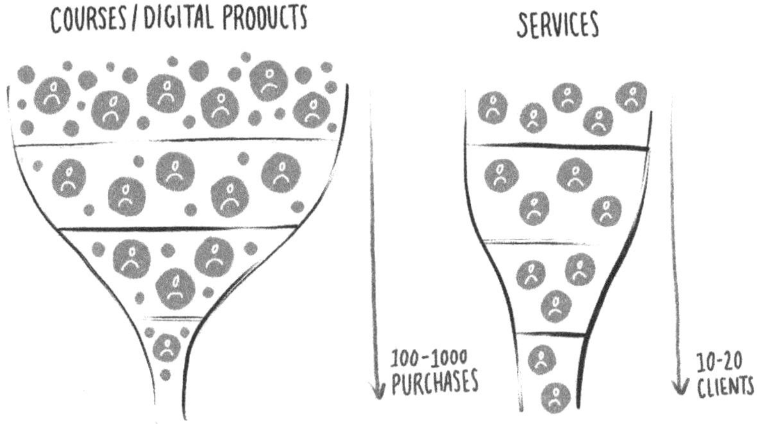

At a 2%–3% conversion rate, you'll need 3,000 people to visit your sales page or see your email. And if only 50% of your list reads your email? You will need upward of 6,000 new subscribers to your list each year.

There's no way you can have relationships with 6,000 people. The only way to build up the sheer number of people needed on your list is through leveraged distribution on social media, content creation, collaborations with other established audiences, and (most likely) ads.

Your goal here is scaled relationships.

But let's say you run a delivery-based business, where you need to work with 10–20 clients per year. If about half of the people you talk to in discovery calls book with you, you only need to have conversations with 20–40 potential clients per year (that's 2–3 sales calls per month).

Your goal here is conversations and connections.

The twenty clients you have probably send referrals your way. (I certainly go out of my way to send referrals to my trusted partners.) Some of your clients renew. You do a few podcast interviews, guest teach in a community, or host some workshops to invite more connections into conversations. You build relationships with forty people in the communities you engage with. It may take time, but the relationships compound.

One of my clients needs only three customers every year, and many of those clients renew for a second year. She will always fill her business through curated conversations and relationships—not through content creation as an attraction mechanism.

Wildly different business models require wildly different numbers and tactics.

So let's add up the time you (might) spend on content creation:

- Let's say you spend 30–60 minutes to create each daily post and graphic.
- You take another 30–60 minutes each day to engage on the socials to boost the algorithm (and to connect with real humans).
- You pass lots of time checking each post for vanity metrics (no shame; I do this more than I admit).
- You then spend two hours on a weekly newsletter or podcast.

In the end, you might be spending ten hours a week on content creation! And unless you get really efficient at repurposing that content, its impact on the socials will be very short. Growing your newsletter or podcast still requires getting in front of new people.

Are you seeing your client roster grow in exchange for those ten hours?

Or would you be better served by spending those ten hours per week doing some or all of the following:

- Inviting two colleagues or people you find interesting to thirty-minute connection calls
- Emailing your past clients with podcasts or articles you know they'll love

- Creating a limited audio podcast series outlining your best points of view that new listeners can binge when they hear about you
- Inviting people into an experience of your service (paid in either money or their time)
- Participating in aligned communities and building relationships
- Hosting a monthly masterclass or roundtable
- Publishing a monthly newsletter
- Writing long-form posts for your website with optimized SEO

In a relationship business, content should be the "soft landing," whereby people who hear about you can learn more about you and how you work to see if you're a fit. Through social media and your website, blog, or newsletter, potential clients can see your most recent posts, understand your point of view, and see you demonstrate your authority. That content isn't what brought them to your world, but when they arrive, it lets them know they're in the right place.

I recommend choosing one activity from each stage: Connection, Consideration, Conversion, and Champion. If you're primarily focused on relational marketing, ensure you have an outreach activity at each stage as your base. As you gain experience and the outreach flywheel starts humming, add on one or two additional activities that you can maintain, investing in both broadcast methods and discovery assets.

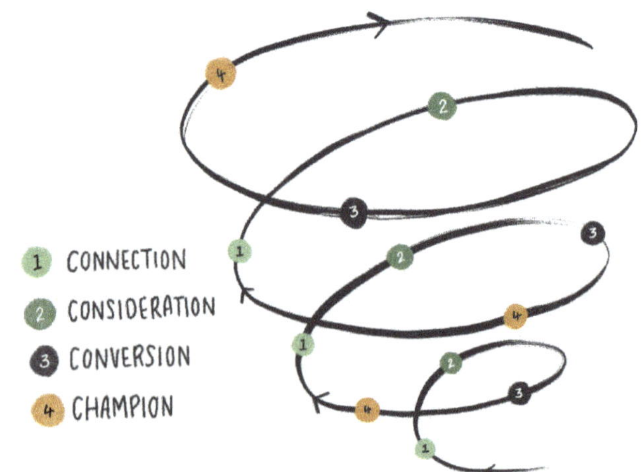

SUMMARY

Leaving the Marketing Game isn't about finding better ways to get more followers—it's about aligning your marketing approach with your business model. We select activities we enjoy that help us meet new people, build trust and relationships, showcase how we work, and effectively guide clients through the sales process. We expand our ecosystems beyond potential clients to include referral partners and other aligned humans who can connect us to collaboration opportunities. We move beyond broadcast marketing as the default option, incorporating both more immediate and higher-power approaches like outreach and discovery. By moving away from the "followers and funnels" approach, we can skip the facade and build a client conversion system that works for us.

Reflection Questions 

1. Does your business model require relational marketing, traffic marketing, or to land somewhere in the middle of the spectrum?
2. What are your primary activities in the Connection stage?
3. What are your primary activities in the Consideration stage?
4. Do you run a simple or complex sales process? How do you plan to invite potential clients into your Conversion process?
5. How can you turn clients into repeat customers?
6. How do you support your clients and raving fans as your Champions?
7. Do you need rapid results in your client conversion process, or are you focusing on power and long-term results?
8. What activities can you cut from your marketing efforts to focus on fewer, better commitments?

Want to map your marketing approaches? You can get your own "Marketing Map" template in the *Leaving the Casino* workbook or from the downloadable resources at deeperfoundations.com/casino

We spend time automating all of the workflows or delegating to an assistant without asking this fundamental question: What really needs to be done in the business? And do I have the honest capacity to take this on?

CHAPTER 8

Efficiency—The Time Management Trap

YOU'VE MADE IT PAST the Pricing Game and the Marketing Game, tuning out the advice to "charge your worth" and "grow your audience at all costs." But running a business still takes more time and effort than you ever imagined. The to-do list that used to live on a Post-it note is now a never-ending conveyor belt of tasks, each one more urgent than the last. You're spending nights and weekends just trying to catch all of the balls in the air … and more than a few in your business (not to mention your life) are crashing to the ground.

This is not the laptop lifestyle or freedom you were promised!

As you walk through the Casino, you pass by the craps tables, and you can't help but notice the excitement: players placing chips all over the table, betting on multiple numbers and outcomes simultaneously. The dealer encourages you to spread your bets, promising bigger wins if you cover more ground with each round. The appeal is clear—why bet on just one number when you can save time and get the same result by betting on everything at once?

That's the **Efficiency Game** in a nutshell: Time block your calendar down to the second, automate every repetitive task, and create systems that will do the heavy lifting for you.

You're told you can hack time itself—by doing more, faster, and all at once. The promise? Freedom, ease, and time to finally focus on what matters most.

Here's what the dealers say to keep you at the table of the Efficiency Game:

"You just need this perfect tool!"
"Block your calendar to the minute!"
"Automate it all!"
"Work smarter, not harder!"
"Every second counts!"
"The four-hour workweek is real!"

All over the internet, a wave of productivity and time management advice hits you squarely with its singular commandment: Do more in less time.

The influencers selling you the dream of efficiency are often playing a different game entirely. Their business model is not built on selling services, where delivery requires consistent time and energy investments. Instead, they sell courses, frameworks, and tools that promise freedom and ease—but only because they've already built their business models around selling at a broad scale.

They market the idea of a low-effort, high-reward business. What they don't show is the effort—and often the upfront hiccups—it takes to create and sustain these systems. Developing systems for marketing and course operations takes years of content creation, hundreds of hours of delivery, and relentless online visibility. And these systems don't build themselves. Behind every automation is an entire team: copywriters crafting email sequences, content creation teams editing those videos and creating the thumbnails, and operations managers chasing after team members to hit deadlines. Their "efficiency" is backed by massive up-front investments of time, money, and resources that can take years to pay off.

They show off perfectly polished plans, a consistent publishing schedule, and time to "be the CEO." But what's not acknowledged? That there's a team buffering any hiccups in their systems. Automations don't work? There's hired help to repair it. Broken links? That's someone else's job to fix it while the CEO is doing their deep work.

And what about being efficient outside of the business? Many of the male productivity gurus either have no children or turn over the mental load of running the home to women, either as the primary partner or as a paid caregiver. That productivity advice about "the optimized morning to make you successful" goes out the window if you have young children or other care responsibilities or are primarily responsible for keeping your house in order.

It's no wonder the Efficiency Game resonates with so many—when you're drowning in tasks and feeling stretched too thin, the promise of doing more in less time feels like a lifeline. But beneath the surface of these quick fixes lies a deeper issue: the pressure to do too much, too fast, with systems that may not truly serve you.

We're facing an **unsustainable level of information flow, with more fractured attention than ever.** We're buried under a mountain of responsibilities, from client work to operations, and trying to multitask increasingly fractures our attention. The onslaught of information coming at us—from emails to social media notifications to *dings*—has never been higher, as discussed in Johann Hari's book *Stolen Focus*.[43] Particularly for women, our time resembles "time confetti," a term coined by author Brigid Schulte: "What time is like for most women: fragmented, interrupted by childcare and housework. Often women are so preoccupied by all the other stuff that needs doing—worrying about the carpool, whether there's anything in the fridge to cook for dinner–that the time itself is what sociologists call 'contaminated.'"[44]

We've long been sold the dream that **efficiency will help us do more with less.** In the 1930s, economist John Maynard Keynes suggested that technological enhancements would make us so productive that we could support ourselves with only fifteen working hours per week and that we would then be faced with the challenge of how to occupy our

---

43 Johann Hari, *Stolen Focus: Why You Can't Pay Attention—and How to Think Deeply Again* (Crown Publishing, 2022).

44 Brigid Schulte, "Brigid Schulte: Why Time Is a Feminist Issue," *The Sydney Morning Herald*, March 14, 2015, https://www.smh.com.au/lifestyle/health-and-wellness/brigid-schulte-why-time-is-a-feminist-issue-20150309-13zimc.html.

leisure time.[45] Clearly, that hasn't happened. Time-saving devices like microwaves and laundry machines were supposed to make our homes more efficient. Yet, the hours we spend on housework haven't changed since the 1950s.

What *has* changed? The standard of living and the expectation to keep up has increased. The same is true in business: It's not about having a "six-figure business"; it's about being a "seven-figure mentor" or even a "billion-dollar creator." Automations and workflows often lead to greater expectations in various areas (e.g., how quickly we respond to emails), both from our clients and from ourselves. When processes become more efficient, we tend to fill the time with additional tasks—more efficiency drives more demand.

The belief that **visible activity equals impact**—or what author Cal Newport calls "pseudo-productivity"[46]—has been the primary way to measure employee and organizational performance since the Industrial Revolution. To improve factory performance, Frederick Taylor introduced principles of scientific management to optimize factory output, such as counting widgets, timing tasks, and standardizing hand movements. In the modern knowledge economy, this translates to the idea that the more tasks we complete or the more automations we set up, the higher our output—and therefore our outcomes—will be.

But this mindset can trap us in the cycle of "doing" vs. the discernment of what really creates impact.

Ultimately, **American culture glorifies work and even overwork,** stemming back to the Protestant work ethic that equates productivity with morality. Today, that belief has evolved into the pervasive idea that rest must be earned—and only after you've maximized your efficiency. There's the pressure, the constant drive to maximize efficiency before taking a break. Time management techniques like task batching and the Pomodoro method promise to help you "earn" leisure, but they often reinforce guilt around rest.

---

45 John Maynard Keynes, "Economic Possibilities for Our Grandchildren," 1930, PDF file, accessed March 25, 2025, http://www.econ.yale.edu/smith/econ116a/keynes1.pdf.

46 Cal Newport, *Slow Productivity: The Lost Art of Accomplishment Without Burnout* (Portfolio, 2024), 22.

Entrepreneurs have gone viral with posts about how success demands relentless focus and sacrifice, including videos about how one famous entrepreneur didn't go to weddings in his twenties to get in more hours of work time and outpace his competitors. Rest becomes a fleeting aspiration because this underlying belief remains: If you're not working, you're falling behind, both guilty of resting and simultaneously guilty of not resting!

While the appeal seems high, there's yet again a cost to playing the Efficiency Game. The price we bear for trying to be ruthlessly efficient is burnout and rigidity, not to mention the tangible costs in time and money. And the house rules distract us from the real work to be done—**being honest with your capacity, taking on the work that really matters, and honoring your energy.**

The promise of efficiency often comes with a hefty price tag. Every new tool, software subscription, or system you adopt adds to your expenses, with costs that quickly increase over time. That $20/month task management tool or $50 automation software may seem manageable at first, but multiply that by several tools you're only partially using, and the expenses start to pile up. If you're not able to implement or maintain these systems yourself, you may also find yourself hiring expensive consultants and admin support just to keep everything running.

Systematizing too early—or too much—can create *an unintended rigidity* in your business. Every time you make a change to your offers, pricing, or marketing strategies, you'll find yourself trapped in a web of outdated automations and workflows. Updating one process means troubleshooting and fixing countless interconnected systems, consuming hours of your time and energy. You may feel unable to pivot or experiment because every adjustment requires an overhaul of your systems. I've heard many business owners say, "I can't sell this offer until I have the funnel or workflow set up," only to spend weeks building infrastructure for something that may not even sell.

The pressure to be hyperefficient often leads to packed schedules and rigidly prioritized task lists. When every moment of your day is time blocked and optimized, you leave no room for the unexpected—delays, last-minute client needs, or personal emergencies.

This lack of margin can create a fragile system, one that collapses the moment life doesn't go according to plan.

Over-scheduling also erodes your ability to think, rest, and create. Without white space, you sacrifice spontaneity, creativity, and the capacity to reflect on what your business truly needs. And you run the risk of burning out your most precious business resource—you and your nervous system.

When your capacity is overextended, what's the first thing to go? The activities that sustain and grow your business, like marketing, sales, and business development. Your clients come first, so you absorb the brunt of overwork, stretching yourself thinner and thinner in a relentless cycle.

Ultimately, by overestimating our capacity and commitments, thinking we can "productivity our way out," we end up trapped in an overwhelming cycle, desperately looking for a better strategy.

But we don't have to be left with a set of manual tools or a wide-eyed look of "what am I supposed to do today in my business?" Instead of buying into the Efficiency Game, we grow by doing the following:

- Understanding where to focus our time for the greatest business impact
- Aligning our energy and priorities with our natural rhythms and capacity
- Systematizing processes at the right level to support our goals without overengineering
- Identifying and avoiding the traps of optimization that don't serve our business

In this chapter, we'll cover how to approach building efficiency with intention rather than play the game.

LEAVING THE EFFICIENCY TABLE

The biggest myth we're sold? We can do it all, and we can do it all at once. We can show up on all of the marketing platforms, *and* sell individual services *and* groups *and* courses, *and* we can blog at the same time, *and, and, and!* And to take on all of those projects at once, we spend more time moving tasks around our calendar, like arranging the deck chairs on the Titanic. We look for tools and hacks to make things easier. We might even try to hire all of this work out to someone else (which we'll cover in the next chapter on the Hiring Game).

We spend time automating all of the workflows or delegating to an assistant without asking this fundamental question: *What really needs to be done in the business? And do I have the honest capacity to take this on?*

To leave the table, we need to do more than optimize and add in systems and automations.

We need to rethink what actually needs to be done, align those tasks with the time and energy we have, and prune anything that doesn't drive power and directly impact our business growth. Only then can we build sustainable systems that support growth instead of adding to the chaos.

We'll cover four ways to evaluate your time and increase effectiveness without playing the Efficiency Game:

1. Your Real Time Budget
2. Energy Alignment
3. Process, Prune, Prioritize—Then Plan
4. Systematize to the Level That Matters

YOUR REAL TIME BUDGET: HONORING LIMITS

We're often sold an image of entrepreneurship that feels like a fantasy: working a few days a week and delegating client work and marketing, all while magically scaling the business.

But here's the reality—sustainable businesses require thoughtful allocation of your time, energy, and focus across key areas. There's no shortcut around it. We need to match that time allocation to our business model to ensure we have the ability to meet our revenue needs with the time we've allotted to delivery.

Trying to contort yourself into an ideal weekly schedule that doesn't honor each of these needs means you're going to be overwhelmed and burned out.

Your time is your most valuable resource, but how you allocate it depends on your business stage, model, and goals. Here's

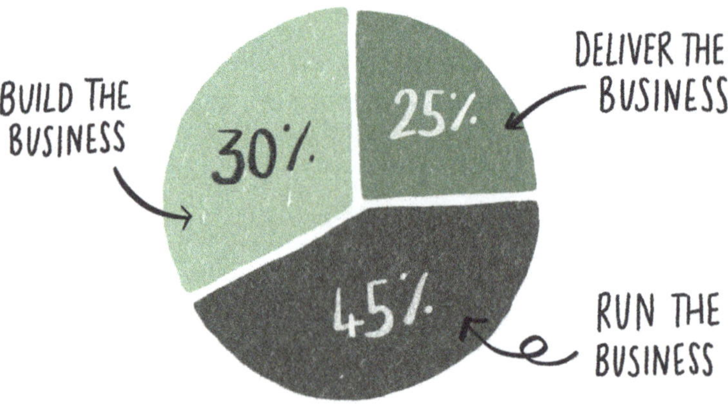

a general guideline for allocating your time, focusing first on delivery-based businesses.

Delivering the Business: Projects and/or Content Creation (50%—60%)

This is the core of your work—delivering for clients or creating salable assets or marketing content. This includes all time spent on delivery, including prep and session follow-up. For delivery-based businesses, this should comprise roughly 50%–60% of your total business working time.

- "I'm creating content for this community I run."
- "I'm delivering for this retainer client."
- "I'm making a new course and setting up sales automations."
- "I'm writing my next book and/or my paid newsletter."
  (For Edu-Tainers where this is a core business model.)

If you run a business that doesn't need as many clients or sophisticated systems (e.g., a Craftsman business model that only takes on 2–3 retainer clients for a long time), you might spend more than 50% of your time doing client delivery, as there's simply less marketing to be done. But if your business relies on a consistent flow of new clients, I recommend taking this as a guideline and evaluating how to make the financial math work for your business by changing your offer scope, price, or target market. Otherwise, you'll end up working yourself into the ground: overworking on delivery, scrambling to have time for marketing, and never building the assets and foundations that make business growth easier.

Running the Business: Ongoing Activities to Maintain Momentum (20%—30%)

These are the activities you do regularly to continue bringing in clients or customers, managing your business operations, and tending to your business systems. You want to manage these long-term responsibilities over time, and they often don't have end dates. As a delivery-based business, this should comprise 20%–30% of your total business working time.

- "I send my newsletter out each week."
- "I run this event each month."
- "I monitor ads and conversion on my products."
- "I review my financial books each month."

Common areas often fall into specific business departments. I call these the business "tending" activities—because, as any gardener knows, you're never done with watering, feeding, or weeding.

- **Marketing:** Any regular/ongoing marketing efforts like a newsletter, a podcast, or social media posts
- **Sales:** Making connections and building your relationships; pipeline management; proposal writing; contract management
- **Finance:** Monthly bookkeeping; quarterly taxes; regular forecasting and financial planning
- **Delivery:** Communications for an ongoing product or service like a community or subscription; scheduling clients
- **Admin and Planning:** A monthly or quarterly review and goal-setting process; cleaning out emails

Building the Business: Defined Projects to Strengthen Your Foundational Business Systems (10%—20%)

This time is dedicated to projects that grow your business and your business-building systems so that you can implement or improve the functions and activities you'll run on an ongoing basis. These formed initiatives have a fixed end date and specific tasks. You're able to say, "I've completed all of the steps to reach a certain result." This will likely comprise 10%–20% of your total business working time.

- "I'm establishing a new welcome sequence to nurture newsletter subscribers."
- "I'm implementing this process to make running this event easier."
- "I'm launching this smaller product by this date: Here's what's included and how I'm launching it."

I call these the "root" building projects, as they are the improvement efforts that strengthen your business foundations and allow your business to grow stronger. However, at only 10%–20% of your working time, you can't take on too many projects at once or you risk stalling out and making progress on none of them.

If you're a creator?

Substitute the time spent doing delivery with time dedicated to creating your salable collateral or marketing content.

Instead of spending your time delivering to clients, you'll likely spend it creating content, delivering speaking engagements, and creating products, courses, or tools.

You'll also spend even more time on "Run the Business" marketing: creating YouTube videos, social media content, and marketing emails. As some famous YouTubers say, you'll move from a 9-to-5 job to a 24/7 job. You'll essentially replace the time you spend on client delivery with client acquisition. The number of customers you need is often much higher, sometimes exponentially so.

Those business leaders who say they're coaching just two hours a week? What you don't see behind the scenes is the time they're spending managing their teams, handling sponsorship logistics, and creating the content. You also don't see the time they're spending photographing their vacations or being omnipresent on social media, immersed in messages and ongoing chatter. And you definitely don't see the fact that their brains are always thinking about the next content, the next video, the next way to make money.

SHIFTING PROPORTIONS OVER TIME
In the Early Stages

You're spending a lot more time on building literal foundations in your business, fostering relationships, and securing your first customers to build up to a sustainable client roster. You'll spend roughly one-third of your time on each area: delivering client work, running your marketing and sales systems, and building foundational business systems. The goal here is to build momentum and establish your business.

As You Grow

As your business grows, you'll start to shift the ratios, with half of your time spent doing delivery while retaining at least 25% of your time for sales and marketing and 20% for business admin and building. You may shift even more of your time to client delivery and away from marketing, but only if you can afford to grow your customer base slowly based on your business model. (And you'll need to be super potent in what you choose to do for marketing—no spending hours making videos or intricate posts that disappear in the feed.)

When Scaling with a Team

As you bring on a team and move toward an Agency model, you'll start to reduce the amount of time you spend doing client delivery and replace that with managing your team while also setting aside a substantial amount of time for marketing and sales. Bringing on a team doesn't mean you necessarily end up working less. It just means your time shifts from delivery to business development and team management.

MATCHING YOUR ENERGY LEVELS

Time allocation sets the size of the container, but how you fill it depends on your available energy. Not all work requires the same mental or emotional effort, and if you've ever tried to write a high-impact proposal when you're drained, you know how true this is. Matching the right tasks to your energy levels ensures you're productive without burning out.

Matching the right tasks to your energy levels isn't just about efficiency—it's about sustainability. It allows you to do your best work when you're at your best and protect your well-being when you're not.

Here's how to think about your energy in tiers.

Tier 1 Energy: Strategic or Creative (10%—20%)

This is your best energy and should be dedicated to your big-picture, deeply creative, and most visionary work. This could be designing a new offer, creating marketing assets, or systematizing a process that will create future leverage. Strategic work is where long-term growth happens. Protect this time during your peak energy hours—maybe that's every morning, on Mondays or Fridays without meetings, or even once a month. For me? I have my strategic time on Saturday mornings at my coffee shop.

If we don't set aside time to do the important but not urgent tasks, we end up on the never-ending burnout treadmill.

Much of your "build the business" project work (the 20% of your time) should be scheduled during your Tier 1 energy periods.

Tier 2 Energy: Standard (50%)

Standard energy represents the time during which you can maintain reliable, sustained effort during your business hours and should be dedicated to your standard work. This fuels the bread and butter of your business—client delivery, content creation, sales calls, and marketing. It should be spent on work you plan for (e.g., making that YouTube video or writing your next campaign), but it can also include urgent tasks like drawing up a last-minute proposal or addressing an unhappy client.

Yes, I'm saying it here: Your clients don't get your best energy!

This energy should be spent on a mix of both "run the business" and "deliver the business" work—the work you need sustained energy to do but not your peak energy.

Tier 3 Energy: Maintenance (10%)

Maintenance energy represents the period of your days, weeks, or month when your energy is at its lowest. These time periods should be dedicated to the administrative, behind-the-scenes work that keeps your business running—like email processing, calendar management, bookkeeping, or minor admin tasks. This is also a mix of the "run the business" and "deliver the results" work.

Tier 4 Energy: Margin and Rest (20%)

Leave 20% of your business hours as buffer time. You or your children or your family will get sick. The kids will inexplicably be out of school yet again. Something at home will break and need your attention, or your internet will go down for a day. Some tech will go haywire in your business, or you'll want to hunker down during your menstrual cycle or the new moon.

Maybe you'll get an unexpected new client proposal or an urgent visibility opportunity to respond to! Or perhaps you'll want room to enjoy an unexpectedly sunny day or accept an invitation you don't want to pass up.

The point is, leave buffer time in your business! Something will pop up, and without margin, every surprise becomes a crisis. With it, you have the freedom to handle unexpected challenges and embrace spontaneous joys.

Matching tasks to energy levels is nonnegotiable. If you try to do deep strategic work when you're mentally drained, you'll struggle. If you use your best energy for admin tasks, you'll miss out on your most productive hours.

Here's where energy alignment and your time budget work together: Tier 1 energy fuels your business-building efforts, Tier 2 energy periods ensure you deliver results and continue to bring in new clients, and maintenance work performed during Tier 3 periods keeps the business running smoothly.

But without margin, even the best plans will eventually fail. So the next step is even more crucial—clearing space by pruning excess work.

PROCESS, PRUNE, AND PRIORITIZE: CLEARING THE PATH

Now that you've mapped out how to allocate your time and match it to your energy, it's time to address what's actually filling that time. Most entrepreneurs aren't overwhelmed because they aren't working hard

or efficiently enough; they're overwhelmed because they're trying to do too much. You might already be noticing that even if a process has been made "easier" through templates or automation, you simply don't have the time or energy to do everything on your list.

Ultimately, you're dealing with volume—the sheer number of obligations competing for your time and attention. As Cal Newport writes in *Slow Productivity*, "By volume, I'm referring to the total number of obligations that you're committed to complete—from answering a minor question to finishing a major project. As this volume increases past a certain threshold, the weight of these efforts can become unbearably stressful."[47]

This is where the real work begins: **processing what's on your plate, pruning what isn't creating impact, and prioritizing what truly matters.** Only then can you create a plan that works.

---

47 Cal Newport, *Slow Productivity: The Lost Art of Accomplishment Without Burnout* (Portfolio, 2024), 48—54.

Before you even think about optimizing, you'll need to eliminate the tasks and projects that don't meaningfully move your business forward or that you no longer have the capacity for. This isn't about squeezing more out of your day or making tasks more efficient through automation—it's about doing less, more effectively.

When I go through this process myself, I often think of a quote by Greg McKeown in *Essentialism: The Disciplined Pursuit of Less*:[48] "Essentialism is not about how to get more things done; it's about how to get the right things done."

Step 1: Process

To start pruning, you first need to **process everything you're trying to get done in your business.** That means collecting everything together—digital task managers, notes, journals, emails, text messages, social media DMs, your calendar.

Then, group these tasks into the following categories:

- **Ideas:** The dreams and unformed ideas you want to take on.
    - ✧ "I want to grow my newsletter."
    - ✧ "I want to make running this event easier."
    - ✧ "I want to sell a smaller product to increase conversion."

Until you know exactly what you want to implement, what success looks like to you, and the steps you need to take, these ideas remain just that—ideas. They should be cordoned off in a way that allows them to germinate and grow without cluttering your mental load or task list.

Then, list existing responsibilities, which is everything you're currently doing in your business, organized by domain as described below. This has been adapted from Tiago Forte's PARA approach.[49]

- **Build the Business Projects:** Formed initiatives with a fixed end date and specific tasks that you're already working on or planning to start within the next month or so.

---

48 Greg McKeown, *Essentialism: The Disciplined Pursuit of Less* (Crown Business, 2014).

49 Tiago Forte, *Building a Second Brain: A Proven Method to Organize Your Digital Life and Unlock Your Creative Potential* (Atria Books, 2022).

✧ "I'm implementing a new welcome sequence to nurture
newsletter subscribers."

✧ "I'm launching this smaller product by this date."

- **Run the Business Areas:** Ongoing activities you do regularly to keep
your business running. Group these by function.
  - ✧ **Marketing:** A newsletter, social media, or a podcast
  - ✧ **Sales:** Connecting with potential clients and partners
  - ✧ **Operations and Admin:** Task management, email processing, and
  team coordination
  - ✧ **Finance:** Monthly bookkeeping, taxes, and forecasting
- **Deliver the Business Activities:** Your client-facing work, including prep
and follow-up. Group these by client or program.

Step 2: Prune

Pruning doesn't just mean eliminating tasks—it means refocusing on the
core actions that compound over time, driving results and momentum. By
identifying what's cluttering your mind and schedule and investing in what
works, you'll avoid becoming overwhelmed and unable to focus.

Where should you look to prune? Start with evaluating your current time
allocation across building, running, and delivering.

When it comes to *building the business* projects, taking on too many
ideas or new initiatives can stall your progress. You can get trapped in
the cycle of perpetual learning and endless research and end up stuck in
preparation mode without making traction. Juggling multiple projects
at once often leads to context switching and mounting administrative
overhead. You end up with "zombie projects," the projects that linger
somewhere between started and finished that compete for your attention
(and clog up your to-do list). You never break through the adaptation curve
of new tools or systems, and your efforts fail to deliver the efficiency you're
aiming for.

In *running the business*, trying to keep too many plates spinning
regularly can create problems. You're trying to produce the podcast *and*
the YouTube, write the email newsletter *and* the daily social media, manage
regular outreach *and* your free community—it's just too much while you're
also delivering for clients. Your calendar fills with activities keeping you on

the constant hamster wheel, leaving you no time to assess what's working, prune inefficient systems, or refine your processes. Instead of improving weak spots, you're stuck in a loop of repetitive work that keeps your business running but doesn't make it easier or more effective over time. Without time to pause and evaluate, the operational side of your business becomes a bottleneck, hindering growth.

Delivering the business can easily take over everything else if you're not careful. When client work dominates your time, "build the business" and "run the business" activities—like refining your marketing, engaging in authority-building efforts, or implementing financial systems—always fall to the bottom of the list. This often leads you to a feast-or-famine cycle where you're scrambling to find new clients or playing catch-up on finances.

Questions to help you prune whole tasks, projects, or even areas in your business include the following:

- **Does this lead to getting more clients or growing the business?** Really look at the data to see where your results are coming from.
- **Have you outgrown this task or process?** What worked in the past may not be serving you anymore.
- **Is the time or cost investment worth the return?** Evaluate whether other tasks could deliver similar or better results with less effort.
- **Is this a "should" that you resent?** Be honest about whether this is an obligation you've imposed on yourself due to external expectations.

Make the Most of Your Time: Think in Multipurpose Assets

As you grow your business, nothing you do should serve just a single purpose. Particularly when your time is stretched across these three domains of your business, always think in terms of how one activity can fuel multiple processes. Market research on a new offer is actually marketing because you're talking to people and reminding them of what you do. A client deliverable can turn into a workshop or tool you send to prospects. A newsletter post can also become a blog entry. A client question can spark an idea for a YouTube video or an illustration that can be used in a training.

Multipurpose assets ensure that you're never starting from scratch, and they reward you with ongoing returns on your initial investment of time.

Maximize the Return on Investment

Additionally, you can improve the return on your time and effort investment of the activities you keep in one of two ways: by making your activities more effective or by reducing the time you spend on them.

- **Making your current activities more effective:**
    - ◈ If you're networking in a community, don't just lurk. Schedule follow-up calls, deepen relationships, and create partnerships.
    - ◈ If referrals drive your best leads, focus on nurturing your referral sources through consistent, personalized outreach.
    - ◈ If guesting on podcasts works for you, don't just stop at the recording. Make sure you're following up with the host and optimizing the landing page listeners visit.
- **Reducing your time investment:**
    - ◈ Publish shorter newsletters or shift to a biweekly schedule for higher-impact pieces.
    - ◈ Skip consistently creating new content in favor of creating seasons (with breaks) or including some "reruns" of best content, as new audiences haven't seen your full catalog.
    - ◈ Cut back on social media posting or eliminate underperforming platforms altogether.
    - ◈ Wind down free communities if they're not generating leads or engagement.

I've been there—trying to do everything, everywhere. I joined multiple communities; juggled Instagram, LinkedIn, and Twitter; and wrote a weekly newsletter. At first, I didn't know what worked, but eventually, I realized that doing everything at once meant doing most of it poorly. So, I pared down. I quit most social platforms and focused on what really moved the needle.

In every core activity, you can optimize what already exists instead of chasing more. You don't need fifty different marketing strategies—you need the core ones to work harder for you.

Ultimately, pruning is about subtraction. Cut the tasks and projects that aren't delivering results. Double down on the ones that do.

Ask yourself:

- How can I maximize the impact of what I'm already doing?

- Can I increase my skill so that each repetition gets better results?
- Can I increase my efficiency so that each repetition takes less time?
- Can I increase the frequency of effective actions to build momentum?

You'll find that you can do better by doing less. By focusing on the essentials, you create a ripple effect whereby each task builds on the last, freeing up time and energy for long-term growth.

Once you've pruned, take a critical look at what's left. **Do you have enough time and energy to handle these tasks effectively?**

Are you maintaining some protected time for business-building projects? Have you dedicated an appropriate amount of time to running the business, specifically for ongoing sales and marketing activity? If you truly can't cut out any more activities without harming the business foundations or stunting its growth, it's time to automate, delegate, or outsource some activities in the business (we'll cover this in the next chapter).

Pruning unnecessary tasks is about creating breathing room, but once you've made space, the next step is just as crucial: identifying and addressing the biggest bottlenecks in your business. Without this step, even a streamlined task list can still lead to a stagnant business.

Step 3: Prioritize

Now that you've created that necessary space, ask yourself: What do I take on first, particularly for business-building projects? If you've ever stared at a seemingly endless list of tasks and projects, unsure of where to begin, you're not alone. The truth is, most of us are pulled in multiple directions because we're not solving the core problem—our bottleneck.

Think of your business as a flow-through system, moving from marketing and sales to delivery and operations. Somewhere along that flow, there's often a choke point—a place where work gets stuck, slowing down progress and creating inefficiencies elsewhere. Maybe you're not booking enough sales calls, which means you're constantly scrambling to find clients. Or perhaps your client onboarding process is clunky, leaving you bogged down in admin instead of delivering your services. Whatever the case, the bottleneck is the one area where solving the problem will unlock momentum across multiple parts of your business.

Addressing anything but the bottleneck is like adding a spoiler to a car instead of a faster engine. The spoiler might look shiny, but anything that isn't making the car go faster isn't an effective use of your time and energy.

Find Your Bottleneck

Your first step in prioritization is to **identify the bottleneck.** Where do you see friction, delays, or backlogs? What keeps causing the same problems over and over again? Or, what's holding you back from future growth? Fixing the bottleneck isn't glamorous, but it's effective. Once addressed, it improves the performance of the whole system, unlike fractured efforts that don't create impact.

For example, let's say you need more clients. To know where to focus our business-building efforts (the real bottleneck), we have to look below the surface and ask more questions.

Are you getting prospects that don't convert or no prospects at all? If you are getting prospects and sending proposals and they aren't converting, the bottleneck might be either strengthening your messaging or increasing your sales skills and qualifications process.

If you aren't getting prospects, how many new people are you meeting who might be, at some point, ideal clients? If you're meeting lots of people who seem like your ideal clients but are not interested in working with you, the bottleneck would be in the middle stages of the client conversion process.

If you're not meeting new people regularly, what is holding you back from doing so?

- You might not be confident about who you're working with (client knowledge).
- You might not know what you're selling (revenue and profit suite).
- You might not know your point of view (authority).
- Or, you might not have enough people in your network to talk to (client conversion, specifically ecosystem building).

Once you've established the areas constraining your business, you can start to put projects in place to address the root cause of the presenting symptoms.

Prioritizing Your Projects

Maybe you want to work on a few tasks or projects simultaneously within the core bottleneck you want to address. Before taking on multiple projects at once, especially large projects, strategically consider the composition of your "build the business" projects.

It's tempting to take on multiple large projects at once, but this often leads to feeling overwhelmed and making slow progress. Most small business owners can only handle one or two large or high-complexity projects at a time while maintaining their daily responsibilities. Incorporate *small, quick wins* where possible and intentionally plan for larger projects during seasons when you have more time to focus. Prioritize *high-impact efforts*—those that drive revenue, efficiency, or long-term growth—and set aside projects that are "nice-to-haves" but don't lead to sustained impact.

Also, don't solely focus on making operational improvements or on building something new, as you'll need a mix of both. Alternate between **foundation fixers**—projects that fix broken systems, reduce friction, and improve operational efficiency—and **growth enablers**, which build on your strengths, like a new offer or new marketing approach. If you spend too much time fixing foundations without taking on growth initiatives, your business growth may stagnate. But if you focus only on growing without fixing underlying operational issues, you'll struggle to sustain that growth.

How does this philosophy show up in practice? Here's an example of a long-term goal in my business that steadily moved forward, but over a longer time period than you might expect. I knew early on that I wanted to implement a Teacher business model and launch a YouTube channel. But birthing that final vision took over a year.

I first wanted to improve my video setup: new camera, new lighting, new audio equipment. I then had to rearrange my entire office for a good video background, including getting the guest bed moved out from behind my desk, ordering a new sofa, and then sprucing up the background by ordering *so much décor* and having my dad paint my office wall. (Sure, I didn't have to do this. But I was all in!) Then, I needed to free up time and cash to hire a YouTube editor, so I ended my engagement with my social media team, concluding with a final project to create a static Instagram grid. Finally, I had to find and interview a YouTube editor, and we spent a month creating the look and feel of the video editing.

Each of these projects took about two months to implement, but they all stacked on each other to create momentum over a year. And now, I have a small but growing YouTube channel!

Embracing the Backlog

As you prioritize, recognize that your capacity is finite. You can't fix everything at once or take on every exciting growth opportunity. This is where discernment comes into play. Look at your current workload and determine what's feasible within the time you've protected for business-building projects.

If you find yourself taking on too many large or complex projects at once, it may be time to revisit your list and be even more surgical in what you choose to actively work on. The goal is to maintain a balance—steadily progressing on fixing core issues while continuously making improvements for growth.

You'll inevitably encounter projects or ideas that you can't tackle immediately. And that's okay. Instead of letting them weigh you down, capture them in an idea backlog. This could be a Notion database, a journal, or even a wall of sticky notes. The important thing is to revisit these ideas regularly, during quarterly reviews or when you've completed current projects.

Not every idea will remain relevant as your business evolves, but capturing them ensures you're never starting from scratch. As you move forward, you'll be able to draw from a well of insights and prioritize what your business—and the market—needs from you most at any given time.

PLAN YOUR EFFORTS: BRINGING IT ALL TOGETHER

By this point, you've aligned your time budget, matched your tasks to your available energy, and pruned down your activities to what's essential. You've prioritized projects based on impact and complexity, and now it's time to put this into action through intentional planning.

This isn't about crafting the perfect "Ideal Week" template because let's be honest—there's no such thing. No two weeks are ever the same, and as we discussed earlier, life will inevitably throw surprises your way. But that doesn't mean you can't approach your calendar with intention and flexibility!

The Arc of Time

Before we start with any kind of time alignment, think about the time horizon you're considering and planning for based on your personality, health, and business goals. If you're prioritizing flexibility or time in your Zone of Enoughness, you may find that you need to review a longer horizon for the ebbs and flows of projects and work—alternating months or weeks of heavier project or client work with months or weeks of rest. Alternatively, you might like the routine of days and weeks that look very similar, with more of a steady consistency to your work. (Reference your Zone of Enoughness questions about time and flexibility from Chapter 5.)

Every day doesn't have to look the same, nor does every week or month. Instead, consider these different approaches to arranging your time.

Seasonal or Yearly Arcs

During the year, you may have seasons of heavy client delivery and seasons of rest or business-building projects. If you're a tax professional, I wouldn't imagine you'll have much business-building time during the heart of tax season. But you can invest in new initiatives during the slower months. You might have a "micro-plan" for the week and a much more macro-plan to build, run, and deliver across the year. This is the time to plan for sabbaticals or extended time away.

Once your business is established and there aren't so many immediate bottlenecks to focus on, you may end up regularly revisiting one set of systems (e.g., sales and marketing, cash, people and processes, or vision) each quarter so that all get tended to and improved.

Monthly Cycles

If you menstruate or align with the moon's cycles, you may choose to orient your time and tasks to a weekly rhythm within the month. Your best visibility and creative time for sales and business-building projects might be planned for the full moon, and your margin and maintenance time may be aligned with the new moon.

Weekly Theme Days

You might choose to align weekdays with certain activities. For example, on days with lots of client work and meetings, I can't do any strategic thinking. So instead of trying to do sales and marketing, client delivery, and my best business-building work every day, I theme my days: Friday is for podcast recording and Tier 3 maintenance activities (so I have fewer meetings); I film many of my courses on Wednesdays; and Mondays are when I focus on business-building projects that don't require me to be on camera. Tuesdays and Thursdays are standard client delivery days.

In all of these approaches, you do have to maintain your "run the business" work to at least a minimum viable level. If you take an entire season off from meeting new people and generating new interest in your work (without a solid discovery engine from Chapter 7), you might end up in a revenue roller coaster. You also can't ignore administrative details for too long; otherwise, you'll end up with an overloaded inbox and some missed opportunities and income.

Align Your Time, Tasks, and Energy

Step 1: Block Your Margin First

Before you schedule anything else, protect your white space. At a macro level, block holidays, vacations, and planned time off. Within a week or month, set apart time for rest, meals, and breaks—and don't underestimate the importance of a chunk of unscheduled time at the end of each week or month. This margin is your buffer for when the unexpected happens (and it will) or for when you simply need the breathing room to recover or reflect.

Step 2: Schedule Your "Build the Business" Projects

Identify your Tier 1 strategic energy periods—the time when your focus and creativity are at their peak. This is when you'll work on high-leverage activities like developing new offers, improving processes, or creating valuable marketing assets. Protect this time from distractions, meetings, or any routine tasks that could drain your focus. Select your next business-building project(s) so that you know what to work on during this time. Be cognizant that this time might ebb and flow if your client delivery workload is inconsistent based on your arc of the year or season.

Step 3: Fill In "Run the Business" and "Deliver the Business" Activities

Use your Tier 2 standard and Tier 3 maintenance energy periods to handle ongoing responsibilities. These include everything from performing client delivery to sending newsletters, managing finances, and handling admin tasks. The tasks should fit naturally into the times when you have steady but not necessarily peak energy. For routine "run the business" activities (e.g., writing your newsletter, sending relationship-building emails, or recording your podcast), consider blocking off your calendar so that you see the time commitment you've made, even if that block shifts from week to week based on other obligations.

Step 4: Adjust and Adapt as You Go

If you notice that "run the business" or "deliver the business" tasks start to creep beyond their boundaries, consuming your margin or strategic time, that's a signal to prune further. Go back and reassess what's truly essential and what can be streamlined or eliminated.

On the flip side, if you're struggling to make meaningful progress during your "build the business" time, you may need to break projects into smaller, more manageable chunks. It's okay to adjust your timeline—business building is a long game, and slowing down is often the most sustainable path forward.

This isn't about sticking rigidly to a schedule or squeezing productivity from every minute of the day. It's about creating a sustainable rhythm that allows you to achieve your goals while honoring your capacity. As your business and life evolve, so will your plan. The key is to check in regularly, adjust when necessary, and give yourself grace when things don't go exactly as planned.

Ultimately, the most important plan is one you can actually follow—one that balances progress with rest, ambition with ease, and delivers not only results but also sustainability.

SYSTEMATIZE TO THE LEVEL THAT MATTERS

By this point, you've cleared out unnecessary activities and prioritized your projects with a focus on what truly drives impact. You've seen what you can sustainably absorb with your time and energy. Only now should you focus on making the remaining processes in your business more effective and efficient.

But here's the caveat: **Over systematizing can be just as dangerous as doing too much.** Complex, rigid systems often create fragility instead of freeing up time. The goal isn't to automate everything—it's to improve effectiveness where it counts without overcomplicating your operations.

Focus on the Purpose Before the Tool

Before jumping into automation or investing in tools, take a step back.

What's the real purpose of the system you're building? Where does friction currently exist, and is it worth fixing?

Not every inefficiency needs a tech solution. Sometimes, simplifying the process or adding a human touch is more effective

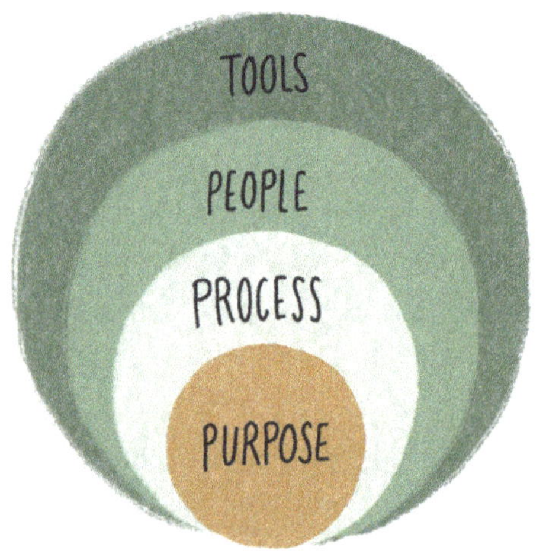

than automating it. The juice should always be worth the squeeze.

Define what you really need first by outlining the purpose, the process, and the people—and then expand to the tools and tech.

Purpose: Get clear on why this process exists and what it's supposed to achieve.

- Why am I doing this process or task in the first place?
- How often is it used?
- Does it contribute to business objectives (e.g., revenue, client experience, or reduced costs)?
- What does success look like when this process runs smoothly?
- What level of process quality is appropriate based on what I charge?

Process: Map out the steps to see where improvements can be made.
- What signals the beginning of this process?
- What marks the end of the process?
- What are the key steps of the process, and are any steps unnecessary or overly complicated?
- Are there decision points or times when manual intervention is needed?
- Who is responsible for making those decisions, and are they clearly defined?

People: Identify who or what will execute this process.
- Who is responsible—an internal team member, an external contractor, or a system?
- Does this process require someone to act in real time or outside of normal business hours?
- Is a level of oversight required, or can the process be delegated or automated without risk?

Once you have a clear understanding of the purpose, process, and people, only then should you consider the tools. The goal is to enhance the work—not overengineer it. Think of tools as enablers, not solutions.

Choose the Right Level of Systemization

Finally, before trying to automate with a tool or workflow for efficiency, see if a less rigid approach will solve a majority of the inefficiencies with little to no build time and effort.
- **Coworking and Rituals:** Sometimes, you don't need a complex system. You just need accountability and a routine. For example, a

weekly coworking session can help you stay on top of tasks you tend to avoid.

- **Processes and Templates:** If you find yourself doing repetitive tasks, create a checklist or template. This doesn't require tech—a simple document can reduce cognitive load and improve consistency.
- **Manual Workflows:** Not sure how long a process takes or worried about errors? Start with a manual workflow where you initiate each step yourself. For example, manually mark a client project as "complete" before triggering follow-up tasks.
- **Automations:** Automate when tasks have clear steps, straightforward logic, or minimal risk. Automation should serve you, not introduce additional layers of complexity. For instance, my video recording software automatically uploads to my storage system, saving me time on manual uploads. Similarly, a client inquiry might trigger an automatic email response and populate my customer relationship management (CRM) platform, but I retain control over personalized follow-ups.

Not everything should be automated. Processes involving creativity, judgment, or sensitive client touchpoints often benefit from human oversight. Automate repetitive, low-risk tasks like data entry, file organization, or reminders, but for high-stakes activities—like client outreach or strategic decision-making—maintain a level of flexibility.

Systems should reduce friction, not introduce it. The best systems adapt to your business needs without requiring constant troubleshooting or maintenance. By systematizing only what truly matters and leaving room for human flexibility, you'll free up time, protect your energy, and ensure your business continues to grow sustainably without unnecessary complexity.

SUMMARY

Efficiency isn't about pursuing more and trying to jam everything in through slick automations and workflows. We're ultimately pursuing the most impactful efforts, in accordance with our energy, that appropriately help build, run, and deliver our business. Define your working time for strategic, standard, and maintenance work based on your energy and leave time for margin. Process and prune your responsibilities: Determine where you're over-indexing across building, running, and delivering and find out which activities aren't generating results. Prioritize projects that address your bottleneck first and only systematize what matters—and to the appropriate level.

Reflection Questions

1. How many hours should you plan to work in a given week or month considering your time parameters in the Zone of Enoughness?
2. How many hours are you spending on building, running, and delivering the business? Are you over- or under-indexing in one of these zones?
3. What are your best energetic time slots for Tier 1 strategic, Tier 2 standard, and Tier 3 maintenance work? Do these change across the week, month, or season?
4. How much Tier 4 margin time do you need to incorporate, and do you need that margin incorporated every day, week, or month based on your flexibility requirements?
5. What activity or process can you prune from your business or make more powerful? (Identify at least one thing to prune!)
6. What projects should you prioritize this season to address your business bottleneck?
7. What remaining processes can be systematized, and what level of systemization do those processes require to generate the most impact with the least effort?

> You can get the "Process, Prune, and Prioritize" template in the *Leaving the Casino* workbook or in the downloadable resources at deeperfoundations.com/casino

In an expertise-based business, your team doesn't just execute tasks; they become an extension of your brand, values, and customer experience.

CHAPTER 9

Hiring—The Low-Cost Labor Lie

AS YOUR BUSINESS GROWS, so do the demands on your time and energy. In the beginning, you handled everything—because you had to. From delivery to strategy, sales, and administrative details, every task fell on your shoulders. You wore every hat, put out every fire, and juggled every ball. But by now, you're growing weary of the urgency, the constant grind, and the feeling that there's no end in sight. You've already pruned many of the tasks that didn't need to be done in Chapter 8, when you left the Efficiency Game. But you're still left with more to do than you have the capacity for. Wouldn't it be nice to have some help?

At first, the **Hiring Game** feels like blackjack, with straightforward, simple rules to follow: Split on certain cards, hit when you're under a target, and stay when you're over. The rules for the Hiring Game? Hire when you hit a certain revenue level, outsource tasks that drain you, and "buy back your time."

The influencers at the Casino table call out to you, promising freedom and ease:

"Hire before you're ready!"
"Stay in your zone of genius!"
"Delegate that sh*t!"
"If you don't have an assistant, you are the assistant!"
"You can hire a VA for $5/hr overseas!"

The house rules of the Hiring Game are clear: Hire as early and cheaply as possible, delegate everything you don't want to do, and watch your business thrive.

The promise of the Hiring Game is undeniable: the freedom to step out of the day-to-day details you despise, the ability to focus on the visionary work that only you can do, and the status that comes with being a "real" business owner—a leader with a team. The proof? Look at the influencers selling you the secrets. They boast about their team members, who handle everything from client work to marketing, all while they focus on "big picture" strategy, work three-day workweeks, or take vacations (which, of course, they post as social media highlights).

But the secret to their success isn't just delegation—it's often a mix of rampant overwork, exploitation, and mismanagement of their employees. Many influencers sell you on the dream of delegation while running their own teams with ever-shifting deadlines, poor communication, and a lack of clear direction. They promise "freedom" while relying on underpaid VAs, misaligned contractors, or burnt-out employees to keep their businesses running.

And when you struggle to replicate their results, who steps in to help? The same influencers, ready to sell you courses, templates, and coaching programs on how to hire and manage a team like they do.

It's easy to sit down at the table and play the Hiring Game. After all, the promise is tempting: Hire help, lighten your load, and finally get the breathing room you need to focus on what truly matters. When you're stretched thin and overwhelmed, it feels like hiring is the only way to break the cycle. The pressures to play the game often push us to bet before we're truly ready.

It is seen as a **power move and a status signal** to have a team. It's a sign that you've "made it." In the traditional business world, having someone else answering your emails, managing your schedule, or handling administrative tasks is practical but also signals success and legitimacy to others. For many small business owners, there's real pressure to appear larger than a one-person operation. We're told to create an email for "admin@" even when it's just us, to write "we" on our website, or to hire team members to prove we're capable of taking on bigger projects. A team can also represent real capacity—having more people in the business means you can take on larger contracts, expand your scope of work, or increase your client roster.

You may be facing the **dual burdens of running a business and managing your home.** Many entrepreneurs face this scenario, especially if you have a more flexible schedule than your partner or live by yourself. You're already carrying the weight of running your business—managing clients, marketing, operations, and delivery—and then you close your laptop only to start your "second shift" at home. The second shift, popularized by Arlie Hochschild,[50] is the concept of managing the entire emotional and mental labor of the household. Whether it's arranging daycare, navigating healthcare, or just making dinner and doing the endless loads of laundry, the perpetual list of responsibilities adds up. The Hiring Game is so tempting because it promises that there will be someone to finally help you carry the load at work.

Running a business can feel **isolating and lonely,** especially in a world where many traditional forms of community have faded away and we're increasingly spending time online on little screens. Religious spaces, neighborhood connections, and third spaces like libraries, coffee shops, or community centers—places where people naturally gathered—have dwindled over time, a decline Robert Putnam discusses in his book *Bowling Alone.*[51] The COVID-19 pandemic accelerated this shift, moving much of our lives and work into virtual spaces. For entrepreneurs conducting business online, we can go days without leaving our house or having a real conversation with a flesh-and-blood human being. We no longer get to chat at the water cooler with colleagues; instead, we're often sitting alone at a desk, communicating through screens.

To make matters more isolating? If you run a business solo, you have no one else to bounce ideas off of or share wins with. The promise of a team—real people to collaborate with, share ideas, and lighten the load—feels like a way to create a sense of belonging and shared purpose in an increasingly disconnected world.

---

50 Arlie Russell Hochschild and Anne Machung, *The Second Shift: Working Families and the Revolution at Home* (Penguin Books, 2012).

51 Robert D. Putnam, *Bowling Alone: The Collapse and Revival of American Community* (Simon & Schuster, 2000).

Finally, **it's easier than ever to hire talent at low costs or flexible
schedules,** especially with the rise of technology and access to global
talent pools. Many VAs and specialized contractors in lower-cost regions
have built their expertise to meet the needs of small businesses. Platforms
like Upwork and Fiverr make finding specialized talent easier, without
the commitment of full-time employment. Chat tools, video conferencing,
and task managers allow for communication and collaboration across
time zones. And as I'm writing this, you might even start to "delegate"
to a combination of a human and AI agent. Delegating at the click of a
button, with low-cost tools to collaborate, dramatically decreases the
barrier to entry of the Hiring Game.

But we don't realize the odds of winning this game or what it
truly requires.

The Hiring Game advice doesn't come with a serious evaluation of
your actual needs and ability to support a team member on an ongoing
basis. The idea that hiring will help ("Growth solves all problems!")
is a risky gamble that involves the lives and livelihoods of other real
human beings.

Expanding your team takes you from a position of managing yourself
to managing others. And in your expertise-based business, your team
members are an extension of you, your brand, and your business. How
you lead and manage *anyone* in your business—regardless of whether
they are a contractor or employee, full-time or part-time—is a reflection
of you and your values.

While all of the online business gurus are teaching you to "hire before
you're ready" or "just outsource it," very few are talking about how
doing so puts you in a position to impact the lives of others. They're not
discussing the nuances of hiring and onboarding, building relationships,
or being a strong manager. They might not be providing strategies for
how to have difficult conversations with an underperforming team
member or thoughtfully end the relationship with a contractor when
the business dynamics shift. Moving from a sole business owner to an
employer is an identity shift. Hiring changes your business model and
transforms your role and responsibility, like we've discussed in Chapters
1 and 4. Signing a contract doesn't automatically make you ready to lead.

Without a thoughtful plan to hire, you're likely to end up feeling confused, resentful, and burdened in new ways as an employer or manager. Too many business owners hire before they are ready or expand their team without the necessary systems, structures, and core leadership skills in place; then, they end up having to let that team member go a short time later—their initial issues no closer to being solved.

Without a clear plan, hiring can exact a price that you're not expecting to pay.

- **Financial Costs:** Hiring isn't cheap. The monthly invoices for payroll processors, software seats, and tools to collaborate quickly add up. Many of the roles you're encouraged to hire for early on (e.g., a VA or a "marketing assistant") aren't directly revenue generating, putting pressure on you to increase your client roster or marketing and sales activity just to cover costs. If your team is underutilized with client work, continuing to pay them means often you shortchange your own pay or profit. If you're not careful, you can burn through cash trying to keep up.

- **Reputational Costs:** In an expertise-based business, your team is an extension of you. If you don't have the right systems in place to manage client delivery, you may risk your reputation with clients through missed deadlines, inconsistent quality, or customers feeling like they are just a number, lost in the crowd. I've been on the other end of that myself, expecting the same level of service and communication that I was receiving from the founder and then being disappointed with the quality degradation of the product or service (often while paying a *higher price* to account for the owner's cost of paying team members).

- **Emotional Costs:** Instead of the freedom and relief you imagined, you might feel more burdened. The emotional and mental load of leadership—communicating expectations, providing feedback, managing performance, and navigating team dynamics—requires a skill set that is rarely taught to small business owners. You might struggle with finding a balance between control (it's your business!) and providing autonomy and not wanting to feel like a micro-manager (they are capable adults!). Without preparation, hiring can feel like trading one type of overwhelm for another.

- **Values Costs:** Hiring without a plan can lead to perpetuating harmful systems of underpaid labor, misaligned priorities, and disorganized workplaces. A lack of appropriate systems or clarity can create frustration for your team members, who might feel underutilized, overworked, or simply lost about what's expected of them. The promise of "buying back your time" can quickly turn into spending *more* time managing misunderstandings, redoing work, or addressing unmet expectations. If you're not careful, you risk replicating the very systems you set out to avoid.

But the answer isn't "don't hire," even though I have laid out a lot of reasons hiring shouldn't be a knee-jerk response. To leave the Hiring Game, we need to approach hiring with intention and preparation. Done skillfully, it can create a broader foundation in your business for impact and resilience for you as a founder. This takes doing the following:

- Understanding when your business is truly ready to hire and what tasks or roles will have the greatest impact
- Evaluating the types of roles that align with your business needs, budget, and long-term goals
- Building systems and processes to ensure that team members are set up for success and that your leadership reflects your values
- Preparing yourself for the shift from managing yourself to managing others, including the mindset and skills required to lead effectively

This chapter will help you navigate the decision to expand your team with clarity, purpose, and sustainability, ensuring you build an employee roster that enhances your business without compromising your values instead of gambling on hiring before you're ready—or out of desperation.

LEAVING THE HIRING TABLE

The decision to hire transforms your role in your business. You're no longer just managing yourself—you're managing others too. In an expertise-based business, your team doesn't just execute tasks; they become an extension of your brand, values, and customer experience. How you lead and manage these hires reflects directly onto you.

Before diving into the hiring process, it's essential to take a step back. When leaving the Efficiency Game in Chapter 8, you created a comprehensive list of the activities you perform to run your business—ideas, "build the business" projects, high-level "run the business" areas like social media marketing, client scheduling and bookkeeping, and "deliver the business" client work. That list gives you an honest look at everything you're currently managing. Hopefully, you've taken the opportunity to prune whole activities that aren't working or necessary for your business and added some systems to optimize the remaining activities.

But hiring isn't just about offloading tasks. It's about deciding what truly needs to stay under your control, what can be delegated, and when it's the right time to bring someone else into your business. To make these decisions effectively, you need a framework that not only considers your skills and preferences but also evaluates the strategic importance and complexity of the tasks you're delegating.

That's where the **Hiring Matrix** comes in. Unlike popular delegation frameworks that focus on passion and proficiency, the Hiring Matrix provides a practical lens for identifying what to delegate, what to keep, and how to prioritize based on your business's unique needs. It categorizes activities by their functionality (Core vs. Adjacent) and complexity (Simple vs. Complex), providing clarity on where to focus your efforts and how to delegate responsibly.

Before we dive into the Hiring Matrix, let's explore some frameworks you may already be familiar with: the Zone of Genius, the Freedom Compass, and Buy Back Your Time. This illustration of their benefits and limitations will demonstrate the need for a more nuanced approach for small, expertise-driven businesses.

COMMON FRAMEWORKS AND THEIR LIMITATIONS

Popular delegation frameworks offer helpful starting points for prioritizing your work. They encourage you to focus only on tasks that align with your passion and proficiency, suggesting you delegate the rest or simply restructure your business so that you can stop performing activities outside your ideal zones. Let's look at these frameworks one by one.

Gay Hendricks's "Zone of Genius" framework, introduced in *The Big Leap*,[52] has captivated entrepreneurs with its simplicity. The premise is straightforward: Identify the work that you excel at and deeply enjoy—your Zone of Genius—and delegate or eliminate tasks that fall into other categories:

- **Zone of Incompetence:** Tasks you're not skilled at
- **Zone of Competence:** Tasks you can do but that others can do just as well (or better)
- **Zone of Excellence:** Tasks you're highly skilled at but don't energize you

According to this framework, if you spend most of your time in your Zone of Genius, you'll achieve not only success but also deep satisfaction.

Michael Hyatt's Freedom Compass[53] introduces a similar concept but with two dimensions:

- **Passion:** How much you love doing the work
- **Proficiency:** How skilled you are at the work

Tasks that fall into the overlap—high passion, high proficiency—form your Desire Zone. Hyatt advises focusing on this area to maximize productivity and fulfillment. The remaining tasks fall into the other zones identified in the framework:

- **Drudgery Zone** (low passion, low proficiency): Delegate or eliminate these tasks.
- **Disinterest Zone** (low passion, high proficiency): Outsource these tasks if possible.
- **Distraction Zone** (high passion, low proficiency): Avoid these tasks unless you're willing to build the skills needed to perform them.

---

52 Gay Hendricks, *The Big Leap: Conquer Your Hidden Fear and Take Life to the Next Level* (HarperOne, 2010), 29–36.

53 Michael Hyatt, *Free to Focus: A Total Productivity System to Achieve More by Doing Less* (Baker Books, 2019), 48–55.

Dan Martell's book *Buy Back Your Time*[54] presents a delegation strategy aimed at freeing entrepreneurs from tasks that consume time without directly creating value. His approach starts with identifying tasks you dislike or that feel repetitive and outsourcing them to regain time for higher-impact work. He suggests hiring for "$10-per-hour tasks" first and gradually moving up to more complex roles.

While these frameworks provide helpful tools for prioritization, they can mislead you into delegating too early—or delegating the wrong things in general. They suggest you should first delegate or outsource tasks outside your zones of genius or desire.

But almost every early-stage, expertise-based business owner finds some of the core functions potentially onerous or tedious. You may not be good at or passionate about them, but these **core functions include messaging, marketing, sales, and financial management—things you, the business owner, absolutely need to do.**

At the beginning of your entrepreneurship journey, of course you're not proficient or skilled at these functions. These are skills that you didn't learn when becoming an expert in your craft, and they are also skills that have been warped through exploitative practices. When marketing equals posting short-form videos multiple times a day and sales equals spammy cold emails and DMs, of course, you want someone else to take it on. You probably think, "I just want to see clients and do what I got into business to do!"

But in expertise-based businesses, these core functions are foundational. These areas are often challenging *because* they're complex and require iteration—not because you lack passion or proficiency.

While working within your passion and proficiency or "genius" zones sounds ideal, delegating too early can prevent you from understanding how your business really works. Without mastery over the foundational areas of your business, you may lack the skills and resilience you need to make changes to your business should the market change. Many of the tasks that fall outside your natural comfort zone—like refining

---

54 Dan Martell, *Buy Back Your Time: Get Unstuck, Reclaim Your Freedom, and Build Your Empire* (Portfolio, 2023), 86.

messaging, building sales skills, or developing financial fluency—are the very ones that drive revenue and long-term growth.

These frameworks, particularly Buy Back Your Time, also presume that your business has established systems and processes, making delegation straightforward. In reality, many small business owners haven't dialed in the specific steps and success metrics for those processes, especially if they're still iterating on those core functions, dialing in their marketing, pricing and offer structures, and delivery processes. Outsourcing tasks without clear processes and expectations can create more work, confusion, and frustration on both sides.

Let's look at some examples of what can happen when foundational functions are outsourced or delegated without clear process steps and expectations.

Instead of improving our messaging and our skill at marketing, we hire social media agencies that end up creating generic content that tanks engagement. Or we bring on a copywriter too early, spend too much, and end up with a voice that doesn't sound like us—and then we never even put the words on our website. We throw money at ads or ad specialists before we've dialed in our offers and messaging through real customer conversations.

In sales, we get lured by lead gen firms promising "30 appointments a month" with unqualified leads who don't even know who we are. Or we hire VAs to do scripted "social selling" in the DMs, filling our network with strangers who never convert. The time spent coaching them or sitting in unaligned sales meetings ends up outweighing the time we were trying to save.

When it comes to finances, we outsource to a bookkeeper or CPA and expect them to explain the numbers. Or, worse, we hand things off to a VA and wonder why nothing adds up. Without understanding our own finances, we're left scrambling to pay bills or taxes and frustrated when we can't make informed business decisions.

All of this can happen without realizing—until it's too late—that you **cannot outsource the core parts of your business that directly contribute to the growth of the business.** Even if you're not proficient or particularly passionate about them, these are your areas of purview—at least until you've become good enough and practiced enough to turn those functions into a structured, well-functioning system.

Because ultimately … *no one will care as much as you about your business.*

No one knows your business better than you do. This means that you—the person actually working with clients in the business—are the best person to write about, sell, and improve your products or services.

So instead of being quick to hire out areas in which we're neither passionate nor proficient, let's evaluate outsourcing and delegation decisions through a different lens: the Hiring Matrix.

THE HIRING MATRIX OVERVIEW

The Hiring Matrix builds on the aforementioned frameworks but shifts the focus to the context and stage of your business. It categorizes activities and tasks not simply by your passion or skill but by their functionality and complexity within your business.

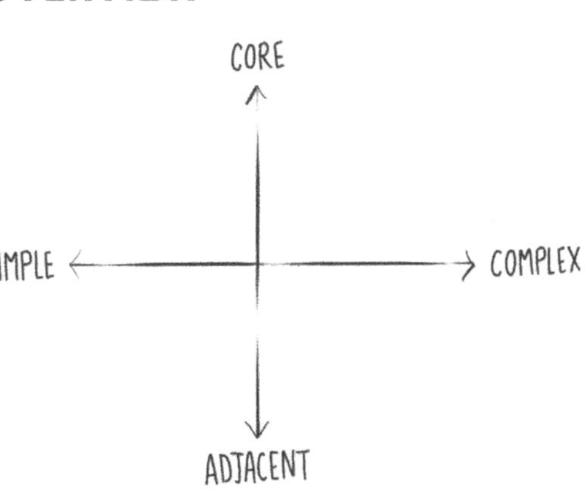

- **Functionality: Core vs. Adjacent.** Core activities are essential to your business's identity, strategy, profit, and client success. Adjacent activities (e.g., podcast editing or SEO research) support the business but are less critical to how it directly makes money.
- **Complexity: Simple vs. Complex.** Simple tasks have straightforward, repeatable processes. Complex tasks require nuance, decision-making, and expertise.

Let's get into more detail about the meanings of **Core**, **Adjacent**, **Simple**, and **Complex** activities.

Core Activities

Core activities are directly tied to your business revenue and client success.

- **The Strategic Vision for Your Business:** Only you can decide what type of business you want to run. How much money do you want to make? What form of delivery makes sense for you? How many hours a week are you working, and how large is your team? These decisions are core to your strategic vision.
- **Your Brand Message, Voice, and Positioning:** You must define what your business stands for at its essence. You have to first develop the foundations of your brand messaging, voice, and positioning before someone else can create marketing or brand materials on your behalf. If your business lacks a strong internal voice or point of view, you can only imagine the headache that will arise when you try to bring in an outside person to create on your behalf.
- **Your Marketing and Sales Process:** Until you know exactly how to identify, connect with, and convert new clients consistently, you can't hire someone else to figure that out for you. No one else will tell your story or speak about what you do with passion and conviction. No one else has your network, expertise, and connection to the product or service, especially when you are still refining your messaging, offers, and pricing. If you outsource sales before you've clarified those elements of your business and brand, you're going to end up on a lot of sales calls with questionable—or completely wrong—conversations. (Or end up on no sales calls at all!)
- **Your Intellectual Property:** Until you've distilled and documented how you do what you do—what makes up the "special sauce" of your work—hiring anyone to support you in any core client delivery will be challenging.
- **Your Financial Health:** Having accounting and reporting tasks performed by trained professionals is smart. Relying on them to make decisions in your business, or even to tell you when things are going awry, is not. You are responsible for the financial health of the business and can't outsource your business strategy.

Adjacent Activities

Adjacent activities support your business but aren't directly tied to generating revenue.

These activities might include tasks like podcast pitching, editing YouTube videos, conducting SEO research, or setting up your project management systems. They might also cover the outputs or extensions of your core functions, such as translating your brand into graphic templates for marketing materials or having your taxes prepared once you hand over clean books that you understand.

While important, these activities don't have a direct impact on bringing in income; they enhance your operations and visibility but don't drive immediate results. For example, a well-designed project management system might make your workflows smoother, but it won't directly land you new clients. Similarly, paying taxes is essential, but optimizing your tax preparation won't increase your revenue. You can run a successful business without investing significant time or money into most of these adjacent activities early on, especially when resources are limited, as long as your Core revenue-generating functions remain strong.

Simple Activities

Simple activities include tasks or processes with clear instructions that have standard inputs, documented rules or process steps, and expected outcomes.

These tasks can be followed with a straightforward process or even automated. The output expectations are clear and, for the most part, don't vary.

Simple activities are typically administrative enablers that support both Core functions and Adjacent projects. Examples include the following:

- **Sales:** Researching client prospects or adding inquiries to a CRM
- **Delivery:** Scheduling client sessions or sending recordings
- **Finances:** Creating invoices or following up on past-due payments
- **Marketing:** Scheduling social media posts or uploading podcasts to hosting platforms

Complex Activities

Complex activities or processes are not as straightforward to perform as Simple activities because of the amount of nuance, different inputs, or human knowledge and/or interaction required. Some level of intervention is necessary, even if the underlying task seems administrative.

These activities require creativity, strategy, and a bit of finesse—things that can't just be boiled down to a checklist or handed off without serious thought.

- **Client Delivery:** Designing and delivering creative or strategic solutions tailored to individual client needs
- **Custom Proposals and Pricing:** Crafting personalized proposals and determining pricing that aligns with both client goals and business profitability
- **Copywriting:** Writing high-impact website copy or sales pages that effectively communicate your message and resonate with your audience
- **Asset Development:** Creating assets for your business, like worksheets, assessments, and process overviews, that can be used in client delivery or sales
- **Pitch Development:** Preparing tailored podcast or PR pitches that align with your brand and effectively target specific audiences
- **Financial Planning:** Developing detailed financial forecasts to support strategic decision-making and business growth
- **Legal Preparation:** Drafting or reviewing contracts and conducting tax planning to ensure compliance and protect your business interests

Complex processes can become simpler over time. We first standardize our packages or pricing structures, then our offers, and then our outreach templates for customization—and, in the end, we can more clearly identify our target clients to make outbound research easier.

We can create templates, client worksheets, and videos to explain and teach our frameworks. Ultimately, we can "productize" our service so that it's turnkey for someone else to deliver it or for you to deliver at scale, should you choose to do so.

But as the business owner, you must have the time and patience to document your thinking, the willingness to create training materials, and the determination to standardize these Complex processes (it's not for everyone!) to make them simpler for others to execute.

POPULATING THE MATRIX

You're now ready to start layering your initial list of tasks and activities onto the matrix. Here's how it'll look:

- Core and Simple? Top left.
- Core and Complex? Top right.
- Adjacent and Complex? Bottom right.
- Adjacent and Simple? Bottom left.

First, look at the original list of ideas, projects, and recurring tasks in your business. You may need to break down your projects and recurring activities even further than just the high-level items.

Let's use "guesting on podcasts" as an example. Here's a list of the specific actions that must be performed to accomplish this activity:

- Developing your point of view, topic ideas, and ideal audience
- Turning your point of view into a podcast pitch
- Creating an initial list of shows to pitch
- Emailing the hosts with the pitch
- Following up with the hosts
- Coordinating scheduling
- Posting audiograms and graphics on social media

Developing your point of view, topic ideas, and ideal audience is Core *and* Complex work—only you can do this, and it's going to require thought and research.

Writing a podcast pitch and creating an initial pitch list are Adjacent and Complex tasks. They require creativity and strategy but are not central to how your business makes money.

The remaining items—like emailing the hosts, following up, coordinating scheduling, and posting on social media—are both Adjacent and Simple. Someone who's not part of your business could follow repeatable steps with clear outcomes to accomplish these tasks.

Repeat this process for all of the tasks you'd love to no longer have to perform in your business. Once you've plotted all of the tasks on the matrix, you'll see what is necessary for you to personally prioritize and what can be delegated. Then you can plan to either complete those tasks or hire for them.

HIRING DECISIONS THROUGH THE MATRIX LENS
Prune Before Delegating

You might find that many items in your business constitute "busy work" that you want to delegate:

- Scheduling social media posts
- Repurposing long-form video into short-form video
- Social selling in the DMs on social media
- Sending and manually following up on invoicing
- Making graphics for social media posts
- Setting up complex email automations and funnels.

Others constitute even more substantial tasks or projects:

- Creating a weekly podcast
- Running a free or paid community
- Publishing a twice-weekly newsletter

But before delegating, this is a friendly reminder to go back to Chapter 8 and review the Efficiency Game. First ask, honestly, *do you need this task or this process in your business?*

Early in my business, I hired a VA to help me manage a free community that included content and events (because I thought I needed one—I was sold that marketing to my own community was the right strategy for me). What I discovered? I didn't have a large enough network to make a community work early on. I was spending quite a bit of time and money organizing events and repurposing content that only my raving fans saw, and I wasn't spending any time on meeting new people.

I tried having the VA help me create social media graphics and graphics for my blog posts … until I realized that I didn't actually want graphics for my blog posts. And having static posts on Instagram wasn't growing my business. I was paying the VA to do tasks that weren't growing my business, and managing these tasks actually kept me from doing the building work.

So I shut down the community, ended up leaving my graphics-based social media platform, and invested that time and money into other tasks.

Who to Hire

Once you've identified the tasks that fall outside your Core and Complex zone, the next step is determining how to effectively delegate them. The Hiring Matrix not only helps categorize these tasks but also guides you on who you need to bring into your business.

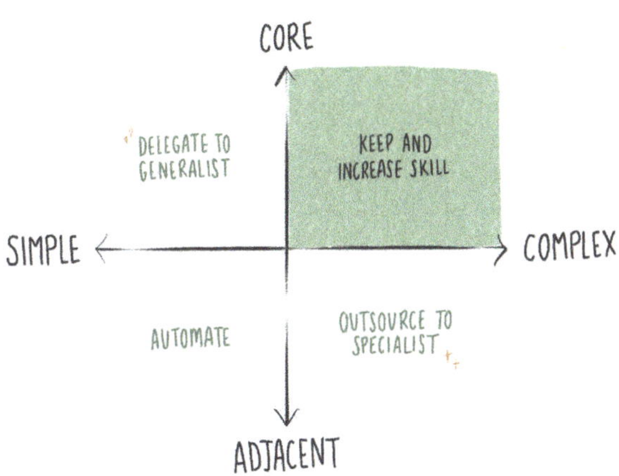

Specialists for Complex Needs

Specialists provide deep expertise in specific areas, making them ideal for the Complex tasks that require nuanced understanding and tailored approaches. These are the professionals you turn to when you need strategic insight, system implementation, or niche problem-solving. Examples include accountants for tax strategy, legal advisors for contracts, SEO consultants for website optimization, and branding agencies for comprehensive design work. Specialists often arrive with their own tools, processes, and frameworks, reducing the requirement for oversight and training on your end.

Generalists for Simple Support

For tasks that require human intervention but aren't deeply complicated, consider hiring a generalist. Online business managers or VAs can handle a range of uncomplicated, repeatable activities provided you've documented processes and set clear expectations. They thrive when performing well-documented tasks, executing on well-scoped projects, or filling in gaps across multiple areas. However, without strong documentation or defined outputs, even Simple tasks can become unnecessarily complicated, so ensure these generalists are set up for success.

Automation and Efficiency Tools

Not every task requires a human touch. Tools and automations can handle repetitive, rule-based activities with precision and reliability. For example, instead of hiring someone to manage invoicing or scheduling, you can use software that automates these processes. Tasks like logging prospects into a CRM, sending reminders, or creating routine reports are often better suited for lightweight systems than for human delegation. However, setting up these tools may fall into the Complex and Adjacent bucket, making a short-term specialist a smart choice for implementation.

Balancing In-House and Outsourced Support

Deciding between in-house and outsourced hires often depends on the task's complexity and your capacity to manage. Outsourcing to firms can be particularly efficient for Adjacent activities like ongoing accounting, podcast production, or website design. These providers typically come with established systems and onboarding processes, saving you from having to develop these frameworks yourself.

For Core and Simple tasks tied directly to revenue or client outcomes, however, you'll want to keep tight control, whether by hiring for these roles for your team or working closely with contractors. Even if these tasks are Simple, they are critical to your business's stability and growth. Delegating them to an external firm or an unmanaged team member can lead to missed opportunities or costly errors.

Enlisting Support for the Core and Complex Activities

Nothing changes the fact that many Core and Complex tasks may fall outside your current skill set. Instead of immediately delegating these tasks (and risking wasted time, energy, and money), you might consider seeking support that helps you build confidence and competence in these areas. Addressing the underlying challenges—whether they stem from a lack of skill, capacity, or desire—can set you up for long-term success.

A **skill gap** refers to a lack of training or knowledge in an area or task. For example, you might not know how to set up your bookkeeping system to better understand your financials. Remember, just because you launched a business doesn't mean you immediately know how to do everything required to run it, and there's no shame in asking for help. I have an MBA, and even I hired someone to set up my bookkeeping system and show me how to use it! I've hired experts to help me grow my skill in copywriting, storytelling, podcasting, and sales—worth every penny—and I have grown my skills along with my revenue.

To close a skill gap, seek out targeted learning opportunities, such as working with a mentor, enrolling in a course, or using templates and examples to develop your own approach. For instance, a sales coach might provide scripts and guidance to help you structure and lead effective sales conversations until you build confidence.

A **capacity gap** arises when you don't have the space to take on more Complex tasks, especially when you're also learning a new skill. If you're tempted to delegate Core and Complex activities because you're overwhelmed, revisit streamlining your workload even further rather than delegate prematurely. Eliminate the mental overload of switching between tasks and be even more deliberate with pausing or removing entire activities (particularly Adjacent ones) from your workload to create more space for what truly matters.

Finally, if you're dealing with a **desire gap**, reflect on how you can reframe your mindset. If you don't want to do something you believe you're bad at or experience "imposter syndrome," I say, "Of course, you're not good at this yet. You've never been trained to do it!" Often, discomfort with certain responsibilities, like managing finances or engaging in sales, stems from societal narratives or personal biases rather than an inherent weakness at the task. We can reframe sales from being pushy to building genuine relationships. We can reframe a belief that you're bad at finances to a belief that investing in your business's financial fluency is better than the return you'd get on the stock market.

By thoughtfully addressing these gaps—through learning, simplifying your workload, or reframing your mindset—you'll be better equipped to manage Core and Complex tasks, ensuring they are handled effectively until you're ready to delegate them responsibly.

SHIFTING ZONES OVER TIME

As your business evolves, tasks that once felt Complex can become Simple, and activities that seem Core now might eventually become Adjacent. For example, early on, writing sales emails or creating social media content might feel highly complicated because you're still defining your voice, message, and audience. Over time, as you refine your messaging and create templates or reusable assets, these tasks become more straightforward and easier to delegate. Similarly, client onboarding might initially feel Complex because you're codifying your "secret sauce" and developing templates and processes—but as you standardize your process with clear workflows and automated tools, it can move into the Simple category, making it easier to delegate or even automate completely.

What you consider Core can also change. If you shift business models, as explained in Chapter 1, from a delivery to a creator model, then live client work might be something only done sporadically, with most of your revenue coming from courses, books, or cohorts.

Similarly, something that's Adjacent might become Core: Pitching for speaking engagements might have been handled by an agency at the start, but if you're becoming a keynote speaker as a dedicated stream of income, you'll most likely want to bring that back in-house, as it is central to your revenue.

Recognizing these shifts allows you to adapt your hiring and delegation strategies, ensuring you always focus on the activities that drive growth and align with your long-term goals.

READINESS TO HIRE AND LEAD

Now that you've mapped your activities on the Hiring Matrix and identified potential opportunities for delegation, the next question isn't *who* and *what* to hire for but *when* and *how*. Hiring is not just about offloading tasks but about taking responsibility for guiding, leading, and ensuring the success of your team. Before you take this step, it's essential to revisit your readiness—financially, strategically, and operationally.

Know Your Business Before You Delegate

You don't need to be an expert in every area of your business, but fluency is nonnegotiable. If you're hiring a specialist, you need to understand enough of their role to set expectations and evaluate outcomes. It's a "trust but verify" situation: If you don't know what to expect and lack basic knowledge of the role, you risk mismanaging resources or failing to measure success.

Generalists thrive with well-defined systems and processes. If your tasks or projects aren't yet documented or streamlined, handing them off prematurely will only create more work for you. Also assess whether there are enough repeatable activities to justify the management responsibility of delegating to someone else. Take the time to structure your workflows, clarify expectations, and set up processes to delegate tasks and manage the outcomes.

The Commitment of Leadership

As discussed in Chapter 4 on the responsibility you want to carry, delegation is not about offloading tasks that you dislike. It's about aligning responsibilities with your business priorities and ensuring every role supports your long-term goals. Do you have the financial stability to sustain a hire, with at least three months of their pay set aside? Most importantly, are you prepared to dedicate time and attention to onboarding and ongoing management?

Even with the right hire, leadership requires preparation and continuous effort. Onboarding, training, and collaboration take time, especially when tasks are not yet standardized. Even experienced contractors or specialists require oversight. Be prepared to provide feedback, review their work, and maintain regular communication to align their contributions with your business goals.

Growing Without Hiring

No matter what the Casino tells you, you can grow your business without hiring first. Revisit the earlier chapters on the Pricing Game, Marketing Game, and Efficiency Game to evaluate how to make your business even more potent and profitable before you take up the responsibility of leadership.

When You're Ready to Hire

Many resources are available to help you onboard, lead, and manage your team once you're ready to hire. I'm following my own advice and sending you to specialist resources with much more information than I have.

Look for resources that espouse clear communication, thoughtful delegation, and frequent feedback.

Some of my personal favorite books and thinkers in this space include the following:

- Lia Garvin: *THE UNSTOPPABLE TEAM: A Simple Formula for Managing Your Team, Reducing Overwhelm, and Increasing Revenue* and *The New Manager Playbook: A Simple Guide for Leading with Ease*
- Johnathan and Melissa Nightingale from Raw Signal Group
- Frances Frei and Anne Morriss: *Unleashed: The Unapologetic Leader's Guide to Empowering Everyone Around You*

These resources are linked in the bibliography.

SUMMARY

Hiring doesn't follow a one-size-fits-all formula. Bringing someone into your business changes how you work and lead and what you're responsible for. Hire too soon—or for the wrong tasks—and it can drain your time, energy, and resources instead of expanding your capacity. However, the Hiring Matrix offers a more grounded approach, helping you sort your business activities into Core, Complex, Adjacent, and Simple zones rather than hire based on what you dislike or struggle with. From there, you can build skill in the areas that matter most and develop smart strategies for delegating or outsourcing what falls outside your core responsibilities as the business owner. This framework supports sustainable growth and ensures that hiring decisions truly strengthen your business.

Reflection Questions 

1. What major activities in my business are Core and Complex?
2. What activities fall outside of the Core and Complex category—such as Core and Simple, Adjacent and Complex, or Adjacent and Simple?
3. What activities do I want to hire for that I should actually prune instead?
4. Where might I benefit more from skill building than outsourcing in my Core and Complex work?
5. What activities should be automated or outsourced to a specialist?
6. Do I have enough remaining tasks and a sufficient budget to support an internal hire in a way that's sustainable—for them and for me?
7. Am I prepared to take up the responsibility of leadership at this stage of my business?

You can find the "Hiring Matrix" template in the *Leaving the Casino* workbook or in the downloadable resources at deeperfoundations.com/casino

The appeal of passive income is clear—but the price is sky-high.

CHAPTER 10

Resiliency—The "Passive Income" Promise

YOU'VE BEEN STEPPING BACK from playing their game. You're recognizing the time, team, marketing and sales, and pricing approaches and strategies that work for *your* business, vision, and goals.

But you still have worries. Even if you've hired a small team, it's still just you out there. You want to keep your business growing but also want to be able to absorb the shocks and know your business won't shut down if something happens where you need to step away.

Then, just as you've nearly reached the exit of the Entrepreneurial Casino, you pass by a roulette table right as the dealer spins the wheel on the **Passive Income Game**. As the ball spins and slowly begins to spiral, your mind does too—if you ever had to stop working, stop creating … you might stop getting paid.

"You want a business that can operate without you while still making you money, right?" the dealer asks. "Your job as a CEO is to work yourself out of a job. To keep growing while working less!"

"Launch your course—and make money while you sleep!"
"Open a community and get that recurring revenue!"
"Serve one to many and stop trading time for dollars!"
"Build your evergreen offer!"
"Teach others how you did it!"
"Build a team so you don't have to deliver the work!"

The house rules are clear: Decoupling income from your time is easy through "passive income" strategies.

These solutions all promise that you'll be able to step away from your business and rake in the cash on autopilot. All of the advice is targeted at removing you from the day-to-day delivery.

The web celebs boast about how they have endless free time and a clear calendar, how they have constant *cha-ching*s on their phone. They tell you the secret: Form groups, communities, and courses. Teach people how you do what you do, how to achieve the success that you created in your business. Or "productize" your service. Streamline it down to a step-by-step process with accompanying worksheets and videos so that your clients can DIY it or your work takes less time.

Trust them! Buy their programs to learn how! This is how they're so successful with no meetings on their calendars!

But these influencers' real secret? Spending hundreds of thousands of dollars on ads and affiliate marketing. Having a team that works five or more days a week so that they can remove themselves from the day-to-day business. Scaling up to so many students that they can't serve well, damaging their reputation for repeat business. In the best cases, they've served hundreds of students first in order to curate a product and messaging that serves and sells at scale.

Is that what you want? It sure makes sense to want to spin that wheel given what you're likely facing.

If you live in the United States, **your ability to fund vacations, leaves, and rest** is often tied to your ability to pay for it. Without a social safety net providing universal healthcare, disability insurance, or paid leave, entrepreneurs are left to fund these necessities on their own. This is especially pressing for those who face unexpected health challenges, parental leave, or caregiving responsibilities. Passive income feels like a way to solve this problem: a path to earning money while you step back from the business. What's not disclosed are the hidden costs to build and maintain the engine that keeps traffic coming to your business when you're away, as the algorithms are never stable and markets are always changing.

For neurodivergent entrepreneurs, those with chronic illnesses, or primary caregivers, **passive income promises the flexibility traditional**

systems fail to offer. The rigid structure of jobs (and some business models) that require meetings, live delivery time, and strict deadlines doesn't account for fluctuating energy levels, the need for breaks, or working in ways that align with nonlinear, hyperfocused productivity. If you have a business that relies on live delivery or client calls during the "standard workday" to get paid, this can be precarious—a medical appointment or school holiday can drastically alter your ability to deliver the same efforts day to day.

Having something that "sells on autopilot" or not tying your revenue to your ability to deliver live seemingly gives us some of that protection— you build a stream of income that doesn't rely on you being consistently healthy or available to deliver that service, especially if you have limited delivery time due to a chronic illness or care responsibilities. Of course, those promises don't disclose the extensive upfront work required, the constant updates to content or offers, and a level of promotional effort that can burn out even the most organized entrepreneur.

Another form of passive income sold to those most vulnerable is the MLM scam. Specifically targeted to women, **MLM schemes often trap women seeking both flexibility and financial independence**—not through selling products but in recruiting others to your team and having them sell (and recruit, and recruit, and *recruit*). They pose as the perfect solution for women juggling caregiving responsibilities, offering what seems like an ideal blend of income and flexibility. They claim you can set your own schedule, work from home, and earn unlimited income by promoting products you believe in and recruiting others to join your team.

But most MLM participants end up spending more than they make: pressured to purchase inventory, attend training events, buy sales coaching, and recruit others into the system.[55] Many women end up not only losing money but also damaging relationships with friends and family along the way. If you're in the online space, you might find this very similar to the "coaches coaching coaches to coach coaches" business models, and in fact, the "MLM to coaching pipeline" is a well-trodden

---

55 Emily Lynn Paulson, *Hey, Hun: Sales, Sisterhood, Supremacy, and the Other Lies Behind Multilevel Marketing* (Row House Publishing, 2023).

path. The influencers who make the most money are those teaching you how to coach others to make money rather than actually delivering a service to an end customer.

The appeal of passive income is clear—but the price is sky-high.

If there was ever a time when the Passive Income Game was a reasonable play, that time is over. The era of "if you build it, they will come" in online business has sadly ended. (Similarly, the MLM scam always ends up with completely saturated markets when they simply run out of people to try to recruit.) Trying to build a volume-based business like a course or digital product is more than adding an arm or some new leverage—you are essentially starting a whole new business that needs fundamentally different things than a delivery-based business.

Buying into the Passive Income Game, you're probably changing your audience, your customer maturity, and your marketing message to appeal to a new buyer. Your message at each stage of the customer journey needs to be adapted, particularly as you start depending on larger numbers of people who don't yet know you and your work well enough to make the math work. And as your business changes, you'll need different marketing and sales approaches, as mentioned in Chapter 7 on the Marketing Game.

Additional fees include the cost of community or course platforms, the cost of any additional marketing software, and, of course, the cost to get enough new eyeballs to make the math work. You would need to take the time and opportunity cost to create that course and the associated marketing assets, which is risky if you're switching audiences or having to build one from scratch.

To achieve success with the leveraged delivery models the business influencers are teaching you to run, you need to have a substantial audience size and be constantly fueling traffic to your work. You must also have a validated message and offer so that people will both buy in and want to recommend it to their friends to create the flywheel effect.

"Passive income" that relies on a constant stream of new purchasers is never passive.

Something has to drive new eyeballs to your work consistently, and that something requires time or money and must work in the current market environment. Social media algorithms are always changing, ad policies are constantly evolving, and what worked a year or two ago to drive traffic may not work anymore.

There *was* a "sweet spot" to build attention online for cheap, boosted by the algorithm—but that time has largely passed. In recent years, there have been changes to iOS privacy settings impacting Meta ads, the Google search algorithm has changed, and social media platform algorithms and AI have dramatically changed how to reach customers. Moreover, ad costs have increased, making these models substantially less profitable unless we are willing to throw even more money at them and not burn out our audience.

Consumer tastes and buying patterns also change. At the height of the COVID-19 pandemic in 2020 and 2021, all types of courses experienced a boom as everyone got online—and many consumers were home with some extra stimulus cash in their pocket. But in 2022, the course bubble burst as people got back to their routines and their pocketbooks got lighter thanks to rising interest rates and the threat of a recession. The market swings, and a particular content format may go in and out of style quickly.

The costs of playing this game continue to add up. If your passive income source is a subscription or membership, you'll need to keep creating new content or products for your membership, trying new strategies to minimize churn, and keeping your buyers engaged—all the while also enrolling new customers.

If your idea of passive income is building a team to run the day-to-day activities of your work, be prepared to shell out a pretty penny of your profit for a seasoned operator who can take management off of your plate.

Ultimately, playing the Passive Income Game leaves you dumping time, money, and attention into audience building, complicated technology, and course creation, often leaving you with less time to build more profit into your delivery-based business.

Instead of betting big on the illusion of passive income to buoy and protect you, you need to build a resilient business—one designed to thoughtfully help you ride the ebbs and flows of running a business over time. The key elements include:

- Reducing the "key person" risk by codifying key portions of your business
- Evaluating alternative delivery structures that accommodate flexibility without building a different business entirely
- Incorporating resilient marketing strategies that leverage your existing efforts and assets
- Building the ultimate source of resilience: cash

This chapter will help you design and incorporate strategies that ensure you can stay in business for the long-term instead of buying into the dream of passive income or being trapped in a 24/7 marketing and delivery cycle.

LEAVING THE PASSIVE INCOME TABLE

It's important to acknowledge that your business does come with "key person" risk. At some point, you will need to take time away from your business or have schedule flexibility for illness or caregiving, family needs or personal investments, and planned yearly vacations to rest and recover. You need to be able to do these things without risking what you've built while being able to keep funding your life.

But the best way to do that is not to "create passive income" by adding in another arm of your business that fractures your operations or dilutes your message across too many different types of buyers.

Instead of playing the Passive Income Game, build real resilience into your business. Construct buffers of time, energy, and attention so that you can incorporate flexibility and "give" into your business for when it matters.

Resilience might also be more personally satisfying and better for your long-term sustainability. When you stay involved in active marketing and delivery, you're more attuned to the needs of your clients and the shifts in the marketplace. And most importantly? Maybe this is the work you love to do! When you're removed from the work via so-called passive income, does that reflect the way you like to do business?

In this section, we'll discuss different approaches to resilience, including your delivery method, marketing and sales, and internal operations. We'll evaluate the type of resilience you need and what tactics might make sense to incorporate into your business.

Last but not least, we'll talk about the ultimate resilience builder: a financial cushion.

DEFINING YOUR PROCESS: CREATE REPEATABILITY AND A STANDARD APPROACH

At first, your work with clients may be totally customized to them. As you gain more experience delivering your service, you start to see patterns and can begin developing a standard set of tools you use with clients and in your work.

But if your working process only exists in your head, it becomes difficult to take time away, bring in help, or make your work more sustainable over time.

Developing a repeatable process and standard toolkit for how you work is one way to reduce the "key person" dependency. This might look like:

- Documenting the onboarding questions you ask in a standard template
- Recording videos to use with clients that explain your philosophy and approach
- Developing standard email templates to use with clients
- Developing a standard graphic template and creating "grab-and-go" client tools and a resource library

As you continue to grow, your marketing might start to leverage any intellectual property you've developed, including forms and audits. You may choose to productize at least a part of your service so that it can be delivered in a standard fashion and potentially by other team members.

You might not be able to develop a custom strategy for a client without live communication, but the more you see similar patterns, problems, and questions and develop a formal approach and standardized toolkit for responding, the more you de-risk your business from being just you.

When I was building my practice, I worked as a contract coach for an established productivity company. Each week, the company hosted a live preplanning call for clients. For years, the founder led those calls himself—he had everything dialed in: the slides, the script, the Q&A frameworks.

Eventually, as the company grew and the founder needed to step away, whether for international travel or paternity leave, they brought in contract coaches to lead the calls. Because their methodology was clearly documented and their philosophy well trained, I could confidently step in. I knew how to answer questions in the company's voice, follow the structure, and deliver the same experience. Clients got consistent results, and the business could run smoothly without relying on the founder being there every time.

You might never want to bring on team members or fully productize your service and sell it as a course, and that's okay.

But consider how codifying your approach might impact how you work with clients: You save time by having key resources documented in a standard toolkit. You're actually delivering value more quickly by having frameworks to work from instead of reinventing your approach for each client.

Developing these frameworks and tools can be a source of fulfillment and growth as well, pushing you to think more deeply about how you deliver the work and see concrete results from your efforts. Personally, I love the fact that I can mark progress in my business with the frameworks and tools I've built.

You might spend less "live time" instructing or setting scope, as some of that information can be shared asynchronously. And, depending on your business, you may be able to build in some more leveraged business models like groups, courses, or training without having to construct an entirely new business.

This standardization doesn't just apply to delivery. You can systematize many parts of your business and have a team help you with operations—but only when you have processes in place.

In fact, documenting your intellectual property and delivery methods is the only way to diversify to the brand model from Chapter 1, including licensing, franchising, and certification programs. Maybe then someone else really will be able to sell or deliver on your behalf!

RESILIENT DELIVERY

Depending on your background, you might have built your business to resemble the models you once worked with.

Coming from an agency background? You might have started selling based on a retainer model.

Coming from a coaching or therapy background? Maybe you started selling based on an hourly structure.

Coming from a consulting firm background? You may be structured around a full five-day workweek.

But perhaps it's time to revisit *how*—and not necessarily *what*—you deliver in a way that works better for you and for your clients.

From Projects to Intensives

Instead of a long project in which there's plenty of time for a client to get distracted or change scope, you could structure your work as a short intensive. By guiding the client through the process of collecting material upfront, an intensive process can help mitigate scope creep and schedule delays and also return results in less time. And because you can condense the project management overhead, projects are often shorter, and you can build buffer weeks or months into your schedule.

From Retainers to Recurring "VIP" Days/Intensives

The point of the VIP day/week is to do a whole chunk of work in one sitting, like an intensive. While VIP days as a business model can be challenging to sustain (specifically the part where you have to bring on new clients 2–4 times a month), a recurring VIP session is a nice delivery model for ongoing delivery needs.

Instead of a standard retainer—where you are "on call" all month responding to client needs and being pulled into revisions and meetings (and risking being treated like an employee)—you can formalize and condense your approach. For example, once a month, you could batch create all of the business's marketing needs or record a whole day of podcasts. This approach can help keep the project management overhead down because the work is being completed in one day while freeing up your schedule.

From 1:1 Calls to a Client Studio Approach

Particularly if your service involves a transfer of knowledge or frameworks to clients, you can start incorporating a client studio approach, creating "mini courses" for your clients for specific steps of your work. You create templates, tools, and even videos with clients live, based on what they need. You then use these tools with future clients and update your explanations and frameworks based on questions they have.

After a few rounds, you have turned your expertise into an asynchronous tool that can get your clients results and no longer have to deliver all of the information live. You might even sell it as a standalone product—without having to build something new from scratch.

From Hourly-Based to Subscription

Professionals who traditionally charge by the hour—which means an hour worked is an hour billed—might change this structure to a subscription model. For access to monthly accounting, forecasting, and yearly tax prep, an accounting firm might charge a flat monthly fee that also includes access to office hours and calls. While some periods of the year will be heavy in delivery (e.g., year end and tax deadlines), there will be lower seasons—without the lower revenue. This model might also apply to lawyers, who can provide legal advice and review on a subscription model, that comes with a priority access line and turnaround time, but without being penalized for being efficient in the hours you work.

From Agencies to Referral Partners and Collaborators

Maybe you want to take on larger projects without bringing on another team member whom you have to keep fully utilized year round. In this case, you might consider a collaborator model—finding trusted partners that work on parts of the project you don't have the skills or capacity for, without bringing them fully into your agency. When the project is over, you don't have to keep finding work (for them and for you) if you need to take a step back.

From Live Masterminds to Asynchronous Feedback or Voice Memos

Many times, to scale to larger groups, the advice is to start a group call for training and feedback. But another option is to provide asynchronous document reviews or feedback via a voice memo or private podcast. This approach retains the individual dialogue and feedback but removes some calls from the calendar.

Resilient delivery isn't about doing less or moving your business model away from service provision—it's about designing delivery that honors your energy, protects your time, and ensures your business can keep running even when life happens.

RESILIENT REVENUE

As your business matures, you may want to grow your revenue without increasing your workload or fracturing your focus. But jumping to a new business model or selling something entirely different can dilute your positioning, confuse your audience, or overextend your team. The revenue strategies discussed in this section allow you to extend your earning potential from inside the business model you've already built, without starting from scratch.

Land and Expand Services

Your core service is just the beginning. From a higher-touch anchor like coaching or consulting, you can extend your value with lighter-lift offers that meet your clients where they are. Think of these as extensions, not pivots. You might offer internal trainings for a client's wider team, follow-on implementation sessions, or long-term community access for alumni. These offers often aren't marketed publicly—they're offered after trust has already been built, allowing you to expand your client value over time and supplement your income without as much upfront delivery effort.

Sell the "By-Product"

The templates, checklists, videos, or custom tools you've built for client delivery don't have to live in a drawer. When you turn those behind-the-scenes assets into standalone offerings—like a workshop recording, a specific playbook for one part of your process, or a template—you can generate revenue from what you've already created. This doesn't require new positioning or an entirely new audience. You're simply making what already works for clients available in a more accessible format, capturing additional value without diluting your core offer.

Marketing Assets That Pay

Some offers aren't your core service—but they still earn revenue for you as an asset. A live training might primarily build trust with potential clients, but it can also generate nontrivial income. A community might start as a low-commitment entry point but become a powerful place for conversions. A recorded workshop can be designed to increase commitment and identify future clients, but its sales can still add up. These marketing assets serve a dual purpose: to grow your ecosystem while also creating meaningful revenue.

Boosters and Bundles

These are low-effort, evergreen additions that increase the value of your core offer without requiring live time or a new sales strategy. Think resource libraries, swipe file vaults, mini courses, or add-on toolkits. These assets can be bundled with your core offer or made available as upgrades—and while they're simple to maintain, they often carry a high perceived value for clients. You're not creating something new; you're enhancing what already works, giving clients a smoother path and giving yourself a buffer of leverage.

Affiliate or Sponsorship Add-Ons

If you're frequently referring clients to a trusted provider or consistently using a particular software tool, you may be able to incorporate referral, affiliate, or sponsorship revenue. This might look like a referral fee when a client hires a collaborator you've recommended or a small commission when someone purchases a tool you regularly use.

You might also negotiate a sponsorship for a workshop or newsletter from a brand that aligns with your work. These small, additive revenue streams don't require you to build a full creator-based business model—they simply make the most of the trust and traction you've already built.

From Delivery to Licensing or Certification

Eventually, you may want to step back from the room without stepping back from the impact. By codifying your methodology into a teachable, transferable system, you can license your intellectual property to others or certify practitioners to deliver it under your brand. This approach lets you serve more people, create a new revenue stream, and maintain ownership of your work, even as others carry it forward. It's a powerful way to multiply impact without multiplying effort.

All of these strategies share one thing in common: They allow your business to keep supporting you, even when your capacity changes. That's the heart of resilient revenue.

RESILIENT MARKETING

As we discussed in Chapter 7 on the Marketing Game, some marketing approaches require consistent effort in terms of outreach and content creation.

But there are ways to make your marketing work on your behalf without direct, daily effort.

Playlist-Style vs. Feed-Style Content

Feed-style content is what we generally think of as posting on social media feeds. One minute the post is there—but after the scroll? It's gone. Sometimes you saw something you wanted to read, clicked away, and then the piece disappeared!

Feed-based content is depreciating: The minute it's published it loses its value. Sure, some people who land on your page might scroll back to see what you've posted, but most probably won't.

Email newsletters that aren't turned into blog posts? Same deal. That newsletter might land in someone's inbox on a day they are busy, and they never read it. New subscribers who find you probably won't go back and look at your archives (even if you share the archive link). You have to keep showing up to keep throwing "marketing" in their face.

But playlist-style content can work for you long-term, even when you take a break.

Playlist means that your material should be easily navigable and live in a permanent place online. It shouldn't be peppered with other activity or disappear within twenty-four hours. You can re-use "feed-based" content like emails as blog posts on your site or a public newsletter archive—or even turn your social media posts into a podcast!

Someone hears about your podcast? They can listen to all of the episodes they want just by choosing those in the playlist.

Someone is recommended one of your YouTube videos? They can watch multiple videos in a row, spending tons of time with you without your having posted anything new.

Someone finds a blog you posted on your site? They can go down the rabbit hole of your beliefs and philosophy and come to you fully sold—without another piece of content having been posted.

Someone subscribes to your newsletter? You can send them a "best of" series or an ongoing nurture sequence of your best pieces, even if you're not publishing new content.

With playlist-style content, you can repurpose that content and regularly publish it, staying visible on feed-style platforms without the pressure to keep making new content.

"Evergreen" Authority-Building Content

There's a reason books are an outstanding way to build authority. Once you've written a book, it can be shared and recommended by friends—and without you having to publish any more content, they can go from being unaware to becoming a customer. A book is the ultimate "publish once, utilize everywhere" asset that can work on your behalf for years to come.

Regina Anaejionu[56] champions the work of evergreen content with a "Radical ROI." In her work, she outlines four pieces of content that will certainly return on the investment:

- **A Core Tenet Essay:** A signature piece, essay, or guide that expresses "a deeply held belief around an inequity or an underlying reason for a problem, or, a clear idea of how the world (or life, or certain systems) should be for a particular community." Author and consultant Jay Acunzo[57] calls this the "stake in the ground" premise assertion essay.
- **The Email Runway:** An evergreen email series or educational email course that fills gaps for one or more of your best-fit client profiles. This can also just be a nurture sequence of your "best of" or foundational content that's sent alongside your standard newsletter after any welcome sequences.
- **The Shapeshifting Course:** A philosophy- or framework-based course that helps to educate your clients or shift their perspective.
- **The Idea-First Homepage:** A home page that leads with your ideas and your body of work.

These assets can carry your work for years to come. The essays can be shared or gain traction in search results and the courses used in collaborations, bundles, or summits. You can run lean thought leadership ads to these pieces, and the email runway ensures that evergreen content—which runs without you having to rewrite it or stay connected to social media—closes all of the safety, education, and belief gaps your clients may have when they first find you.

I once saw a Google Doc written by coach Ross O'Lochlainn[58] about how to be "open every day" without launches and what most sales funnels do wrong. Within a week, I had enrolled in his free mini course where he shared his philosophy of long-tail conversions, bought his $100

---

56 Regina Anaejionu, "Radical ROI," accessed March 23, 2025, https://byregina.com/radicalroi.

57 Jay Acunzo, "You Can't Own Your Audience—But You Can Own an Idea in Their Minds," last modified January 5, 2024, https://jayacunzo.com/blog/you-cant-own-your-audience-but-you-can-own-an-idea-in-their-minds.

58 Ross O'Lochlainn, "Open Every Day," accessed December 30, 2023, https://conversionengineering.co/open-every-day-book/.

offer design course, and ultimately spent about ten hours learning from him. I enrolled in multiple programs he ran, but I don't even know if he has a social media account. He'd been able to set up evergreen, playlist-style content that didn't require him to do any new content creation for the first few weeks I was in his world.

Lean Ads, Email Referral Campaigns, and SEO

Of course, the trick is to get new people in your world to hear about your methodology, find your playlist, or see your tenet-shifting essay.

This evergreen, pillar-style content can work on your behalf for years by being found in searches or shared by colleagues. You can also amplify that effort through low-spend ads that point directly to your core piece (and not an offer)—because you aren't advertising a "freebie" or "lead magnet" but ultimately a piece about your philosophy, you end up getting a cleaner list of people who want to hear from you, not just get access to your free template.

For years, email marketing had zero discoverability built in. But now? Email providers are implementing referrals and network building into their platforms. Some allow creators to recommend other newsletters—this way, when a person subscribes to someone else's newsletter, they have the option to subscribe to yours too. Or you might create a referral campaign within your newsletter itself, with new tools that allow subscribers to earn rewards by sending your newsletter to other people.

You can also use paid recommendation networks, which allow you to pay another creator directly for sending you engaged subscribers without having to navigate the Meta ad network.

Partnerships, White Labeling, Referrals, and Marketplaces

Finally, resilient marketing works best when you're existing as part of an ecosystem—because if you need to take time away, your ecosystem can be marketing for you on your behalf.

Cultivate strong referral relationships and partnerships. In the most transactional sense, you can have affiliate partners—people who use their audience (and their marketing) to send you business and get paid a portion of your revenue for each sale in return. For some of the larger affiliate-based programs, affiliates make more money affiliating for someone else's business than they do from selling their own products!

Or you can have more relational referral relationships. Stacey Brown Randall,[59] referral specialist, has shown that within a few years, her clients can get triple-digit numbers of referrals annually from cultivating strong referral relationships.

And don't sleep on marketplaces and partners, particularly for tech firms. If you're able to get in early to a service and tool and be listed as a "preferred partner," that can pay dividends. The partner or software service is doing the heavy lifting of bringing you traffic, and you're benefiting from the marketing.

Maybe you don't even do the marketing and instead "white label," where you deliver your services as a part of someone else's offer.

Some strategies are designed for businesses in the earliest stages: turning your work into playlist-style content, cultivating referral relationships, and engaging in free email referral networks (especially with colleagues you know).

Other strategies are best tailored to more established businesses, once you're clear on your message and know that the assets you create are stable enough to last: the evergreen content, core essays and mini courses, and paid ads.

But, ultimately, all of these strategies are designed to help find, educate, and convert new clients. Some of these might sound like a funnel, but the intent is different. You're not trying to shove everyone through a passive income pipe. You're building real assets that can work on your behalf and give you flexibility on when and how else you market.

THE ULTIMATE RESILIENCE: CASH

The ultimate resilience is having cash or access to credit in your business. Having a cash or credit buffer is a great way to fund time away from the business, to say no to misaligned projects or clients, and/or to

---

59 Stacey Brown Randall, *Generating Business Referrals Without Asking: A Simple Five-Step Plan to a Referral Explosion* (Morgan James Publishing, 2018), xxi.

invest in people who can help run the day-to-day operations while you're focused on something else.

And it's not just about profit—it's about cash flow. What if you need to pay a big tax bill now, but the cash to pay it won't come in for weeks? That's a cash flow problem, not a profit problem.

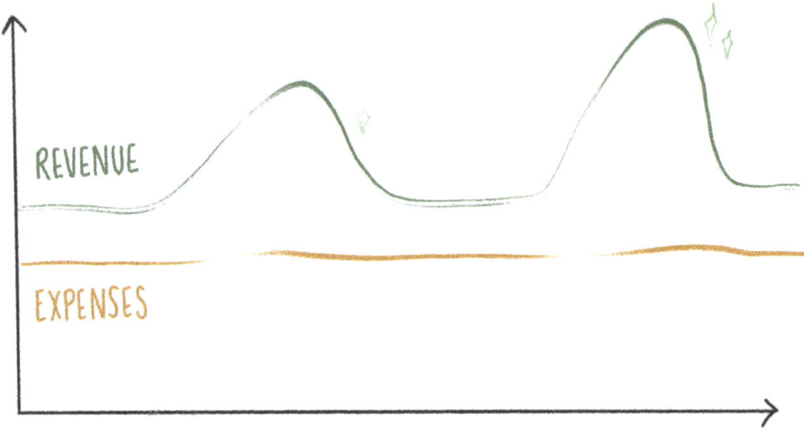

While your overall business might be profitable in total, lumpy or spiky cash flow can still add stress to your operations. You might want to pay yourself a stable salary but are only taking clients in the spring or fall. Maybe you need to have a capital outflow to secure a venue for a retreat but won't get registration fees for 6–12 months. Or perhaps you're working on a project with sixty-day net terms but need to pay your contractors within thirty days.

If a major disruption hits your business—whether it's a global crisis or a sudden policy shift that restricts your primary service—you'll need cash reserves to navigate the transition, pivot your model, and rebuild your income stream.

These are all times it's helpful to have a cash buffer or access to a line of credit. This is not the "run up your bills and never pay down your debt" type of credit—rather, it's to give yourself the resilience needed to navigate choppy waters with cash flow.

Here are a few ways to build financial resilience into your business.

Set Aside Money for Taxes

Depending on your tax structure, you'll need to set aside money for taxes. If you are an S corporation, a large portion of your taxes will be collected through your payroll process. But you'll need to set aside a dedicated percentage of your revenue each month to pay taxes and a higher percentage if you're a sole proprietor or LLC. And don't let the tax "advice" on social media fool you—it's not worth it to spend money on things you don't need to "save on taxes" or to take questionable deductions.

This is an area to invest in financial support with a strong tax accountant or fractional chief financial officer who can understand your whole personal and business financial landscape to help you save on—and save for—taxes.

Build Your Expenses Buffer

First step—pay yourself. Once you're consistently paying yourself, work to build up *at least* three months of operating expenses and owner's pay in your checking account(s), with another chunk of savings if your business is wildly seasonal.

Operating expenses are the day-to-day costs of running your business, including team payroll, software and legal/accounting payments, marketing expenses, and any business investments you're making. This also includes the amount you want to pay yourself each month. And your owner's pay is either what you pay yourself through payroll or what you draw from your business and transfer to your personal accounts, averaged out over time.

Particularly at the outset of your business, you will want to reinvest money in certain areas of your business to move more quickly, such as branding support, website, or business education. But don't overinvest and jeopardize your ability to save or take all of the money out of your business unless you have to. Building up an expense buffer early, even with small deposits, can create a needed hedge against swings in your business.

Financial Forecasting

Maintain a forward-looking financial forecast. Look at your upcoming client roster and project pipeline, including potential renewal dates or expiry dates. Forecast your expenses, such as your team's expenses and any one-off nonrecurring payments. Add in your projected tax liability and then see if you have warning signs about expenses being higher than revenue in upcoming months—do you have the cash to weather that pattern? If you don't or won't have enough cash, you'll know in advance so that you can increase your sales, reduce your expenses, or change the timing of either of those elements through preorders or changing payment terms.

This aspect is particularly important for "lumpy," seasonal, or launch-based businesses. Ideally, you're not relying on future payments to pay off expenses you outlay today—you're saving the cash from the last launch to fund the investments for this one. Or if you want to have more flexibility and only take projects every other month or take summers off, you can plan for that in your forecast.

Line of Credit or Capital

Additionally, you can take out a line of credit or secure access to capital. Debt shouldn't be a fix for consistent profitability problems, but having a backup plan to bridge funding can be the difference between staying in business and having to miss payroll, lay off employees, short pay vendors, or shut down altogether. There are different sources of loans and credit, including some that are personally guaranteed against your personal assets and others that can be forgiven.

Always talk to a financial professional before investing in outside funding. But securing loans or credit in advance of when you need it can be a way to weather short-term revenue or expense disruptions or make necessary investments without having to implement structural changes to your business.

WHAT KIND OF FLEXIBILITY AND RESILIENCE DO YOU NEED?

Not every business owner needs the same level of flexibility and resilience. Therefore, the strategies you implement might differ from those others employ. Here are just a few examples of how you might incorporate

these resilience and flexibility approaches based on what you need in
your business.

Variable Work Across the Year

You might live in a country that takes a month off each year—or a
whole summer! Or, you may structure your year around sabbaticals or
offseasons or need to take time away to work on a creative project. In this
case, you might lean on different delivery structures that aren't monthly
retainers or ongoing coaching while creating a financial forecast that
accounts for the gaps in your work. Evergreen marketing and playlist-style
content will be a great asset: When people find you when you're off work,
they'll get to hear about you without you being at your computer.

Calendars with Fewer Calls

You may have children at home or adult caregiving responsibilities,
which makes having a lot of fixed meetings on the calendar challenging in
case you have to frequently reschedule those meetings. You're optimizing
for flexibility, not necessarily for sustained periods away from the business.
As such, you want to build structures that incorporate more asynchronous
communication or ensure your business model isn't relying on a heavy
proportion of calls that you personally lead.

Chronic or Immediate Health Concerns

When you need to build in resilience for your health, are you doing so
for chronic issues that exist today, for future health requirements, or to
prepare for parental leave or other shorter-term situations? The issue at
hand dictates the kind of resilience you need to create.

You may want to design work around a schedule that also has fewer
calls and more flexible deadlines. This might mean focusing less on "live"
delivery and more on flexible projects or moving to more course- or
community-based business models. You'll also want to invest more in the
resilient marketing category so that you don't have to spend as much of
your limited time and energy creating new content.

Maybe you need a schedule with more contained deadlines over
a week, instead of over a day, to give you both flexibility and a
dopamine-driving deadline.

Or perhaps you want to keep doing client work but hire a team that can do more time-specific or repetitive (read: more boring) tasks in your business.

If you know in advance about upcoming leaves (e.g., for a major surgery or parental leave), you may want to add in or incorporate services that can be delivered by others, create digital products or courses, or set up a cash and content buffer. Instead of spending cash on trying to build a huge audience for digital courses or communities, you may instead want to use that money to purchase disability insurance.

Drive for Novelty

Maybe "resilience" for you means getting to change up your offers or marketing based on the season—or your season of life! In this case, you'll want to look at your whole portfolio of offers and marketing. What stays as your ballast, your steady core offers—and what scratches the itch for new and fun marketing and delivery? You don't have to have just "one signature offer" to have resilience. You can incorporate novelty into your business in a way that doesn't detract from the delivery and marketing of your core service.

SUMMARY

You don't need to chase the passive income promise to build a resilient business. Instead, resilience comes from how you deliver, earn, and market in ways that support your focus and flexibility. The first step is codifying your approach and process to reduce "key person" risk and give you more options for delivery and revenue opportunities. Resilient delivery models reduce your reliance on scheduled calls and a busy calendar without changing your business model, allowing you to build revenue streams that support your core offer without splintering your focus. Instead of relying on nonstop content creation, you can use resilient marketing strategies like evergreen assets, playlists, and partnerships. And, ultimately, resilience means building a cash buffer that gives you space to breathe, pivot, or pause when circumstances shift.

1. Where in my business have I already codified my methods—and where is it still all in my head?
2. What parts of delivery require me to show up live, and what could be delivered differently or by someone else?
3. What delivery shifts would give me more flexibility—without losing the quality or connection my clients count on?
4. How can I add value to my clients or add to my revenue without creating an entirely new business model?
5. Where can I rely more on long-term, low-lift marketing strategies instead of chasing short-term visibility?
6. How long should my financial runway be to help me feel spacious and steady, especially in times of uncertainty? (You may want to go back to the Zone of Enoughness framework.)
7. What kind of flexibility do I need in this season of life, and is my business structured to support that?
8. What does a resilient version of my business *feel* like—not just in numbers but in rhythm, spaciousness, and energy?

Want to bring more resilience through standardizing your delivery? You can find the "Repeatable Processes" template in the *Leaving the Casino* workbook or in the downloadable resources at deeperfoundations.com/casino

Conclusion: When You've Left the Table

YOU'VE DONE IT! YOU'VE walked out of the Entrepreneurial Casino.

The air feels different out here—crisper, cleaner. For the first time in what seems like forever, you can hear yourself think. You can hear the birds chirp!

The relentless noise, the flashing lights, and the intoxicating promises of the Casino are behind you, and in their place is an unfamiliar quiet. It's exhilarating but unsettling too. What will you do with this freedom?

As Brené Brown says in *Braving the Wilderness*, "The wilderness is an untamed, unpredictable place of solitude and searching. It is a place as dangerous as it is breathtaking, a place as sought after as it is feared. The wilderness can often feel unholy because we can't control it, or what people think about our choice of whether to venture into its vastness or not. But it turns out to be the place of true belonging, and it's the bravest and most sacred place you will ever stand."[60]

The Casino is always waiting, its neon lights flickering on the edge of your consciousness. It's designed to lure you back in, promising quick fixes, shortcuts, and certainty.

The reality is, to stay out of the Casino, with your feet firmly planted in the earth in your place of true belonging, you'll need to make some changes—not because you're cutting ties with your past life but because you're choosing discernment. You'll need to pay attention to what you listen to, whose advice you trust, and where you turn for validation.

---

60 Brené Brown, *Braving the Wilderness: The Quest for True Belonging and the Courage to Stand Alone* (Random House, 2017), 36.

You must redefine success on your own terms, rooted in the size, style, and scope of the business that feels right for you. This journey isn't about chasing someone else's version of success but aligning with your pace, your seasonality, and your cycles.

You don't have to go back.

Step by step, root by root, you'll implement the foundations that allow your business to grow sustainably, guided by your navigational beacons from the Big Questions. And as you do, you'll come to see that leaving the Casino isn't a one-time act; it's an ongoing practice. It's about recalibrating when you find yourself tempted to gamble on tactics instead of investing in foundational practices when faced with the Big Decisions. It's about cultivating your business with the same care and intention as a gardener tending a plot of land, knowing that sustainable growth takes time, patience, and trust. It's about returning to what you've built and what you've planted and remembering why you started.

This journey isn't meant to be walked alone. Finding fellow travelers who share your commitment to thoughtfully building a right-sized business will help you stay the course. Seek out physical and virtual communities and spaces aligned with your values, read books written by some of the resources I mention here, and work with mentors and teachers who teach sustainable principles and curate communities of those who want to build differently—though these groups probably don't exist on social platforms! The effort to find the others is worth it.

If you'd like to join my world as we build sustainable businesses, I encourage you to explore the Deeper Foundations offerings.

"True belonging doesn't require us to *change* who we are; it requires us to *be* who we are," Brown reminds us.[61] Surround yourself with others who value integrity over spectacle, depth over shortcuts, and sustainability over endless growth. They'll remind you that you're not alone on this journey—and that you never have to walk back into the Casino to find direction, especially at a price you might not want to pay.

---

61 Brené Brown, *Braving the Wilderness: The Quest for True Belonging and the Courage to Stand Alone* (Random House, 2017), 40.

I want you to know: I've walked this path too. This is the work I do every day—helping entrepreneurs like us realign with our visions, connect with each other, and build businesses that thrive outside the noise and hustle of the Casino.

So take this moment to breathe in the fresh air of possibility. Feel the sunshine on your face, the wind guiding your steps toward what's next. The path ahead is yours to create, to walk with intention, integrity, and the agency to grow a business with deep roots.

Bibliography

BOOKS:

- Baker, David C. *The Business of Expertise: How Entrepreneurial Experts Convert Insight to Impact + Wealth*. Rockbench Publishing, 2017.
- Bentley, Demir, and Carey Bentley. *Winning the Week: How to Plan a Successful Week, Every Week*. Matt Holt Books, 2023.
- Blake, Jenny. *Free Time: Lose the Busywork, Love Your Business*. Ideapress Publishing, 2022.
- Brown, Brené. *Braving the Wilderness: The Quest for True Belonging and the Courage to Stand Alone*. Random House, 2017.
- Burgis, Luke. *Wanting: The Power of Mimetic Desire in Everyday Life*. St. Martin's Press, 2021.
- Burkeman, Oliver. *Four Thousand Weeks: Time Management for Mortals*. Farrar, Straus and Giroux, 2021.
- Cialdini, Robert B. *Influence: The Psychology of Persuasion*. New and expanded edition. Harper Business, 2021.
- Dunford, April. *Obviously Awesome: How to Nail Product Positioning So Customers Get It, Buy It, Love It*. Ambient Press, 2019.
- Enns, Blair. *Pricing Creativity: A Guide to Profit Beyond the Billable Hour*. RockBench Publishing Corp, 2018.
- Enns, Blair. *The Four Conversations: A New Model for Selling Expertise*. Gegen Press, 2024.
- Enns, Blair. *The Win Without Pitching Manifesto*. Win Without Pitching, 2010.
- Fields, Jonathan. *Sparked: Discover Your Unique Imprint for Work That Makes You Come Alive*. Harper Business, 2021.

- Forte, Tiago. *Building a Second Brain: A Proven Method to Organize Your Digital Life and Unlock Your Creative Potential.* Atria Books, 2022.
- Frei, Frances, and Anne Morriss. *Unleashed: The Unapologetic Leader's Guide to Empowering Everyone Around You.* Harvard Business Review Press, 2020.
- Garvin, Lia. *The New Manager Playbook: A Simple Guide to Leading Teams with Confidence.* Liminal Work, 2025.
- Garvin, Lia. *The Unstoppable Team: A Simple Formula for Managing Your Team, Reducing Overwhelm, and Increasing Revenue.* Kindle edition. Liminal Work, 2024.
- Gilbert, Elizabeth. *Big Magic: Creative Living Beyond Fear.* Riverhead Books, 2015.
- Harnish, Verne. *Scaling Up: How a Few Companies Make It...and Why the Rest Don't.* Gazelles, Inc., 2014.
- Hari, Johann. *Stolen Focus: Why You Can't Pay Attention—and How to Think Deeply Again.* Crown Publishing, 2022.
- Hendricks, Gay. *The Big Leap: Conquer Your Hidden Fear and Take Life to the Next Level.* HarperOne, 2010.
- Hersey, Tricia. *Rest Is Resistance: A Manifesto.* Little, Brown Spark, 2022.
- Hochschild, Arlie Russell, and Anne Machung. *The Second Shift: Working Families and the Revolution at Home.* Penguin Books, 2012.
- Housel, Morgan. *The Psychology of Money: Timeless Lessons on Wealth, Greed, and Happiness.* Harriman House, 2020.
- Hyatt, Michael. *Free to Focus: A Total Productivity System to Achieve More by Doing Less.* Baker Books, 2019.
- Jaffe, Sarah. *Work Won't Love You Back: How Devotion to Our Jobs Keeps Us Exploited, Exhausted, and Alone.* Bold Type Books, 2021.
- Jarvis, Paul. *Company of One: Why Staying Small Is the Next Big Thing for Business.* Houghton Mifflin Harcourt, 2019.
- Kimmerer, Robin Wall. *Braiding Sweetgrass: Indigenous Wisdom, Scientific Knowledge, and the Teachings of Plants.* Milkweed Editions, 2013.
- Kimmerer, Robin Wall. *The Serviceberry: An Economy of Abundance.* Zando, 2024.
- Konrath, Jill. *SNAP Selling: Speed Up Sales and Win More Business with Today's Frazzled Customers.* Portfolio, 2010.

- Lebrón, Trudi. *The Antiracist Business Book: An Equity Centered Approach to Work, Wealth, and Leadership.* Row House Publishing, 2022.
- Martell, Dan. *Buy Back Your Time: Get Unstuck, Reclaim Your Freedom, and Build Your Empire.* Portfolio, 2023.
- May, Katherine. *Wintering: The Power of Rest and Retreat in Difficult Times.* Riverhead Books, 2020.
- Mazur, Michelle. *The 3 Word Rebellion: Create a One-of-a-Kind Message That Grows Your Business into a Movement.* Communication Rebel Books, 2019.
- McKeown, Greg. *Essentialism: The Disciplined Pursuit of Less.* Crown Business, 2014.
- Michalowicz, Mike. *Profit First: Transform Your Business from a Cash-Eating Monster to a Money-Making Machine.* Revised and expanded edition. Portfolio, 2017.
- Millerd, Paul. *The Pathless Path: Imagining a New Story for Work and Life.* Kindle edition. Paul Millerd, 2022.
- Moulton, Rochelle. *The Authority Code: How to Position, Monetize and Sell Your Expertise.* Kindle edition. Be Unforgettable Media, Inc., 2021.
- Newport, Cal. *Slow Productivity: The Lost Art of Accomplishment Without Burnout.* Portfolio, 2024.
- Nohelty, Russell, and Monica Leonelle. *The Author Ecosystems.* Russell Nohelty, forthcoming 2025.
- Northrup, Kate. *Do Less: A Revolutionary Approach to Time and Energy Management for Ambitious Women.* Hay House, 2019.
- Paulson, Emily Lynn. *Hey, Hun: Sales, Sisterhood, Supremacy, and the Other Lies Behind Multilevel Marketing.* Row House Publishing, 2023.
- Perkins, Bill. *Die with Zero: Getting All You Can from Your Money and Your Life.* Mariner Books, 2021.
- Putnam, Robert D. *Bowling Alone: The Collapse and Revival of American Community.* Simon & Schuster, 2000.
- Randall, Stacey Brown. *Generating Business Referrals Without Asking: A Simple Five-Step Plan to a Referral Explosion.* Morgan James Publishing, 2018.
- Raworth, Kate. *Doughnut Economics: Seven Ways to Think Like a 21st-Century Economist.* Chelsea Green Publishing, 2017.

- Schulte, Brigid. *Overwhelmed: Work, Love, and Play When No One Has the Time.* Sarah Crichton Books, 2014.
- Sethi, Ramit. *I Will Teach You to Be Rich.* 2nd ed. Workman Publishing, 2019.
- Stark, Jonathan. *Learn Your Lines: What to Say (and What Not to Say) to Clients.* Kindle edition. Self-published, 2024.
- Tessler, Bari. *The Art of Money: A Life-Changing Guide to Financial Happiness.* Parallax Press, 2016.
- Wickman, Gino. *Traction: Get a Grip on Your Business.* BenBella Books, 2011.

WEBSITES:

- Acunzo, Jay. "You Can't Own Your Audience—But You Can Own an Idea in Their Minds." Last modified January 5, 2024. https://jayacunzo.com/blog/you-cant-own-your-audience-but-you-can-own-an-idea-in-their-minds.
- Anaejionu, Regina. "Radical ROI." Accessed March 23, 2025. https://byregina.com/radicalroi.
- Clouse, Jay. "Creator Science." Accessed March 25, 2025. https://creatorscience.com/.
- Davis, Allison. "Allison Davis: Clarity + Strategy for Thought Leaders." Accessed March 25, 2025. https://allison-davis.com/.
- Diels, Kelly. *We Are the Culture Makers.* Online course, 2022.
- Doctorow, Cory. "The 'Enshittification' of TikTok." *WIRED.* Last modified January 23, 2023. https://www.wired.com/story/tiktok-platforms-cory-doctorow/.
- Hruby, Amelia. "Off the Grid." Accessed March 25, 2025. https://offthegrid.fun/.
- Hy, Khe. "RadReads." Accessed March 25, 2025. https://www.khehy.com/.
- Johal, Jeremy. "The 3% Rule: Engage Customers Before They Need Your Services." Accessed February 24, 2024. https://stickybranding.com/blog/3-rule-engage-customers-before-they-need-your-services.
- Kelly, Kevin. "1,000 True Fans." Last modified March 4, 2008. https://kk.org/thetechnium/1000-true-fans/.

- Keynes, John Maynard. "Economic Possibilities for Our Grandchildren." 1930. PDF file. Accessed March 25, 2025. http://www.econ.yale.edu/smith/econ116a/keynes1.pdf.
- McMullin, Tara. "What Works." Accessed March 25, 2025. https://whatworks.fyi/.
- Nightingale, Johnathan, and Melissa Nightingale. "Raw Signal Group." Accessed March 25, 2025. https://www.rawsignal.ca/.
- Nwangwu, N. Chloé. "Why We Should Stop Saying 'Underrepresented.'" *Harvard Business Review.* Last modified April 24, 2023. https://hbr.org/2023/04/why-we-should-stop-saying-underrepresented.
- O'Lochlainn, Ross. "Open Every Day." Accessed December 30, 2023. https://conversionengineering.co/open-every-day-book/.
- Worts & Cunning Apothecary. "Sliding Scale - Worts & Cunning Apothecary: Intersectional Herbalism + Magickal Arts." Last modified August 11, 2015. https://www.wortsandcunning.com/sliding-scale.

PODCASTS:

- Doyle, Glennon, Amanda Doyle, and Abby Wambach. *We Can Do Hard Things.* Episode 367, "Glennon's Dramatic Social Media Plan with Amelia Hruby." Podcast, December 3, 2024. Audacy Inc., 59:40. https://podcasts.apple.com/us/podcast/glennons-dramatic-social-media-plan-with-amelia-hruby/id1564530722?i=1000678999468
- Holly, Kate. The Space Beyond Scarce. Episode 1, "*Welcome to The Space Beyond Scarce.*" Podcast. October 12, 2021, 59 min., 43 sec. https://podcasts.apple.com/us/podcast/episode-1-welcome-to-the-space-beyond-scarce/id1588805241?i=1000539088134.
- Patterson, Maggie, and Michelle Mazur. *Duped: The Dark Side of Online Business.* Podcast. Accessed March 25, 2025. https://duped.online/.
- Warner, Michelle. Sequence over Strategy. Podcast. "How to Get More Clients with Relationship Marketing." Accessed April 25, 2024. https://www.themichellewarner.com/blog/sos001

Acknowledgments

FIRST AND FOREMOST, I couldn't have written this book without the support of my husband, Philip Sanford. Thank you for believing in my entrepreneurial dreams, being my number one fan, and taking Logan on walkies while I wrote. I love the life we've built together, and I hope this book gives us even more freedom to travel the world together.

To my parents, Mark and Roma Lackey: You fostered my love of reading as a child and have supported me endlessly and unconditionally in my professional and personal pursuits. You saw the potential in me when I didn't always see it in myself.

Thank you to my brother and sister-in-law, Stephen and Katie Lackey, and my niece and nephew, Mary and Thomas. Moving to Charlotte to live near you and put down roots changed my life in immeasurable ways that resulted in the writing of this book.

This book wouldn't exist without my book coach and developmental editor, Rachel Jepsen, who guided me from raw ideas to a coherent, finished manuscript. Your belief in me runs through every chapter. This book is a testament to your confidence in my abilities.

To Fabi Preslar and the SPARK Publications team, thank you for shaping this into a book I'm proud to hold. The amazing illustrations were created by Hollie Arnett, who was able to bring my metaphors to life with a stunning visual identity.

This book has been a personal journey of my business but also a story of my clients and our shared experiences and stories. To Linda Rhyne and Sarah Goelitz, my longest-standing clients: Thank you for the inspiration and support, for the Voxers listening to my occasional overwhelm, and for helping me refine many of these ideas.

Many thanks to my first beta readers, Catherine LaSota and Dr. Matthew Jones, who helped shape both the words on the page and the ways this book is already being applied.

My endless gratitude goes out to the friends I've walked beside in business: Amelia Hruby, Meg Casebolt, Courtney Fanning, Tressa Beheim, Bev Feldman, Diann Wingert, Leanne Knight, Angie Trueblood, Hannah Brandt, Michelle Friedman, Alex Simmons, and Erin Breeden, among others. The final chapter on resilience was written at a retreat with Emily Crookston and Erin Bradford. And to the Stable Hand team, especially Laura and Gracie—your lattes powered many pages.

Much of what I've covered in this book was absorbed by learning from others. I've cited my teachers and mentors where possible, as their teachings and stories have left an indelible mark on my work. Thank you to Andrea Leda, Lindsay Mack, Jay Acunzo, Mel Deziel, Jay Clouse, Regina Anaejionu, Kelly Diels, Ross O'Lochlainn, Meghan Bursiek, N. Chloé Nwangwu, Maggie Patterson, Dr. Michelle Mazur, Lauren Widrick, Jenny Blake, Allison Davis, Tara McMullin, Michelle Warner, Erin Halper and The Upside, Demir and Carey Bentley, Lex Roman, Khe Hy, Paul Millerd, and Tiago Forte. Your influence runs deep.

To the Deeper Foundations cohorts, members, and all of my 1:1 clients: Thank you for trusting me as a guide. Let this book be the permission slip you need to build a sustainable business on your own terms. This book only exists because you attended my events, read my newsletters, pushed me to clarify my approach, and shared your stories with me.

While many of my acknowledgments are for business friends, I've been supported for years by Allison Legg and Anya Lukyanova. From women's training to Portland 2 Coast to the 29029 challenge and more, life wouldn't be the same without my boxty besties.

And finally, to the best boy I know—our dog, Logan. You pulled me away from the keyboard when I needed a break, sat beside me while I edited, and expanded my heart with every walk. You're on every page, even if no one else sees it.

Index

C

The Enoughness Framework (see Enoughness)

Three Sisters   164

Tier 1 Energy   210-211

Tier 2 Energy   210-211

Tier 3 Energy   211

Tier 4 Energy   211

V

Value (see Pricing Approach → Value-Based Pricing)

Value-Based Pricing (see Pricing Approach)

VIP Days   149, 261

Z

Zone of Enoughness (see Enoughness)

Author Bio

JESSICA LACKEY is the founder of Deeper Foundations, a consulting and training firm that helps expertise-based business owners grow and scale sustainable companies rooted in stronger business foundations. She brings a unique blend of strategy and soul to her work, drawing on an MBA from Harvard Business School, a coaching certification from iPEC, and experience at McKinsey & Company and Nike, Inc. Jessica has supported over 200 entrepreneurs through her programs, blending systems thinking, operational rigor, and deep values alignment. She lives in Charlotte, North Carolina, with her husband.

She can be reached at www.deeperfoundations.com

RESOURCES

TOOLS TO HELP YOU BUILD A BUSINESS THAT ACTUALLY WORKS FOR YOU.

MY FREE TOOLKIT includes downloads and companion resources from *Leaving the Casino*—worksheets, assessments, and reflection prompts to help you implement the book's frameworks in your own business.

WHAT'S INSIDE:

- Business Stage Quiz and Guide
- Survive / Sustain / Strengthen and Serve Calculator
- 5 Pricing Approaches Worksheet
- Map Your Marketing Grid
- Process, Prune, Prioritize Worksheet
- The Hiring Matrix
- Repeatable Processes Worksheet

Get the Free Toolkit at
deeperfoundations.com/casino

WANT MORE STRUCTURE AND GUIDED IMPLEMENTATION?

Grab the full *Leaving the Casino* workbook—a practical tool to help you apply what you've learned and build a stronger business on your own terms.

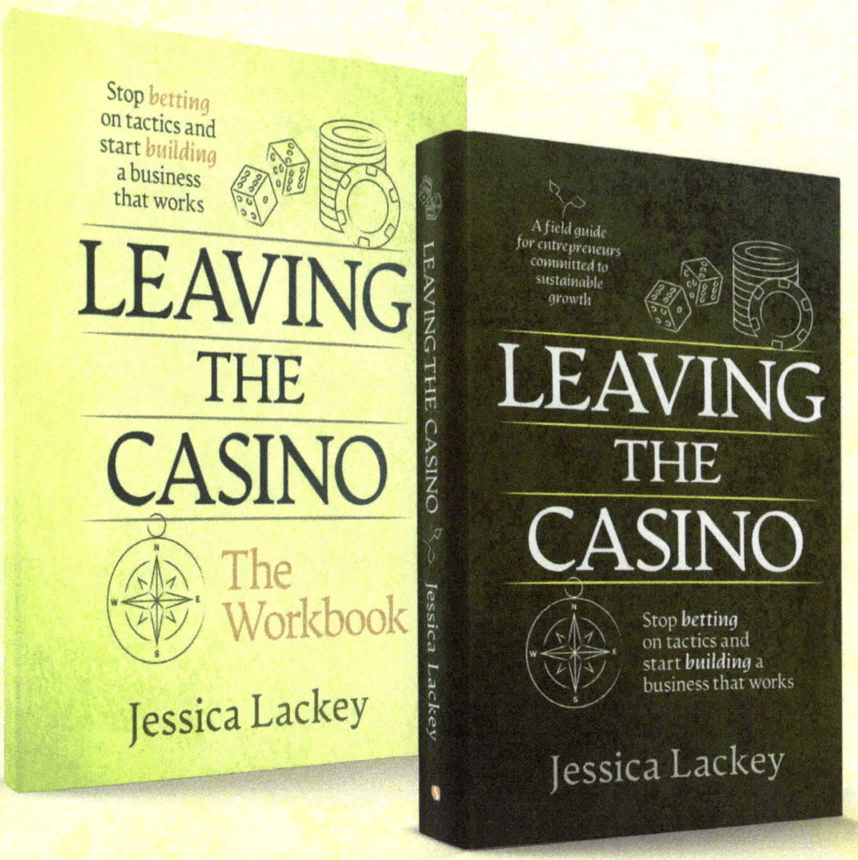